The Fashion Show

BLOOMSBURY VISUAL ARTS
Bloomsbury Publishing Plc
50 Bedford Square
London
WC1B 3DP
UK

BLOOMSBURY, BLOOMSBURY VISUAL ARTS and the Diana logo
are trademarks of Bloomsbury Publishing Plc

First published in India 2018
Copyright © Bloomsbury Publishing Plc, 2018

Gill Stark has asserted her right under the Copyright, Designs and Patents Act, 1988,
to be identified as Author of this work.

For legal purposes the Acknowledgements on p. 210 constitute an extension
of this copyright page.

Cover design: Louise Dugdale
Cover image © BERTRAND GUAY/AFP/Getty Images

A catalogue record for this book is available from the British Library.

A catalog record for this book is available from the Library of Congress.

ISBN: PB: 978-1-4725-6848-9
          ePDF: 978-1-4725-6849-6

Typeset by Lachina
Printed and bound in India

To find out more about our authors and books visit www.bloomsbury.com
and sign up for our newsletters.

The Fashion Show
History, theory and practice

Gill Stark

BLOOMSBURY VISUAL ARTS
LONDON · NEW YORK · OXFORD · NEW DELHI · SYDNEY

Contents

Introduction

The fashion show is deeply embedded within the traditions of the fashion industry. It has also acquired cultural significance within our contemporary society. This book is about the history, theory and practice of the fashion show and of fashion show production. It explores how the show is used as a powerful tool to market fashion products. It is also a practical guide to producing a fashion show, packed with information for anyone who might wish to try their hand at show production. The book focuses primarily on the shows that the fashion industry produces, however, it is written in such a way that the content of the book can be applied to other kinds of fashion shows.

The fashion show is by nature a contradictory beast: its elitist live shows are inaccessible to most, but through digital technology, it has become part of our everyday experience; show production is about creative vision, but it is also about practical production; it feels like entertainment, yet its purpose is seriously commercial; shows are about presenting fashion, yet little of the product on the runway will be worn by the masses; the show has a long tradition, reflecting a bygone age, yet its raison d'être is to present the new.

Fashion shows are transient events, long-awaited, much anticipated and rarely repeated. Planned over many months and costing a small fortune, many last for less than ten minutes. A moment in time, caught in photographs and on film, the atmosphere, the energy, the mood of the moment slips through everyone's fingers, leaving audiences hungry for another taste of that peculiar energy and excitement. Yet the fashion show has worked its magic and fulfilled its most important role, which is to stimulate our desire for the designer or brand, leaving us with strong associations of pleasure and the promise of further gratification when we purchase products.

The fashion show, however, serves other purposes in our contemporary society: it is entertainment, it communicates important creative messages, it is subversive, it is used to make political statements, it launches new careers. The fashion show has acquired cultural significance within our contemporary society. It has become part of our popular culture, part of the zeitgeist of the contemporary scene, as we collectively consume the experience, presented to us in the fashion industry's version of an immersive, multi-sensory performance. It could be argued that the fashion show has become a cultural icon in its own right: the *pose*, the *walk*, the juxtaposition of those who *parade* and those who observe, have all become accepted behaviours with which we are familiar.

For the industry, show time is both exhausting and exhilarating; it is an emotionally charged point in the year. After months of hard work, creative output is presented in a supremely public manner – often internationally. Watching a show that lasts for around ten minutes, industry critics and consumers make their critical assessment and declare the collection well-received or not worthy.

The Internet has changed the relationship between designer, press and consumer forever. Designers and brands no longer have to promote their products to consumers through the filter of the press, sitting front row at the shows. Using digital technology, including live streaming of fashion shows, brands can now sell new product from the runway directly to the consumer, tapping into discontent within the industry about seasonal time lags and an over-proliferation of collections and shows. Meanwhile, trends prompted by changes in society mean that seasonless collections and clothing that is not gender-specific appear on our runways. As the industry shifts and evolves, so its development is partly played out on the runways of the world.

The book provides a comprehensive exploration of the history, theory and practice of shows. The first three chapters of the book are largely theoretical. **Chapter One** examines the evolution of the fashion show from its earliest forms on the streets of Paris and in the elite Parisian couture salons, to the emergence of digital technologies with live streaming and fashion film. **Chapter Two** explores the contemporary contexts of the fashion show, including its many modern purposes, its complex global contexts and social, ethical and environmental issues such as diversity and sustainability. The show is such a powerful marketing tool that the whole of **Chapter Three** focuses on marketing and communication. It investigates how brands use the runway as a vehicle to communicate and it explores how journalism, social media and celebrity endorsement are used to ensure consumer engagement.

The last three chapters of the book are a practical guide to producing a fashion show and are laid out in a logical sequence from pre-production through to post-show activities. **Chapter Four** sets out pre-production work, including developing a creative concept, creating a team, PR, budgets, location and venue, model castings, hair and make-up and set design. **Chapter Five** is about show day and is structured to take the reader through the day, from set-build through to the finale of the show. Finally, **Chapter Six** explores what happens after the designer comes out onto the runway to take their bow. It examines post-production work including backstage interviews, after parties and the role of photography. It looks at how post-show PR activities, including social and other media, are used to maximize every opportunity that the show has presented.

All chapters offer an insight into the specialist area of the fashion show, drawing upon interviews with industry professionals. Further interviews and other material are available online. You will also find Industry Insight boxes throughout the text, which present professional sneak peeks into the industry, with interviews and industry examples. There are now so many fashion shows that it is impossible to include all of the most significant events in this book. Even as you read, somewhere in the world, another spectacular show will be produced. Throughout the book, I have given links to some fashion shows and referenced others. A great way to digest the book is to read the publication while accessing images and footage of fashion shows online.

No one has ever
found a solution
for not doing a
fashion show.
Anna Sui

The fashion show is used
to show the collections of
fashion students. Yemisi
Abraham's collection was
shown in the Regent's
University London
Graduate Show 2017 in
Brick Lane, London, UK.
(© Regent's University
London)

1

The evolution of the fashion show

Chapter One sets the fashion show within its historical contexts. It explores how the fashion show has evolved from its earliest days on the streets of Paris to the phenomenon it has become today. It offers an insight into how the fashion show was influential in the creation of the fashion system and how runway became an internationally recognized method of presenting and promoting fashion. The chapter considers how it has influenced, and been influenced by, contemporary culture, commerce, attitudes to clothing and its presentation in the fashion show.

Figure 1.1 Fashionably dressed people at the Longchamp Racecourse in Paris, France before the Grand Prix De Paris, France in 1866. (Universal History Archive via Getty Images)

Public display and private salons in the 1800s

Street style and style-spotting in the 19th century

Today we talk about *street style* as if it is a modern phenomenon, but displaying new designs on the street and *style-spotting* started a long time ago, and it could be argued that the first fashion shows happened on the street. Long before shows were invented, people liked to walk in *fashionable* places because this was an occasion to show off clothing and to observe what others were wearing. Everyone watched the arbiters of fashion, who were usually the wealthy, royal or famous. Tailors and dressmakers watched the latest *trends* and advised their clients accordingly. Social gatherings such as the theatre were popular, and likewise the races where, as Valerie Steele writes, 'People were as interested in the contest of fashions as in the contest of horses on the turf' (Steele, 1998). It is not, therefore, surprising that Parisian tailors saw an opportunity in early 19th-century Paris to employ young men wearing the latest tailored *fashions* to parade in the fashionable areas of the city and at popular events. In the early 1800s these first models were men because it would have been unseemly for female models to parade in this manner.

Figure 1.2 A French tailor measures a lady's bodice, circa 1700. (Roger Voillet via Getty Images)

Figure 1.3 An early model in a couture house. (W. G. Phillips/Stringer via Getty Images)

The height of modernity

Wealthy people had clothing and accessories made for them by dressmakers, tailors, milliners and cordwainers (shoemakers). Such tradespeople usually visited the wealthy in their homes to show the most luxurious of materials and trimmings, and to discuss the style and detailing of garments to be made. Clothing was sometimes made in miniature on dolls to show how designs would look on the body, and these dolls were also sent out to wealthy customers around the world. The less wealthy bought cloth from drapers and clothing was made in the home or pre-worn clothing was acquired.

With the beginnings of the emancipation of women later in the 1800s, there were two separate but related consequences for what was to become the fashion show. Women were starting to become more independent and it became acceptable for wealthy female customers to start to visit their dressmakers at their premises. This had a radical impact on the display and selection of clothing, moving that process from the domestic scene to the more public couturier's salon. Secondly, female models began to be employed, albeit working in the more private world of drapers' businesses, in dressmakers' premises and in the newly emerging fashion houses. There they wore the latest designs to show clients how clothing might look on the body. In the 1800s, showing garments on a live model was considered the height of modernity. By the end of the 1800s, the use of live models to display new designs would be widely used in Paris and would have spread to other parts of the world. An article in an Australian newspaper about a visit to the Paris House of Worth in 1892 reported: "A grand commissionaire stands inside the door, and you are ushered up the richly carpeted stairs to the salons, or what we would call showrooms. In these are to be seen very magnificently attired young ladies walking about in their own or sample costumes."

Figure 1.4 Hedi Slimane's last collection for Yves St Laurent. (Martin Bureau/ Staff via Getty Images)

The salon show

Models would walk through the couturier's *salon*, and this is still known today as a *salon show*. The salon was one large room or a series of smaller connecting rooms. The fashion show, or the *Opening* as it was called then, was a formal and genteel affair. As the fashion show evolved, it began to borrow ideas from the theatre and later from other forms of popular culture including dance, film and the circus. Photographs of the 1800s show that some dressmakers built small stages in their showrooms, and models would emerge from behind curtains to pose under bright lights. Couturiers began to decorate their *salons* with large mirrors that enhanced the light and the sense of space and occasion. The salon would often be in the couturier's premises, and would resemble a drawing room in a client's house. Salon shows are still produced today, as can be seen in Hedi Slimane's last collection for Yves St Laurent. Held in an 18th-century house and produced in the style of a couture show, model numbers were called out as models emerged and walked through salons while the audience sat on chairs in the tradition of early couturiers' salons.

Figure 1.5 A tableau vivant at an American costume ball,
1872. (Heritage Images/Contributor via Getty Images)

Drawings and photographs show models walking around in front of groups of wealthy society women; walking, pausing and posing for the audience so that clients had the best possible opportunity to view the new garments on the body and in movement. The idea of posing had already entered popular culture, as *tableaux vivant* was a well-liked entertainment. Tableaux vivant means *living picture* and people in costume, theatrically lit, would take up static poses, silently holding those poses while an audience looked on. Tableaux vivant could, therefore, be considered the forerunner of the model's pose, the model silently holding a static position while the audience observed the clothing.

Models in the early shows were chosen for their gracefulness and beauty. They were selected for their likeness to the wealthy clients. The houses thought that customers who could identify with the models would be able to imagine wearing the clothes. The couturier Charles Frederick Worth married Marie Vernet in 1851, having met her while working for the Paris drapers Gagelin et Opigez. Marie Vernet was a model and their son's words about his mother illustrate the desired characteristics of models at that time: 'She was exceedingly successful in this, not only because she had grace and beauty, knew how to carry herself and wear clothes, but because she had great charm and knew how to smile' (Evans, C., 2013).

Figure 1.6 Models in a Parisian fashion house, early 1900s.
(Apic/Contributor via Getty Images)

<table>
<tr><td>

The fashion system

The fashion system is about recognized practices in the design, production, consumption and disposal of fashion. It is about the art of creating fashion and about the business, the marketing and the selling of fashion. It is about the consumer's relationship with fashion and the role that fashion plays within our contemporary culture. The fashion system has a pace and a language of its own. It has a yearly calendar and its nature is predicated upon change.

</td></tr>
</table>

The beginnings of the fashion system

It was in the mid-1800s that the fashion system, as we know it today, began to emerge. Different cities became reputed for the very best in clothing. London's Savile Row became world-renowned for its men's tailoring, and Paris for its couture. Dressmakers such as Worth and Patou became internationally renowned for their craftsmanship, and more importantly for their creativity and innovation, which they also applied to the promotion of their collections. Their businesses became established as *fashion houses*, and a pattern began to be established whereby twice-yearly collections were produced, with national and international customers visiting the couturiers twice a year, thereby establishing the two 'seasons' of autumn/winter and spring/summer, that form the basis of the fashion calendar.

Since the late Middle Ages, guilds had existed so that craftspeople making cloth, shoes and clothing had greater power as collectives over the production and sale of their products. In 1868 in Paris an association called the Chambre Syndicale de la Haute Couture replaced these medieval guilds. In the 1900s this organization set out rules to govern the couture industry, which included the minimum number of outfits to be shown, the number of staff to be employed to create the collections, that there must be two collections a year and that they must be shown on live models.

Figure 1.7 The Cunard ocean liner *Lusitania* at the pier in New York City, 13 September 1907. (ullstein bild/Contributor via Getty Images)

The social scene and internationalization

During the late 1800s and early 1900s, the *social season* was the time in the year when the social elite congregated in cities to socialize and attend glittering events such as balls and dinners. Greater leisure time for some brought developments in culture: music, photography and the theatre, and the fashion show became a central feature of the season. Luggage-making companies such as Louis Vuitton grew their businesses as travelling became fashionable amongst the wealthy. Travelling to Paris from as far away as America, they chose their clothing for the coming season during the Openings from an increasingly well-known group of dressmakers and couturiers. A journey to Paris could take weeks and the society set would pack belongings into trunks ready for a long journey by rail, road or sea. It was soon the custom for men, as well as women, to attend the shows and they would arrive in Paris, seen as the heart of fashion, to view designs that only the wealthy could afford. The Parisian designs they wore around the world spread the latest fashions internationally.

Attending the shows at the Paris fashion houses was one of the activities that demonstrated that you were fashionable, modern and part of the right social set. This is well illustrated by the client list of the couturier George Frederick Worth. Worth created dresses for royalty, including the French Empress Eugénie, and he dressed well-known actresses such as Sarah Bernhardt. Worth designed clothing for the English actress Lillie Langtry to wear both on and off the stage. She did much to promote his designs in the United States, travelling with dozens of trunks filled with luxurious outfits, which were sometimes more of an attraction, and more widely reported, than her performances.

Figure 1.8 Lillie Langtry on the stage. (Popperfoto/ Contributor via Getty Images)

Mass-manufacture, ready-to-wear and the rights to reproduce

While the Openings were part of the social season, they were a serious commercial affair for the couturiers of Paris. The city increasingly relied on the American market, which, because of its size, brought much wealth to the couture industry. However, a new market was emerging. The industrial revolution in the latter 1800s had resulted in the development of mass production and ready-to-wear clothing. With ready-to-wear, the fashion show had a whole new role to play. Soon, in addition to the society set, buyers from stores internationally congregated in Paris twice a year, knowing that garments would sell back home with the *cachet* of having been designed in Paris. In addition to ready-to-wear, a third and very lucrative market soon evolved: selling the rights to reproduce clothing designs. The fashion houses sold *models* or *toiles* to buyers or manufacturers who mass-manufactured the designs in other parts of the world, and especially in America. While couture was still created by hand for the very rich, and the ready-to-wear market sold expensive clothing produced by the fashion houses, the couturiers capitalized on this third opportunity. The designs were often simplified or adapted for mass-manufacturing, but they were still sold with the essential appeal of having been conceived in Paris.

Numbering and naming designs

The fashion show was inevitably affected by the attendance of buyers and manufacturers, and their needs were in some ways different from those of the couture clients. Models started to carry numbers so that clients could identify the clothing they wanted to buy, or the outfits they wanted to buy the rights to manufacture. Couturiers would appear at the beginnings of shows to explain the collections and to point out details and the houses would have *vendeuses* (saleswomen) strategically placed in the salons to give audiences information about the designs. The British dressmaker Lucile was famously attributed with giving models names rather than numbers. According to Valerie Mendes and Amy de la Haye, audiences were 'fascinated and amused' by the names, which gave the garments extra appeal and were an advantage for journalists (Mendes and de la Haye, 1990).

The evolution of the fashion show

The retail show

By the early 1900s, the department store was a popular retail format and the
international buyers adopted the show as a method of promoting clothing in their
stores. Visiting stores was a social activity and retailers put on events, including
concerts, exhibitions and talks and, of course, fashion shows. Retailing flourished
in America; the Ehrlich Brothers' store in New York City is widely attributed with
holding the first American fashion show in 1903. Harrods of London, one of the
world's most famous department stores, showed designs on living models from
1909 and department stores such as Wanamaker's in New York regularly used
the fashion show to attract women to shop with them. Both *being fashionable*
and the *shopping experience* had entered the lifestyles of city dwellers. Likewise,
the fashion show had developed into a method of making a retail store more
attractive, while stimulating the desire of customers to purchase clothing, and by
the 1920s fashion shows were widely held by American retailers.

Figure 1.10 Chantal Fashion House Swimwear Show, Paris, France, 1927. (Keystone-France/Contributor via Getty Images)

A privileged world

In the early 1900s, many couturiers redesigned their fashion houses to create elegant salons that were a blend of theatre and drawing room, with rows of gilt chairs, mirrored walls and stages with curtains from behind which the mannequins appeared. However, the show differed from the theatre in its commercial imperatives and there was a pecking order, with more important clients given preferential seating, the most important 'allotted armchairs with their backs to the light, while the newcomers, or those from less well-known houses,' had 'to be content with hard-seated chairs.' Seats at the shows were fought over as they are today and as Marjorie Hills noted: 'At the popular houses, the crowd is suffocating, and every place is taken long before the first mannequin comes writhing her way between the serried ranks of chairs' (Hills, 1923).

The show and popular culture

During the early 1900s the fashion show continued to take inspiration from popular culture. Invitations and music in the form of live musicians (sometimes whole orchestras) were introduced, as well as refreshments and programmes. The arts were closely linked, with artists such as Picasso designing theatre sets and couturiers designing theatre costume. Having borrowed from popular culture and from film and the theatre, runway itself started to become part of our popular culture. The Openings communicated the mood of the time, reflected in the way that models walked and posed and trends in accessories and hair and make-up. Couturiers had accessories made to complement their collections and employed artists to style hair and make-up. An article in American *Vogue* called 'Paris Openings First Impressions' reported in 1938: 'No doubt about it, brushed-up hair is behind much of what happened at the current Paris Openings. Almost unanimously, Frenchwomen have accepted the brushed-up coiffure.'

The press preview is born

Parisian couturiers repeated the same show to different groups of customers. Some couturiers held what we now call a dress rehearsal, using this to educate their salespeople about a new collection while rehearsing for the event. It was an occasion when the workers of the ateliers saw their hard work on live mannequins. Some couturiers held preview shows for special guests, including the press, whose attendance at the Openings brought both problems and advantages. Their descriptions, photographs and drawings in newspapers and magazines enabled copying. However, the power of the press to promote designers did not escape the couturiers of Paris. Patou started the custom of a *repetition générale* on the night before his official Opening, inviting all the male members of the foreign press, as well as the women (American *Vogue*, Spring 1923).

Because the fashion houses were now selling to three different markets, the shows had to meet the different needs of private couture clients, buyers and manufacturers. Couture clients were sometimes invited to smaller, more select events, and the buyers were invited to a series of shows scheduled according to geographic origin. Those from furthest away viewed the collections first, ensuring that the profitable American market was satisfied.

Lady 'Lucile' Duff Gordon

Couturiers began to enjoy a status different from that experienced before. Dressmakers and tailors, designers and couturiers became internationally famous. One designer, Lady Duff Gordon, who worked under the professional name of Lucile, is attributed with starting many of the elements of the show that we take for granted today (Evans, 2013). It has been claimed, for instance, that she was the first London designer to use live models, and that the department stores copied this practice (Woodhead, 2012).

Lucile's experience of the theatre – while designing costume – had inspired the production of her fashion shows. Mendes and de la Haye (1990) quote from *The Illustrated London News* of June 1908: 'At Mme Lucile's in Hanover Square, there is a charming little theatre where clients of the house assemble to see the latest novelties.' Models at Lucile's shows would first pose upon a stage and then walk amongst the audiences to 'musical accompaniment'. They were given programmes for the shows that listed the running order and that were inspired by the programmes produced for theatrical productions.

The First World War and internationalism (1914 to the 1950s)

The First World War forced some Parisian fashion houses to close and others to change the way they operated. Some couturiers, such as Paul Poiret, were conscripted into the army, and while fashion shows continued to be presented, they were fewer and smaller. As war began, the Openings were postponed and the perception of the fashion season changed: 'A government that needs its railways to transport soldiers takes little interest in new frocks. And steamships on which millionaires pay fortunes for a berth in the steerage look with cold and unsympathetic eyes on boxes from Paris milliners' (Marshall, 1914).

The war highlighted a tussle for prominence in the American market that was to continue for decades. The American government initiated an endeavour to promote American-designed fashion and in 1914, Edna Woolman Chase, the editor of *Vogue*, organized a show to promote New York designers. Meanwhile in Paris, there was concern about losing the prominence of Parisian fashion internationally, particularly in the American market, and an exhibition in 1915 in the United States showed designs by Parisian couturiers such as Paquin, Worth and Jenny. However, as the world emerged from the war, Paris had retained its dominance, for now, as the centre of world fashion.

Celebrity couturiers

Lucile opened salons and produced shows in New York (1910) and in Paris (1911). In New York she is said to have been inspired by 'American hospitality, verve and wealth' and it is claimed that she was 'astounded at the prices rich women were prepared to pay for clothes and happy to beguile them with her elaborate creations and fashion parades' (Mendes and de la Haye, 1990).

Figure 1.12 Fashion models on the runway wearing clothes made from artificial silk at the Holland Park Hall in London on 19 April 1926. (Davis/Stringer via Getty Images)

The Roaring Twenties

The *Roaring Twenties* saw a post-war economic boom. France called it the *années folles*, or the crazy years. There was massive industrial growth, a huge increase in consumer demand and cultural changes as travel, film, music and photography became widely available. Women had greater freedom, epitomized by shorter skirts and bobbed hair, which became the hallmarks of the modern woman. It became more acceptable for women to engage in activities requiring freer movement, such as sport. Music and dance became very popular and a craze for the tango resulted in a natural feel for rhythm and playful, relaxed body movements. Reflecting the mood of the time, photographs from the 1920s show that the way models walked and posed noticeably changed; they moved more freely, were clearly more energized and exhibited more personality on the runway. Photographs illustrate that in some shows models emerged onto the runway as if at the start of the tango.

Marjorie Hills, reporting for American *Vogue*, wrote an article called 'A Seat at the Paris Openings, Spring 1923'. This gives us a fabulous picture of the mood of the time and valuable information about the Openings in Paris as the city prepared for visitors from different parts of the world: North and South America, London, Spain and elsewhere in Europe. Notices were displayed in windows on the rue de la Paix in French and English and 'the newspaper women in the kiosks order a double supply of papers in the English language.' We owe much of what we know today to the accounts of Marjorie Hills, and other journalists of the time, whose situation was anything but enviable. Copying was a major problem. The couturiers of Paris carefully guarded their designs until they were shown at the Openings and then no one could carry pencil and paper into the events. Some companies employed copyists who could memorize the designs at a show and then reproduce them in drawings.

Reporting for American *Vogue*

Marjorie Hills paints an evocative picture of the experiences of journalists and buyers, as well as the changing nature of the show, in Paris in the 1920s:

> In the dark ages of the couture, before Vogue had celebrated its twentieth, not to mention its thirtieth, anniversary, the situation of the journalist, on these opening days, was anything but enviable. Seated on an uncomfortable stool in the darkest or the most glaring corner, paper and pencil prohibited and confiscated if produced, feeling like a worm and looking guilty and uncomfortable, she had the delightful task of learning by heart the two hundred odd models – some of them extremely odd – which filed past her straining eyes. But this state of affairs has been changing, and now, in the great majority of houses, things are very different.
>
> Hark, hark, the dogs do bark, the buyers have come to town! They have come exclusively and uniquely to buy models, and from the first to the fifteenth or eighteenth of February, they are occupied in the perfect orgy of inspection and purchase, which turns a small and select portion of the community into a maelstrom of activity, while the ordinary citizen plods on under his umbrella . . . Paris becomes a huge clothes market, to which provident shopkeepers in the business all repair. (Hills, 1923)

Showing internationally

During the early 1900s couturiers began to travel to show their designs abroad. Some opened salons in different cities, and Lucile, compiling her autobiography, wrote, 'I often wonder how I ever had the audacity to open a branch in Paris' (Duff Gordon, 2012). When she travelled to her branches in Paris and New York she sometimes took her models with her. Patou famously brought American models back to Paris, much to the outrage of the Parisian press. Mannequins were employed by the fashion houses, and worked as fit models in between shows, sometimes travelling with their employers. While the role of Paris as the *capital of fashion* was widely acknowledged, there was revolt against the city as the only arbiter of style. Valerie Steele points out that Poiret 'shrewdly' used 'American models to display his clothes' (Steele, 1998) and it is clear from the constant reference to Paris fashion that the prominence in the mind of the American public of Paris as the origin of new ideas continued for many decades. However, there is also evidence in newspaper reports that London had some prominence, as demonstrated in an article in *The San Francisco Call* in 1912 called 'European Styles Reproduced Here for Smartest Set': 'Every sartorial aid to make the woman pretty, smart and chic in the latest approved fashion of the Paris and London builders of attire'.

In *The Mechanical Smile*, Caroline Evans writes about the differences between Parisian and American fashion shows in the early 1900s. French shows were by invitation only and American shows 'were open to the public who came in their thousands, often paying for entry tickets'. She describes how 'fashion promoters and theatre directors were devising elaborate shows as a form of mass spectacle' (Evans, 2013). In France, the fashion show was part of the very culture of the country, a serious matter, recognized by the population as an important French industry. On the contrary, the mass of the American public saw fashion as an enjoyable activity and the show as a form of entertainment; they enjoyed the glamour of the event.

Having opened her store in New York, and with her penchant for elaborate show production, Lucile is reported to have 'staged fashion spectacles to audiences two to three thousand strong several afternoons a week' in response to high demand. The entertainment element of the events is evident as the report goes on to say: 'Whilst very few women could afford to order a Lucile gown, clearly many derived pleasure by watching and dreaming. Lucile wrote: "So the parade went on, three hours of it . . ."' (Mendes and de la Haye, 1990). It is not surprising that the events were so popular. An account of both the audience and the mood at a showing of her Autumn 1915 collection suggests all of the anticipation of a star-studded event:

> Women in sables, aigrettes, and emeralds fought politely with women in chinchilla, paradise, and diamonds for the best seats. The orchestra started playing. The room was heavy with scent. Programmes cracked between gloved hands. There was an expectant hush, all heads turned towards the entrance, and Madame herself came in. Like royalty she was shown to a chair reserved for her immediately in front of the chiffon-curtained stage. The moment she was seated, the orchestra went into a waltz and the parade of mannequins began. (Mendes and de la Haye, 1990)

The 1930s: Fashion, film and the Great Depression

While the Great Depression had a sobering effect on fashion during the 1930s, a counter-effect was the glamour of film. Elsa Schiaparelli, the first Italian couturier to become an international name, designed clothing for films such as *Moulin Rouge*, acknowledging the influence of film on her work. Schiaparelli approached fashion as an art form and worked closely with many of the artists and photographers of the day, including Jean Cocteau, Salvador Dali and Man Ray. She was part of the Surrealist movement, creating clothing such as the shoe hat. Surrealist artists attended her theatrical fashion shows: 'Working with artists . . . gave one a sense of exhilaration' she wrote, and 'when Bérard walked so lightly into a crowded room . . . the atmosphere became charged. His arrival would immediately become known in the *mannequin cabin*. The show could start' (Schiaparelli, 1954).

Meanwhile in America, Claire McCardell was designing functional clothing, suitable for mass-manufacture. While department stores had been employing designers behind the scenes, now they realized the potential for designer names related to lower priced fashion, and as Rebecca Arnold points out, stores began to use:

> photographs of named designers shown with their fashion collections, encouraging a cult of personality that had previously been reserved for couturiers. This was partly an attempt to encourage home-grown talent while the hardships of the Great Depression made trips to Paris to source fashions too costly. (Arnold, 2009)

As more of the population became aware of designer names, some designers began to produce cheaper ranges of clothing aimed at a cheaper, though still expensive, market.

The prominence in the mind of the American public of Paris as the origin of new ideas continued for many decades.

The 1940s: A Second World War but the beginnings of fashion weeks

The Second World War, a truly global conflict involving the world's most powerful nations, had a large impact on fashion. With the occupation of France, some Parisian couture houses closed. Others struggled on but with business severely curtailed. Schiaparelli, who operated her couture fashion business in Paris, wrote in her autobiography that as the Germans were approaching Bordeaux,

> we had a meeting in the offices of Mme Lanvin. My couturiers, or their representatives, were present at this session held by the light of a few candles . . . No decision was taken that day. The next day we listened to the radio . . . and heard the speech announcing France's capitulation and the terms of the armistice. My work-people, standing white-faced and taut . . . burst into tears. (Schiaparelli, 1954)

Italian companies, which had been selling to American stores, were no longer able to do so. The transport of clothing around the world was very difficult and ships carrying clothing often didn't reach their destinations. The use of large quantities of cloth was frowned upon, as was the purchase of luxury clothing. In the U.K., the government rationed clothing and sponsored well-known designers, such as Norman Hartnell, to design ranges of utility clothing. 'Make do and mend' became one of the biggest mottos of the war and films of the time showed the population how to recycle materials to make new clothes. Fashion shows, no longer purely an industry activity, had entered the realm of entertainment and in Britain they were used to raise money for the war effort.

For America, the Second World War brought major economic and social change, lifting it out of the depression of the 1930s. With little access to Parisian or Italian clothing, American fashion began its real development. Eleanor Lambert, a well-regarded publicist and press director of the New York Dress Institute, was hugely influential in fashion in the United States. Determined to demonstrate the importance of American fashion, she started press week in the early 1940s in New York. She also started the Coty Fashion Critics' Awards for design excellence, which became likened to the 'fashion Oscars'. While it took many years for the international press to fully recognize American fashion, the twice-yearly New York press weeks with their back-to-back shows, interspersed with social events, enabled the press to gather twice a year to see the collections of the major American designers in one place, thereby creating an event that we now call *fashion week*.

Dazzling shows

As cloth and labour were available again at the end of the War, some of the most dazzling shows were produced. For an industry starved of cloth, designers revelled in the excess available, and the New Look created by Dior became one of fashion's most famous images. The mood of excess was reflected in fashion shows of the era. In particular, Paris and Italy produced dazzling performances on raised runways, with sparkling chandeliers and flashing cameras.

While the world still looked to Paris for new directions, the city was no longer perceived to be the only creator of fashion. The US drive for home-grown fashion had finally been successful with American designers such as Claire McCardall and Anne Klein becoming well respected. Meanwhile, immediately after the war, the Italian fashion industry invested in updated manufacturing facilities to modernise and increase production. Based on Italy's traditional crafts, its high quality production, its cultural heritage, and supported by a close relationship with America, it began to sell into new markets and particularly the lucrative American market.

Figure 1.15 The Third
Italian High Fashion Show
in Florence, Italy, 1952,
published in the Picture
Post ('Paris Has a Rival')
on 1 March 1952. (Kurt
Hutton/Stringer via Getty
Images)

The strangest of shows

As the world emerged from the Second World War, one of the strangest of shows
took place. This was the result of an initiative by the Chambre Syndicale in Paris
to remind the world that Paris was the heart of the fashion industry, and that Paris
was back in business. Cloth was in short supply and live mannequins were not
available, but the Chambre Syndicale conceived of an exhibition to replace the
Openings. A collection of designs was produced in miniature by some of Paris'
most famous couturiers: Balmain, Balanciaga, Schiaparelli, Lanvin and many more.
Designs were shown on beautiful two-foot-high wire-frame dolls. The exhibition
of the fashion show was called Théâtre de la Mode and it toured Paris, London,
Barcelona, Copenhagen, Stockholm, Vienna, New York and San Francisco.

The shows that launched Italian fashion into an international arena

Often in the history of fashion, the fashion show has played an essential role in
change. At around the turn of the decade in Italy, a series of shows were used to
propel Italian clothing into a new sphere as one of the world leaders of fashion.
As Valerie Steele observes, a show 'held in July 1952 . . . at the Sala Bianca of the
Palazzo Pitti in Florence . . . is widely regarded as the "birth" of Italian fashion'
(Steele, 2003). The shows that launched the Italian industry were glamorous in
a way that is still synonymous with Italian style, and so Italy entered the fashion
system with the fashion show and seasonal fashion weeks, at the very heart of
that system. Press Week, the forerunner of New York Fashion Week, had started
in 1943 and an equivalent system started in Italy in 1958.

Figure 1.16 Lady Pamela Smith standing beside Coco Chanel, famous couturiere, in Chanel's fashion salon in London, England. Lady Smith was a London society girl who took up a career as a fashion mannequin. (Bettmann/Contributor via Getty Images)

Salon shows and theatrical events

Photographs of fashion shows in the 1950s indicate the continued popularity of the salon show, with its genteel atmosphere and intimacy brought about by the proximity of audience and mannequins: 'it is enchanting to see the elegant 1950s model girls in demure fashion, wearing white gloves and pert hats' (Moss, n.d.). However, other images of the era show a high raised runway, large audiences and a strong sense of drama. In contrast to the salon shows, the audience sits far removed from the models, who parade on the runway like actors in the theatre. The theatre of the show is well illustrated in the events that Coco Chanel produced in a specially designed salon in her premises in Paris. The walls of the salon were entirely lined with mirrors, as was a sweeping staircase down which the models processed. The effect was one of glamour and luxury. Chanel herself would sit at the top of the mirrored staircase, watching the event, and the audience would sit in rows on the traditional gold fashion show chairs. In the audience would be celebrities of the day such as Dali, Diaghileff and Stravinsky. As well as being a talented designer, Chanel was an accomplished marketer and her shows were designed to generate excitement around her brand.

Buying trips to Paris

Martin Moss, managing director of Woollands, one of the foremost department stores in London at the time, wrote about his buying trips to Paris:

> In Paris where the cost of purchasing toiles from couture houses was very high, we would combine our purchases with our leading manufacturers…. We would always attend the second week of the shows when the competitive American stores had already placed their orders. We may have missed some of the initial excitement and the glamorous personalities attending the opening shows, but we received better attention with our modest orders once things had calmed down. In those days a store would be allocated its own vendeuse and she would reserve seats and look after us after the show. There was always much excitement over choosing a toile as each cost at least £250 – a lot of money in the Fifties. By co-operating with our leading suppliers we were able to ensure that we did not buy the same model and we usually would have access to two or three designs from each house. It was often possible to develop several different styles from one toile by clever interpretation. (Moss, n.d.)

Martin Moss used fashion shows to promote Woollands' fashion:

> we were able to build up a comprehensive show, including models from Christian Dior, Hubert de Givenchy, Jacques Fath and other leading designers of that period… This … definitely put Woollands on the fashion map and the press reports were extremely encouraging. (Moss, n.d.)

The international show season

By the end of the 1950s, the twice-yearly seasons of spring/summer and autumn/winter were firmly established, as were the international shows. Collections were presented six months before they were due to be worn, giving couturiers and manufacturers time to produce the clothing and giving the press time to inform their readerships about the coming season's designs. The fashion show had evolved from the intimate presentation of couture to wealthy clients into an international event where audiences also included buyers, the press with attendant photographers, celebrities and fellow artists. The show had become recognized internationally as a method of presenting and promoting new collections and it had also become a form of entertainment, although the mass of the population would not be able to view live industry runway for another half-century. Press reporting at shows meant that information from the runway spread to a wider audience than ever before, strengthening the perception of the fashion show as the source of the latest and most desirable clothing designs. The importance of film (now widely accessible) within popular culture continued to influence the fashion show. Film fostered a growing awareness of the way the body moved and as fashion photographers dabbled in film, the pose of the fashion model became refined, reflected both in editorial photography and on the runway.

Figure 1.17 The British designer John Cavanagh shows a dress to an American buyer, 28 February 1953. He showed in Paris in order to sell to international buyers. (Kurt Hutton/Stringer via Getty Images)

Figure 1.18 Models walk down the runway in the latest fall fashions, Spokane, Washington, United States, on 4 April 1960. (B. Anthony Stewart/Contributor via Getty Images)

Figure 1.19 A Dior fashion show in the 1950s. (Howard Sochurek/Contributor via Getty Images)

Figure 1.20 A Dior fashion show in the 1960s. (Reg Lancaster/Stringer via Getty Images)

It was like a dam bursting with Mary Quant and Alexander. We had the Temperance Seven playing. Vidal Sassoon did the hair and all the top models were there … the music was very important because before that were shows where models had a number.
Vanessa Denza

Youth fashion and pop culture (1950s and 1960s)

In the late 1950s and early 1960s a new trend radically changed both fashion and the fashion show: *youthquake* started in London and rapidly spread internationally. Previously, young adults had aspired to dress in the kinds of clothing that their parents wore. Youth fashion emerged, bold and audacious, produced by young designers. New and revolutionary, it brought miniskirts, tights, false eyelashes and psychedelic prints. The energy of youth fashion broke rules and changed fashion forever. Shows began to reflect the fun, light-hearted optimism of the time, echoing the new pop culture with its rebellious music, art and fashion scene. With more freedom of expression, models danced on the runway, and relaxed audiences tapped their feet, smiled and chatted. Films of shows in the 1960s illustrate the contrast between youth fashion and the sedate salon style shows that some fashion houses continued to produce.

Industry Insight

Vanessa Denza

How did you start to work in fashion?

My Godfather was the head of Condé Nast; he said "why don't you go and do six months in Paris with Vogue". I worked as an intern at Jacques Fath, in the new boutique that was being run by the Princesse de Polignac. I learned to pick the clothes that would sell. Then Martin Moss said to me "Emilio Pucci wants someone to go and work with him in Italy for two months … why don't you go?" But eventually I decided that the only way I was going to learn what I wanted was to go to New York.

What did you learn in New York?

I wanted to learn how to buy. I worked with Lisa Fonssagrives (who was the great model) in Lord & Taylor [department store] in New York. I learned how to answer the telephone, how to address people, the paperwork. Eventually I came back to London. Martin Moss at Woollands [a Knightsbridge department store] said, "I want to start a very young new shop, and there is a designer called Terence Conran, who will design it" and that became the 21 Shop. We stocked the new designers.

Did you do shows in the store?

We did three shows on the opening night of the 21 Shop. Clare Rendlesham (Fashion Editor of British *Vogue* in the late 1950s) was there. Claire had powerful ideas and I remember the shoot we did with David [Bailey]; 15 pages in Vogue; it was revolutionary. We did three shows. By the midnight show there was a queue right round the block, the word just got out: I hit my first year's figures in three months.

Was that a ground-breaking show?

Yes. Nothing like it had been seen. Mary Quant had put on some smaller shows. It was like a dam bursting with Mary Quant and Alexander, and having a show with music. We had the Temperance Seven playing. Vidal Sassoon did the hair, and all the top models were there, and were in the photographs [for the shoot] but mostly Jean Shrimpton. And the music was very new. Mary was important, and the 21 Shop, and then Biba. Biba started in 1963 and Ozzie [Clark] left college in 1965. I can remember him sitting in his square glasses.

The industry was smaller then. The Americans would come over twice a year for the shows. Nobody did shows before that, only showroom shows. I had to buy coats and suits, and all you did was go to the showrooms. The models in the showrooms

Figure 1.21 Mary Quant with models. (Mondadori Portfolio/Contributor via Getty Images)

walked up and down and you picked out the numbers. The models for Quant danced around and they didn't do that couture type of walk any more. This is when fashion shows as we know them today started.

Fashion shows were not the important thing that they are today because PR hadn't become that important. That was all just starting. Buyers, like Lucille Lewin at Whistles, would go to all of the shows to decide what to buy. Designers and clothing companies didn't always do shows and exhibitions; sometimes they would go along to see buyers with their collections in stores, and I used to go and see people like Jean Muir in their showrooms.

Did the style of the models change?

The models Claire chose for the 21 Shop show were modern looking, that is why she got 15 pages in Vogue. The models were of that new look. The hair was new because Vidal was doing it. The dancing and the exuberance were amazing, and the amount of clothes we sold; we would get another 1,000 dresses in and they were gone. Then Biba started and they were turning their stock every two weeks - and manufactured in the UK. Everything exploded: there was new music, the 21 Shop and the fashion shows … it was the precursor of so much.

And what about the press?

There was no PR, even for the fashion show. I had all the journalists coming to me. Veronica Papworth at the Express, Ernestine Carter. They would phone me up "have you got a new story?" We were in the right place at the right time.

For the full interview with Vanessa Denza please visit http://www .bloomsbury.com/stark-the-fashion-show

'I was taken to my first fashion show - Nina Ricci haute couture - in Paris by the White Russian princess, down on her luck, whom I was boarding with in Paris in 1963. I was captivated by the glamour of the gilded salon, the elegant clothes, and the audience of grand ladies.'
Suzy Menkes

Some models, such as Twiggy, Jean Shrimpton and Veruschka, became as well-known as designers, pop stars and artists. Stylists also became celebrities because they too created the look of the moment. Quant said of Sassoon that he was 'a kind of Chanel of hair . . . a total revolutionary' and that it took 'Vidal to visualise the near, sharp, dynamic head-line that would finish the London look' (British *Vogue*, 1992).

The British designer Paul Smith, interviewed about the 1960s, said:

I do genuinely think that the 1960s was a very creative period in Britain. I suppose it was after the horror of world war and the repression and depression of all that horrible time. It was the first generation that had the opportunity to really express themselves without any strings attached. But most human beings on the earth would say that their youth is the most exciting time because it's the first time you experience certain things like falling in love, going to music, or being away from your parents . . . (The Talks, 2013)

Youthquake soon spread to Paris where *Left Bank* and *Beatnik* fashion challenged the traditions of the French fashion industry. Some French designers embraced youth fashion, and this was reflected in the energetic, youthful shows of designers such as Yves St Laurent and Dior. Paco Rabanne, known as *l'enfant terrible*, produced shows with set designs influenced by his work designing costume for the film *Barbarella*, mirroring the 1960s fascination with science fiction and space travel. Within just one decade, more creative, relaxed events became the norm, presaging the innovation in show production that was to come.

Meanwhile in the United States, in 1962 the Council of Fashion Designers of America (CFDA) was formed by a group which included the designers Bill Blass and Eleanor Lambert. Today the group supports the development of both established and new American designers within the global fashion industry while staging the yearly fashion awards and raising considerable sums for charity. The group initially brought together the American designers who until then had been hugely competitive. A decade later competition between designers would take place on a more international level at one of fashion's most glamourous historic events took place.

The 1970s

Competition between the fashion capitals of France, Italy and the United States continued into the 1970s. The importance of American fashion became acknowledged by the international press, an important step for the American industry. In 1973, a show was organized to raise money to restore the Palace of Versailles, outside Paris. The collections of five Parisian and five American designers were shown at a glittering event attended by international royalty and celebrities. The show became legendary for many reasons, including the large number of black models used by the American designers, however its enduring memory is captured in the title it was given by the press: 'The Battle of Versailles'.

As international rivalries continued, one of the biggest influences on the fashion show was to come from a new direction. Japanese designers, who brought with them a radically different aesthetic, needed to show in Europe in order to achieve recognition in Japan. The Japanese designer Kenzo established his practice in Paris in 1970 and in 1973 Issey Miyake was the first Japanese designer to be invited to show at the pret-a-porter shows in Paris. They brought a completely different approach to the design and presentation of clothing, unconstrained by the traditions of the fashion show. Issey Miyake used dancers to present his 'Pleats Please' collection and challenged the traditions of using professional models on the runway, instead selecting members of the public. Often colourful, humorous occasions, his models danced and laughed joyfully. However, the full influence of the Japanese designers was yet to come.

Figure 1.23 Issey Miyake FW 1988 Fashion Show. A fashion model playfully walks along the runway in the latest ready-to-wear women's line by Japanese fashion house Issey Miyake at the 1987–1988 fall/winter fashion show in Paris. She wears a mixed plaid outfit of pants, jacket, and gloves with a bowler hat. (Photo by Pierre Vauthey/Sygma/Sygma via Getty Images)

The 1980s: Fashion was never the same again

Free of conventional ideas about show production, the Japanese designers saw different possibilities. Interviewed in 2011, Yamamoto said, 'In 2002, I decided to show my ready-to-wear collection at the timing of the couture. I did it for three seasons. There were less people attending, so the possibility was there to have smaller places and allow people to actually hear the sound of the fabric. It was a very nice parenthesis' (The Talks, 2011). In March 1982, two Japanese designers, Rei Kawakubo and Yohji Yamamoto, produced shows in Paris that were so far removed from the accepted western aesthetic that they shocked the international fashion press.

The Japanese designers took a holistic approach to the show, using all aspects of show production to present the concept of a collection: clothing, set design, hair and make-up, the way that the models moved, music and lighting. In 1983 Kawakubo presented a show called 'Destroy' which shocked the fashion world. Models' make up was displaced on their faces, tattered garments in black distorted the female form and the models moved differently on the runway. It was a moment that changed runway forever: 'models exiting in groups to cold, flashing lights – was as unconventional as the clothes . . . Kawakubo's vision was simply too extreme a contrast to digest. It is the stuff of fashion folklore that more than a few critics left the space in tears' (Fukai, 2010).

The approach of the Japanese designers continues to influence fashion to this day and others began to communicate the concept of a collection through show production, setting a trend that is still prevalent today. Having fundamentally shaken the west's concept of fashion and the fashion show, the Japanese designers led a new avant-garde, intellectual and art-based approach to fashion.

Figure 1.24 Rei Kawakubo has continued to challenge our notions of beauty and our clothing traditions. Comme des Garcons SS2008 ready-to-wear collection show in Paris, France, October 2007. (Francois Guillot/Staff via Getty Images)

Figure 1.25 Kawakubo's protégé, Junya Watanabe, ready-to-wear collection AW2009. A model in black clothing and black wig poses on a black runway. (Chris Moore/Catwalking/Contributor via Getty Images)

Club culture

While Japanese designers were stimulating a more conceptual, art-based approach to fashion, another influence would ensure that runway became integrated within contemporary culture. The arts had influenced show production for over a century and in the 1980s, the *club culture* movement in London brought fashion and music together through runway more powerfully than ever before. Designers and stylists who were part of the club culture scene carried its theatricality onto the runway through strong music, extreme styling and a drama that was a natural magnet for the press. Through the influence of club culture, fashion and the arts came together on the runway, thoroughly integrating the show into our popular culture. The 1980s also saw shows of a very different kind receive equal press interest, but for very different reasons.

Corporate runway and conspicuous consumption

In the 1980s the marketing of fashion started to become more sophisticated and with it the use of the fashion show. Large organizations bought historic fashion houses, treating them as brands with an inevitable emphasis on commerce over creativity. Bernard Arnault acquired Christian Dior and the Moet Hennessey Louis Vuitton (LVMH) group. Thus began the corporate management of fashion which brought large investment. Designers were asked to harness the runway show to generate excitement that would inject energy into the newly acquired brands and bring a return in the form of profit. Fashion companies began to promote the concepts of *designer products* and a *designer lifestyle*, and the consumer responded with enthusiasm. As Colin McDowell wrote: 'We were to be turned into label shoppers. Designer became a catch-all expression used, misused and abused, in order to label anything with pretensions to exclusivity and originality' (1994). Shows became more extravagant as fashion companies competed to attract publicity. Couture did not make money, but shows were used to generate excitement to sell fashion's lucrative spin-off products: perfume, tights and cosmetics.

Super-shows and supermodels

Celebrities in the form of film stars, musicians and royalty were used to attract press attention and celebrities appeared on the runway. Designers themselves became super-celebrities and consumers were fed photographs of them leading a celebrity lifestyle. The higher profile the celebrities, the more press coverage was achieved. A further outcome of the excess was the supermodel phenomenon. While celebrity models were nothing new, the use of the term *supermodel* reflected the mood of the time. The supermodels became super-celebrities, and the cachet of being a model remains to this day, despite the small amounts that most models earn for runway work. A sad consequence of the huge sums paid to supermodels was the vast increase in the cost of show production which then became the norm, increasing the divide between well-funded brands and young designers.

Figure 1.26 Karen Mulder, Linda Evangelista, Gianni Versace and Carla Bruni at the Versace Fashion Show at the Ritz Hotel on 1 January 1992 in Paris, France. (Foc Kan/ Contributor via Getty Images)

The 1990s: From brash excess to an intellectualizing of fashion

As the 1980s tipped into the 1990s, the supermodel phenomenon was in full swing. The supermodels were treated like film stars and were flown around the world first class. It was rumoured that they refused to rehearse and they demanded to wear particular outfits. One supermodel became renowned for being difficult if someone else wore the outfit that she preferred. They could look disdainful as they prowled down the runways and one of the most famous sayings of fashion was coined by Linda Evangelista when she told *People* magazine that supermodels didn't get out of bed for less than $10,000 a day.

Superstar models killed clothes

The supermodel phenomenon refocused attention from clothing, and while supermodels could lift dull clothing, they distracted from interesting collections. The supermodels also had prominent personalities. The designer Romeo Gigli deliberately chose not to use celebrity models, believing that they overshadowed the clothes. Instead he used 'regular girls'. Other designers, however, paid ludicrously high amounts for supermodels. The Italian designer Gianni Versace was credited with creating the supermodel phenomenon. While unlikely, he did create dramatic shows with an abundance of supermodels. There was huge debate about how much his shows had cost. The obsession with supermodels had other consequences, including the fascination with backstage which continues today.

Backlash

During the 1990s, a backlash against the brash excesses and conspicuous consumption was echoed in fashion shows that took a subtler approach, as epitomized by Rifat Osbek's all-white collection, simply shown, that was widely reported as heralding a new age. (The show can be watched on YouTube at https://www.youtube.com/watch?v=bjD4nvyOymc.) There was growing anxiety about war and recession. The number of American buyers and journalists visiting Europe markedly dropped. As British *Vogue* reported in April 1991: 'amid empty seats of absent American customers and journalists, there was anxious talk of war' and for the Paris couture houses the 'crisis in the gulf is being felt particularly keenly . . . for many have relied on Middle Eastern clients'. There was much debate about whether couture would survive. Balmain closed its couture workrooms and fashion houses increasingly relied on the sale of licensed products.

Figure 1.27 Christy Turlington models for Anna Sui in her SS1994 show. Such was the wealth of the super-brands with their super-shows that young designers struggled to compete. Christy, Naomi Campbell, Linda Evangelista and other supermodels modelled for Sui early in the 1990s in exchange for clothing, thereby attracting the press and helping Sui to establish her name. (Photographer: Niall McInerney, © Bloomsbury Publishing Plc.)

Figure 1.28 Margiela's backlash included using mannequins on the runway instead of models to demonstrate the importance of clothing over models, and at another show men in white lab coats held garments on hangers while the collection was shown on models on a film. (Guy Marineau/Contributor via Getty Images)

Industry Insight

Francesco Brunessci

The journalist Francesco Brunessci worked creatively with Gigli on his shows.

> I remember some very interesting catwalks like the last Romeo Gigli show at the Pershing Hall Hotel in Paris. We talked for hours about the concept and vision of some shows. My position was unusual. I was a journalist, used to working outside the brand but now working inside. I knew what my colleagues wanted to see but I knew that we had to promote the brand. The Pershing Hall challenge was how to create Romeo Gigli's world, which was at the time very poetic, in a hotel in the centre of Paris.
>
> We decided to do something very simple. It was a T with all the chairs around. On each chair with beige cover, just a tulip. Romeo didn't know whether this would be his last fashion show so there was huge pressure. We couldn't let the press know. Romeo's idea was to make all the models dance, but it was impossible to have dancers. First, we found the faces Romeo wanted: classical faces like Reubens, with very light make-up just on the eyes, chignons . . . and the gowns . . . We did a casting to find the faces and at the end we chose all the models that had a background as dancers. We had a dance choreographer and a fashion director.
>
> We could see the hotel's vertical garden. We used natural light with just some lights where the models were in the sweet spot. The result was extraordinary because it was very simple, it was like writing a poem with simple words. As always it finished with a wedding gown. It was in tulle with lots of knots. I watched people's faces during the show and there was huge emotion because it was beautiful. It wasn't a catwalk and it wasn't a dance and it wasn't a typical fashion show.
>
> Romeo was a writer and an artist . . . it was literature, it was telling a story . . . his appreciation of beauty . . . I always remember the hours of rehearsals for the shows to make it as good as it could be. And catering: I remember hours spent finding a decorator in Milan able to fold pieces of paper, and invitations written by hand: a huge number of different crafts people.

For the full interview with Francesco Brunessci please visit http://www.bloomsbury.com/stark-the-fashion-show.

Figure 1.29 Deconstruction and reproducing traditional and period clothes in the 1990s. Linda Evangelista in Vivienne Westwood AW1993/1994. (Niall McInerney, © Bloomsbury Publishing Plc.)

Figure 1.30 The finale of Alexander McQueen's SS1999 show was inspired by an installation by artist Rebecca Horn. Model Shalom Harlow stood on a revolving platform in the centre of the performance space, wearing a simple white dress, while two robots sprayed yellow and black paint on the rotating dress. (Niall McInerney, © Bloomsbury Publishing Plc.)

'I have always found the British Fashion Council [BFC] very supportive. Lee [McQueen] was one of the designers that enabled me to get on well with the BFC. … Some designers would always rather be more creative and show elsewhere … but practically you do have to try to keep people in the right place at the right time. But it did go through a phase in the early 90s where people were dashing all over London, showing in absolutely crazy places.' Kim Blake, who sourced locations with Alexander McQueen for his early shows

The environment

There was growing concern about the environment and this was reflected in the early 1990s in the work of designers such as Martin Margiela. *Deconstruction* of clothing symbolized the wish of younger designers to deconstruct the new form and structure of corporate fashion. On the runway designers such as Margiela played with ideas about recycling, and there was renewed interest in using runway to communicate the concepts behind collections. More fashion companies were being absorbed by the likes of LVMH and while large fashion houses continued to produce expensive shows, small designers were following a different trend. They began to challenge convention, producing shows in alternative locations: old warehouses, disused buildings and the edgier areas of cities.

A new type of fashion show

During the 1990s a new form of spectacle emerged on the runway. Arising from the fusion of fashion and art, and the conceptual approach of the Japanese designers, the impetus was partly the desire to communicate a holistic concept, but it was also an attempt to gain the publicity that the excessive shows of the 1980s had already demonstrated was possible. Young designers, steeped in the zeitgeist of fashion and music of London's street and club culture, applied their creative energies to the design of their shows as well as their collections to attract essential press coverage. The shows of John Galliano and Alexander McQueen were some of the most extreme, generating substantial attention and helping to establish them as legendary designers.

Industry Insight
Kim Blake

In the 1980s and 1990s as designers such as John Galliano and Alexander McQueen emerged from art college, the powerful conglomerates had big budgets to promote established brands. One of the only ways that young designers could attract attention was to stage a stunning, shocking or otherwise newsworthy fashion show. At the beginning of her career, Kim Blake of Kim Blake PR worked with Alexander McQueen on his now famous show 'The Birds'. Kim works with many fashion companies and designers on the PR for their events.

Figure 1.31 Kim Blake.

What was your first show and how did you get into PR?

The only day I bunked off school was to work on an Ozzie Clark show, that was my first taste of fashion. I went to dress. Bianca Jagger was modelling and I thought it was the most glamorous thing in the world. I got an Ozzie Clark suit for doing it. When I started out, I was head of press for Whistles and we did small internal presentations. Lucille [Lewin] used to buy from incredible young designers. Lucille would talk about trends and how pieces should be sold in the stores. Each shop had a loyal customer base and Lucille would give girls knowledge to sell the stock.

Then you started your fashion PR business?

Yes, the first show was for Sonja Nuttall who worked with Nigel Atkinson. Sonja had the girls step in coloured powder on white paper so there were footprints all over: it was beautiful. Then Alexander McQueen became part of my stable, and it was an extraordinary time. With McQueen I saw the fashion show from a completely different angle. The first show I worked on with McQueen from beginning to end was 'The Birds'. We had a limited amount of money, but every model that he asked did it free: everybody wanted to be on board. Everyone had fabulous ideas, but you still have to put it into production. There were no computers and I only had one phone line which was jammed, we had people mobbing our office.

How did you manage the press attention?

I don't think we slept. We couldn't afford security. You had to know everyone who was coming in. Amy from the *New York Times* turned up late and I had to bring her in through an underground car park to get her through the crowds. A friend of mine was filming; it was as basic as that. We all called in favours for many years.

How did you manage post show PR?

It was difficult because a lot of it didn't go into production – everyone wanted the outfits. That collection was created for the catwalk; it was other stuff that sold. That is how catwalk works. When I got home that night, my phone was full of messages from journalists saying it was one of the most amazing shows they'd seen. To start your career on a high like that was incredibly lucky.

Did you get sponsorship?

I was working with young newsworthy designers: not much money, but a lot of incredible creative talent. We also worked in Paris. A lot of young French designers became part of the stable because we could attract the British press. We did New York as well, taking British and French designers out. There was more funding around; or did we manage with a lot less money?

Sometimes you did PR *and* show production?

When someone asked me to PR their show, they might have a producer on board they'd worked with before, or I would say 'I would like you to meet these producers'. In New York, you did PR and show production. The producer would liaise with the designer for castings, and as PR we would probably get hair and make-up in. We were there every step of the way.

Figure 1.32 Alexander McQueen was fascinated by birds and their motifs repeatedly appeared in his shows. Here is McQueen carrying a falcon at the end of the Givenchy AW1997 show in Paris. (Pierre Verdy/ Staff via Getty Images)

How do you keep press lists up to date?

It used to be word of mouth and then there was *Fashion Monitor*. Invitations: most designers have favourite graphic designers. Most of it goes out by email now but you would still send a hard copy to someone like Suzy [Menkes]. We were given the international press lists by the BFC a couple of weeks beforehand. You are given which hotels people are staying in to hand-deliver invitations, that is often an intern job.

Did you seat the journalists?

Yes, I liked to know who had come in. You can't trust that to anyone else. There are always dramas about who to sit where. It is a different front row today. You should be able to get people in quickly and sit them. If you're doing things in the official venues, you know when people are running late. There is always an efficient timeline, so you can tell everyone backstage that you are running late or that everything is on schedule.

As a PR what else do you do before a show?

I used to phone and ask, 'Do you need a car?' Often we would try to sell an exclusive. You would organize backstage interviews. I would phone the press and say, 'There's not much left on the schedule, would you like a slot?' With popular designers, the press would come to you. It was more television backstage. Journalists are off to their next show and would only have five minutes. Interviews backstage were always tight.

What would happen after a show?

Waiting for newspapers to come out. The BFC would put all the press on a board. Nowadays it is all sent out. You had to make sure that you had good photographs. You would have your own photographer or you would buy from Chris Moore. You would select photographs at the end of the show (or overnight before digital) then you would send out the photographs. Now you can do so immediately; it has changed the way everyone works.

Did you start the shows?

Yes, I would say 'everyone's seated, let's go'. During the show, I would watch the press then go backstage. With designers like McQueen I had to have security everywhere. If there were sponsors, you would have a 'step-and-repeat-board'. The designer could stand in front of it to be interviewed. Then, on to the next show. I used to do three a day at London Fashion Week. You had to get the stuff out to press overnight, so not much sleep. You need huge amounts of energy to work in fashion PR at show time. As soon as one show is over, PRs start to look for sponsorship for the next.

Figure 1.33 More costume than fashion and more theatre than runway: Galliano's Orient Express show for Dior, AW1998, with clothing inspired by Henry III. (Guy Marineau/ Contributor via Getty Images)

Spectacle and performance: The late 1990s

Having successfully staged spectacular alternative shows to promote their names, designers such as Galliano and McQueen were ironically offered lucrative jobs in powerful corporate fashion. In 1995 Givenchy in Paris employed John Galliano, and a year later he moved to Christian Dior (while McQueen moved to Givenchy). Their work at these long-established fashion houses involved the creative direction of fashion shows, and with the financial backing of wealthy brands behind them, the fashion world witnessed some of history's most spectacular shows.

Fashion meets fantasy

Galliano's show called 'A Fashion Opera' for Dior's SS1998 collection was shown at the Opera House in Paris. The set was pure fantasy, inspired by Luisa Casati, a flamboyant and eccentric patroness of the arts in the early 1900s. The collection was more costume than fashion and the production more theatre than fashion. Tim Blanks has watched many fashion shows: 'it was a spectacle, it wasn't designed to do anything other really than promote Dior . . . these shows . . . were only staged once . . . so it is in my memory as the most vivid fashion experience I have ever had' (Style.com, 2013). (Watch Blanks reflect on the show in full in the YouTube video by Style.com at https://www.youtube.com/watch?v=0TajifB1KWA.)

In Paris, the shows drawing the most attention were fantasy spectacles; in Italy the likes of Versace and Tom Ford for Gucci were producing altogether more sophisticated spectacles. Responding to a new confidence in women, the emphasis was on overt sexuality: tasteful and elegant in the case of Ford, excessive and flashy in the case of Versace.

Runway as commentary

In sharp contrast to the fantasy shows of Galliano and the spectacles of Gucci, Viktor and Rolf's work in the 1990s approached the role of the fashion show in a completely new way, promoting the new intellectualization of fashion. Rather than creating commercial collections, they produced shows during which fashion was manipulated and commented upon through performance. As Rebecca Arnold observed, 'their designs became one-offs, rare pieces that existed only as comments on the role of the show within the fashion system, rather than wearable garments' (2009). Viktor and Rolf's AW1999/2000 show needed just one fashion model. She stood on a revolving platform as they dressed her in one layer of clothing after another until she was wearing the entire collection. (Watch the show here: https://www.youtube.com/watch?v=MZXR-HkIOrU.) Once again, the relationship between fashion, art and performance was manifest on the runway, as Viktor and Rolf played with both the practices of fashion and the practices of show production. They could be said to have used the show as a means of artistic expression, but Arnold points out their 'work is shown in the context of the international fashion weeks, it is directed to a fashion audience . . . Even when they were not putting their clothing into production, they followed the fashion seasons' (2009).

Figure 1.34 Viktor and Rolf, SS2005, where anonymous models in black helmets walked to the sound of military drums. The second part of the show was as pink as the first half was black. (Michel Dufour/Contributor via Getty Images)

The biggest transformation yet

As Viktor and Rolf's commentaries on fashion were taking place, so too was the biggest transformation in the history of the fashion show since the industrial revolution. Until the 1990s, only the privileged few witnessed runway live as it happened. The technological revolution and the popularization of the Internet were to bring previously unimaginable opportunities to fashion show production and to a worldwide audience of fashion consumers.

As the world entered the new millennium, the fashion show had evolved from the privacy of the couturiers' salons in Paris into a sophisticated spectacle that is a powerful international marketing tool, promoting brands within a global economy. The runway had become a form of entertainment and part of our popular culture. During the early 2000s, technological advances were to bring more far reaching opportunities to fashion and the runway show. With the advent of the Internet the show could be filmed and watched on the Internet by millions around in the world. Yet more exciting, live streaming, experienced during fashion weeks in 2009 and 2010, meant that shows could be watched as they happened: a phenomenon that was to change fashion runway and eventually the fashion industry itself forever. The technological revolution, and its continuing impact on the fashion show will be explored in depth in later chapters of this book.

Activities

01. The evolution of the fashion show

Select images from fashion shows in three different decades over the last century (the 1940s or 1950s, the 1960s to 1980s, and the 1990s or 2010s would be ideal). Compare the different elements of the shows, for instance:

A. The venue

B. The set, including runway, lighting, seating and all other elements of 'the build'

C. The audience

D. The look of the models

E. The way in which the models move and pose

F. Hair and make up

G. The clothing

H. The accessories

I. The relationship between models and audience (and compere or sales people)

J. The 'feel' of the event

02. The fashion show within its wider contexts

Source images of fashion shows during a particular five-year period. For that same period of time, find images of other products from that era: new architecture, book covers, new product designs, vinyl/disc covers, furniture, cars, food and so on. Create a storyboard and paste images onto the board along with any found objects that you can find. Source some music from the period so that you can present both visual and audio materials. You could also create a second board to show the broader context, and this could include images, text and found objects to represent what was happening socially, economically, politically, environmentally and technologically during this period.

03. A different aesthetic

Select images from one of the shows produced by a Japanese designer during the latter 1980s. Compare and illustrate the show, the garments and the styling of hair, make-up and accessories with the shows of other designers from around the world at the same time.

04. A new kind of fashion show

Conduct research into a spectacular show. Examples of designers you might choose:

A. Alexander McQueen

B. John Galliano

C. Viktor and Rolf

D. Vivienne Westwood

E. Gareth Pugh

F. Marc Jacobs

G. Maison Martin Margiela

H. Rick Owens

Research and discuss:

A. The meaning behind the show

B. The different elements of the show production

C. How it was reported in the media

2

Contemporary contexts of the fashion show

Chapter Two sets the fashion show within its contemporary contexts. It examines the various purposes of the show and offers a global perspective of runway. It explains the fashion calendar and the role of the show within the fashion system. It investigates the social, ethical and environmental issues pertinent to show production and importantly, Chapter Two observes how new technologies are being used in conjunction with the traditional format of the show, and more radically, how the use of technology at fashion weeks has started to revolutionize both the runway show and the fashion industry.

Fashion people talk about *moments*: these are points at which fashion shifts, and they are often played out on the runway. Suzy Menkes has said that she lives for 'those moments when there is a sense that nothing after this show will ever be the same': 'Prada had a moment in the mid-nineties, which was the beginning of the ugly aesthetic – the end of sweet colors, and so forth. Rei Kawakubo, of Comme des Garcons, had a moment like that in the late nineties, with those punk-rock clothes, and Helmut had a moment when he did feathers under clear plastic, and another moment when he did his angel-wing collection'.
Seabrook, 2001

Why are there still fashion shows?

People flocked to the early salons in Paris, because attending the Openings was the only way to see new collections. Today, through digital technology, images of collections speed around the world within seconds, so why do we still hold so many live fashion shows? Much of the clothing sold to consumers never appears on the runway, yet the year is packed with shows and industry professionals could spend the entire year attending shows. Suzy Menkes wrote: 'I already spend five weeks at a time hopping between fashion capitals, there is no way that I can spend an extra month in New York – even if that is where the majority of saleable designer clothes are seen' (Menkes, 2013).

Figure 2.1 Marc Jacobs' own label show at New York Fashion Week in February 2011. (Victor Virgile/Contributor via Getty Images)

Lavish productions

Show production is expensive, it takes months to plan, and many shows last for less than 10 minutes. At their most extreme and most expensive are shows such as those by Chanel or Marc Jacobs. The SS2014 Louis Vuitton show was Marc Jacobs' last for the company and it involved a set with a fairground carousel, four elevators, escalators and a fountain. Marc Jacobs' own label show at New York Fashion Week in February 2011 was widely reported to have cost at *least* $1m and it lasted about nine-and-a-half minutes. The set build involved shipping vinyl cloth from California and the production included 63 models, 35 make-up stylists, 50 hair stylists, 70 dressers and 500 guests (Trebay, 2011).

There are other ways of showing collections. Some designers have produced innovative film as an alternative to a runway. The British designer Gareth Pugh's fashion film shown at Paris Fashion Week for SS2011, created with Ruth Hogben and SHOWstudio, created excitement within the fashion community and can be viewed on YouTube. For AW2015 AllSaints showed a film at London Fashion Week, which could be viewed globally through their website and social media, and customers could purchase product immediately. Like runway, films can create excitement and be visually fantastical. So, why are there still so many live fashion shows? Fashion is a complex industry and the answer to this question is equally complex.

Fashion shows are an incredibly powerful marketing tool, and harnessing the power of the runway to promote the fashion product is the primary purpose of the show today.

Johnny Wang

The young London womenswear designer Johnny Wang has produced film as part of his creative output which has been shown on the digital schedule at London Fashion Week.

I did films way back at uni. I made my first film for my interview at Alexander McQueen; it was very much inspired by SHOWstudio and a trip to see Nick Knight's exhibition at Somerset House [London]. That film was a way of showing my work in 3D form and on a model in a setting. Also, I could create something with music because music is so important. It was a way to show the work as a holistic experience. Then when I worked for Phoebe English we did various films. The idea to make fashion films has been constant. More recently for my own brand I did a film for each collection. We had a bit of budget even though it was tight. We were lucky enough to collaborate with sound engineers, stylists, make-up artists and set designers so we had a whole group of people to work on the film to realise a concept . . . also my background in TV production . . . it was natural for me to use film. We showed film at Fashion Week for 2 seasons. I had shown with BFC [British Fashion Council] for a season before. They invited me to show on the digital schedule. Being on the official schedule means your work being exposed to the entire BFC contacts list. For young start-up designers runway is too expensive and the outcome doesn't always reflect the amount of effort.

To read the full interview with Johnny Wang please visit http://www.bloomsbury.com/the-fashion-show-9781472568489.

Harnessing the power of runway

Harnessing the power of the runway to promote fashion products is the primary purpose of the show today. Since the corporate management of fashion in the 1980s, the industry has used the fashion show as one of a range of powerful and sophisticated marketing techniques to persuade the consumer to purchase as much, and as often, as possible. Shows perpetuate the glamour that brands seek to be associated with and they generate the excitement that makes people aspire to buy the licensed products that sell in large quantities. The Italian brands Prada and Gucci developed as leather goods and accessories companies, but didn't sell clothing until relatively recently. Prada showed its first womenswear collection in 1988. Both now have clothing lines, enabling them to present runway shows. Models are choreographed to hold accessories blatantly so that they are prominent in photographs. Such is the power of the fashion show as a marketing tool that Chapter Three is devoted to marketing and PR. However, the fashion show also serves other purposes, socially, culturally and in business, some of which are explored below.

Fashion weeks are times for the fashion community to congregate and communicate

The fashion show is a tradition, woven into the very fabric of the way that the industry works, an essential element of the fashion system. Fashion weeks are the occasions when the fashion community congregates to observe and assimilate new collections, to be part of the zeitgeist and to understand the direction that fashion is taking. Trends, new textile applications and colours are identified and new models are spotted. New collections move things forward incrementally, but sometimes a designer will present something that will truly move fashion forward. It is at fashion weeks that there are what Suzy Menkes called 'those moments when there is a sense that nothing after this show will ever be the same' (Seabrook, 2001).

Shows like McQueen's are very important in this industry. It's a dreamland, a fantasy world – you're seeing something you have never seen before, and that breeds excitement. Fashion needs those kind of visionaries to evolve it into the next phase.

Justin O'Shea, Buying Director at Mytheresa .com, quoted in Harris, 2014

Figure 2.2 The Prada runway show at Milan Fashion Week in February 2013 showing the collection for AW2013/2014. Bag, shoes, sunglasses and belt are all prominently displayed. (Victor Virgile/Contributor via Getty Images)

Communication

Designers present the ideas and concepts embodied in their collections through the medium of the show. We do not see the garment designs in isolation; we see a performance that communicates the designer's philosophy. For some designers, the fashion show is important because it is the only time when they can communicate about a collection and its meaning. Dries van Noten, being interviewed by dazeddigital.com, stated:

> The fashion show is a very important moment for me every time, because it's the only moment when I really can explain what the collection is about. We don't have advertising and it's not that I go to parties often. For me it's more like theatre. The colour of the light, the soundtrack, the way that models move, all these very small elements are what make the imagery clear. That for me is a very important thing. (McCord, 2014)

Figure 2.3 Alexander McQueen's AW1998 show was inspired by Joan of Arc. (Photographer: Niall McInerney, © Bloomsbury Publishing Plc.)

Figure 2.4 The finale of McQueen's Joan of Arc show was a model surrounded by a ring of fire. (Photographer: Niall McInerney, © Bloomsbury Publishing Plc.)

Runway images

Runway images are very important for designers and brands. Sent out to the press, used on websites, in social media, in magazines and books, advertising, store windows, on swing tags, packaging and in myriad other ways, they affirm that the brand is prestigious enough to have a show while communicating important brand messages. Runway photographs have become so important that some designers have these 2D images in mind while working on new collections. The industry uses photographs from the runway during the season, referencing them with journalists, stylists and for production.

Runway for sales

The runway started as a method of selling to the consumer. Today, while the very wealthy will buy what they see live on the runway, the shows are largely intended for retail buyers to determine what to order. While *showpieces* may not be intended to sell in large quantities, if at all, other pieces do and buyers use the shows to choose pieces and to understand the stories around the collections.

Trade shows

Except for sales to the very wealthy, shows have until relatively recently been about business-to-business (B2B) communication. Trade shows are large events, filled with exhibition stands at which fashion companies present their latest collections. Trade shows also feature runway shows where they tend to be pragmatic, with a strong focus on presenting product. Trade shows are attended by buyers, who talk with designers, view new collections and place orders. There are many trade shows around the world, for instance, Pure in London, the Dallas Apparel & Accessories Market and Bread & Butter in Berlin. Like fashion weeks, trade shows focus on specialist areas of fashion, for instance, lingerie buyers might attend the Salon International de la Lingerie in Paris.

Industry Insight

Lou Dalton

Figure 2.5 Lou Dalton. (© Lou Dalton)

The menswear designer Lou Dalton shows two collections a year at London Fashion Week Men's. While Lou will hope for as much publicity as possible, her primary motivation is to show a collection which buyers and consumers will want to purchase. The shows help the buyers decide what to stock for the coming season.

How have your shows helped you to build your business?

I have grown to have a love/hate relationship with the catwalk show of late. These last two seasons I decided to take a wee sabbatical of sorts from the catwalk and concentrate more on product and sales and less about show. Although, as a creative where seasonal collections are the order of the day, it's still key to try and engage as it helps bring attention to the collection, which will hopefully trickle through to the consumer buy. It helps for sure but it's key that one stays focused on what it is we are trying to do and achieve: sell clothes or just get press . . . They are two very different things, press is important but the punter on the street will be the one who will ultimately keep the business afloat.

For you, what is the relationship between selling your collections and sales of the collection?

Unlike some designers and fashion houses, where they will produce two collections, one driven towards sales and one purely for press, I, like many emerging brands, produce one collection which must cover both jobs. Therefore, it is key that you engage the press and the consumer as one. The industry has changed of late, it's far more important to sell clothes than to produce a collection just for press. These days due to financial logistics a return in the form of sales is key.

Figure 2.6 Lou Dalton London Fashion Week Men's, January 2017. (John Phillips/Stringer via Getty Images)

What do you think the biggest changes to menswear shows have been and how has this affected your work as a designer?

A few seasons back the industry and its supporters seemed a little more cash rich but of late, due to company budgets from high street to high fashion being cut, it's unsettling times. It costs a great deal of money to put on a show. These costs get evaluated season on season against the return in sales performance. Of course, this will affect what you do as a designer, how you approach and present your collections. I have always been incredibly determined to maintain a presence within the industry and when tackled with such issues one learns to make changes accordingly and to diversify the business to accommodate all and to allow the business to keep going.

Fashion shows are done for three reasons, which I think a lot of people lose sight of . . . The second one is to sell and that affects how you do your show. If the purpose is to sell, you are going to do your show differently.
Interview with John Walford, 2013

Figure 2.7 The Chanel cruise collection, shown in May 2014 on an island off the coast of Dubai, with a set designed to look like a Middle Eastern souk. (Marwan Naamani/Staff via Getty Images)

Maintaining a consumer base

Chanel's cruise collection, from which the brand makes high sales, has a reputation for being shown in exotic locations: the May 2014 cruise collection was shown on a manmade island off the coast of Dubai. Most commented on in the press was the abundance of Chanel clothing worn by the audience, so that as the 1,000 international guests arrived, the event looked strikingly like a homage to Chanel's creative director, Karl Lagerfeld. Lagerfeld reciprocated by referencing Dubai, including its skyline, in his designs, resulting in a fashion show designed to cement the relationship between the brand and the city.

Retail shows

Retail stores use fashion shows to entice customers into a store, to make loyal customers feel valued and to show new stock. Shows also set a store in the minds of the consumer as an important arbiter of the new and the fashionable. The famous department store Galeries Lafayette, in central Paris, holds weekly fashion shows where customers can watch models wearing the season's latest trends. The *trunk show* was developed in America when designers travelled to different cities with trunks containing their latest collections. Trunk shows started in the early 1900s and if a designer was present, the store would sell a lot more clothing. Today, companies still hold trunk shows, primarily in America.

The benefits of trunk shows are that customers can view a whole collection, see and feel the garments, see them on models and understand how different pieces work together. They feel privileged that they are meeting the designer and hearing from them about the collection, sometimes before it is available in store. Designers such as Donna Karan, Michael Kors and Bill Blass have a big trunk show circuit around America every year. It is a gruelling schedule, but sales can reach hundreds of thousands of dollars in one day. Stores such as Saks Fifth Avenue have been holding virtual trunk shows. With much bigger potential audiences and cutting out the gruelling circuit, these are proving a popular digital form of the traditional trunk show.

Peter Robinson

Peter Robinson, head of press and events at The White Company, talks about a press day show for high street retailer Marks & Spencer (M&S) in the UK:

We did a fashion show as part of our press day, we had a static exhibition at the Old Post Office just outside Victoria . . . we did quite a big production. I think we had 30 to 35 models, each with 3 to 4 looks . . . the purpose was to introduce M&S in a different way, it was quite unusual then for high street retailers to do fashion shows, we had a show producer, a stylist, and it was beautifully lit. People could use that as a tool to call in outfits directly from the show. The Look Book that we gave away at the press day . . . people could recognize outfits from the show.

There was a press release and line sheet on each of the chairs . . . it was almost the way that salon shows work. It looked very beautiful and was quite applauded within the press. It was not the first high street fashion show, but it was unusual at that point, so at that moment everyone watched M&S. As well as inviting the London-based press to that show, we invited signature press from all of the major cities around the UK, also from some of the international cities.

For full interview text, see http://www .bloomsbury.com/the-fashion-show-9781472 568489.

Entering new markets

As brands have opened stores in new cities they have produced shows designed to create excitement in the target market. Givenchy's first show in New York in September 2015 saw creative director Riccardo Tisci work with performance artist Marina Abramović on a show that mixed fashion with live performance. Held on the anniversary of 9/11, the show referenced different cultures and religions. The large set of recycled metal panels and wooden shards was built on a pier on the Hudson River. The audience sat on wooden pallets and comprised industry professionals but also members of the public as the company used the event to promote the brand in advance of the opening of its New York store.

Retailers and press shows

Fashion companies organize press days to show new collections to journalists, and they sometimes incorporate a fashion show. Press days help the media to get a feel for a collection and brands hope that they will feature it in their publications. The press use the brand's images in their publications or call in garments or accessories for editorial shoots.

In-house shows

Fashion companies hold in-house shows to communicate to their staff about a new season's products. Good product knowledge is essential to selling fashion, and runway can explain the story of a collection and show how products work together, the looks they can create and how they can be styled. Everyone loves a fashion show and the event can generate excitement for a new season's range to the people who will work directly with the consumer to sell the brand.

It was quite unusual then for high street retailers to do fashion shows ... People could use that as a tool to call in outfits directly from the show. The Look Book that we gave away at the press day ... people could recognize outfits from the show. Interview with Peter Robinson

Launching new designers

Many universities present their graduates' collections in fashion shows. Some universities present graduates' work in larger events such as Graduate Fashion Week in London which comprises exhibitions, runway shows, workshops and talks. A fashion show is very expensive but enables a young designer to gain visibility. There are organizations that support young designers. One of the most significant is the *ANDAM Fashion Award* in France which supports young designers to produce a fashion show at Paris Fashion Week. The first winner of the ANDAM award in 1989 was the internationally recognized designer Martin Margiela. Likewise, the *H&M Design Award* offered a prize for its 2015 competition of €50,000 and the opportunity to show a collection at Fashion Week Stockholm. In New York, VFILES supports emerging designers to show their collections at New York Fashion Week. In London, *Fashion East* supports three womenswear and three menswear designers each year. Sponsorship includes mentoring, in-house PR and advising. Support for a runway show at London Fashion Week includes show production and a free venue, photographs and video of the show.

Raising funds for charity

The runway show is a good way to raise funds for charity. A fashion show has good entertainment value – people love runway. Companies will often lend clothing to support a charity and famous models and other celebrities may be persuaded to model or attend in the interests of raising funds for the charity. Sometimes a charity fashion show is combined with a dinner and/or an auction. Money is raised through ticket sales or through an auction.

Figure 2.9 Oriole Cullen, Senior Curator at the Victoria and Albert Museum in London, UK (photograph by Amber Rowlands)

Runway as exhibition

Some museums and galleries produce shows to exhibit the work of designers. The Victoria and Albert Museum in London holds fashion shows and the series is called 'Fashion in Motion'. Senior curator Oriole Cullen explains in more detail:

> *The Victoria and Albert Museum is here to bring things to people. The Fashion in Motion shows, with the applause and the clapping, are very different to Fashion Week. There is no pressure for the designers because there is no critique. The shows are about celebrating creativity, about engaging with contemporary design and making it accessible. There are often students in the audience and family. There is a good following; the fashion world follows and supports the V&A and other designers support the shows.*
>
> *Physically 1,600 people come through the door [for each show day]. Most exhibitions at the V&A last for months but logistically, Fashion in Motion can't be for more than one day. But there are other material outcomes. The shows extend the archives. It's impossible to collect every designer for reasons of space, time and budget so Fashion in Motion provides a photographic archive and web-based material. It is about the V&A engaging with contemporary designers to show clothing.*

The Fashion in Motion shows, film of backstage set up and of interviews with designers can be viewed on the Victoria and Albert Museum website here: http://www.vam.ac.uk/page/f/fashion-in-motion.

For the full interview with Oriole Cullen please visit http://www.bloomsbury.com/the-fashion-show-9781472568489.

Runway as entertainment

Finally, whether it is a high-profile industry event, a charity show or a school production, the fashion show is a form of entertainment. The theatrical elements of the show mean that whatever else its purpose might be – with audience and performers, loud music, bright lights and a sense of spectacle – it is always fundamentally also entertainment. Fashion is as much about fantasy and escapism as it is about clothing. As observed in the ID online debate entitled 'Fashion shows are so last year': 'Fashion offers a window into another world of sex and magic and beauty, it offers an escape from the every day and that's why it's so compelling' (Kissick, 2014).

The fashion system and the fashion calendar

There are well over 100 fashion weeks each year worldwide. Fashion week is the name given to a period of roughly a week, when professionals within the fashion industry gather in a particular city to see the latest fashion designs being presented through formats such as fashion shows, films and static exhibitions. Fashion professionals such as buyers, the media, designers and photographers, together with celebrities and other influencers travel to attend and/or work at fashion weeks. Traditionally, women's ready-to-wear fashion collections are shown in fashion weeks, starting in New York and moving on to London, Milan and then Paris (known as the *Big Four*). These are followed by weeks in other cities, including Tokyo, Berlin, Los Angeles and São Paulo. Other *fashion weeks* also sit within the calendar and include menswear shows, haute couture and events which focus on other fashion categories such as swimwear or lingerie. Altaroma is the Italian haute couture fashion week showing demi-couture and neocouture as well as haute couture, and SwimShow in Miami, Florida, in the United States is the biggest swimwear show internationally.

January	London Fashion Week (Men's)
	Pitti Uomo (Florence, Menswear Collections)
	Milan Fashion Week (Menswear)
	Haute Couture (Paris)
February/March	New York Fashion Week (Men's)
	New York Fashion Week (Women's)
	London Fashion Week
	Milan Fashion Week
	Paris Fashion Week
May	Miami Fashion Week (Men's)
	Resort New York
June	London Fashion Week (Men's)
	Pitti Uomo (Florence, Menswear Collections)
	Milan Fashion Week (Menswear)
	Paris Fashion Week (Men's)
July	Haute Couture (Paris)
	New York Fashion Week (Men's)
September/October	New York Fashion Week (Women's)
	London Fashion Week
	Milan Fashion Week
	Paris Fashion Week
November/December	Pre-Fall New York
	Resort

Table 2.1 The most prominent fashion weeks

For over 150 years the fashion calendar operated on a simple system of twice-yearly seasons: Autumn/Winter (AW) and Spring/Summer (SS), with collections (couture, women's ready-to-wear and men's ready-to-wear) shown six months before they were available to the consumer, giving the industry time to take orders and produce merchandise. More recently, and due primarily to changes driven by globalization and digital technology, it became evident that the traditional fashion calendar is no longer fit for purpose. The industry had gradually introduced more seasons, including pre-collections and resort. Furthermore, globalization had resulted in a rise in the number of fashion weeks around the world. The fashion calendar had become packed with both seasons and fashion weeks. In addition, designers and brands had begun to show in more than one city. For those in the industry, more seasons plus more fashion weeks has resulted in fashion professionals experiencing the pressure of fast fashion and multiple collections, together with the desire of consumers to have runway fashion now. Through digital technology, the collections of those who design for major brands are publicly critiqued around the world. They can't make mistakes. The pressure is huge.

Debate has also focused on the consumer, who is now able to view the latest collections from the runway via digital technologies. The consumer has become increasingly confused and frustrated by the six-month wait to buy product and this has resulted in some brands selling directly to the consumer from the runway. Some brands have changed their approach to the calendar, showing just twice a year, showing menswear and womenswear together (or selling androgynous clothing) and, in response to changes in our lifestyles, presenting *seasonless* or *transseasonal* clothing. São Paulo chose in October 2016 to present the first seasonless fashion week, calling it instead SPFW (São Paulo Fashion Week) Season 41. Many of the brands, including Animale, showed product on the runway which was available in stores immediately. In February 2016 Burberry stated that, starting with their September 2016 show, they would sell collections from the runway and make designs available in stores immediately after the shows. They would also only show twice a year and they would present seasonless menswear and womenswear together.

The fashion calendar contains the fashion weeks and other major fashion events that take place each year, organized so that fashion professionals can move from one fashion week to the next. The schedule is arduous, travelling from city to city, from show to show, day in day out, for weeks.

Ready-to-wear fashion weeks starting in September 2014 ran as follows:

04 September to 11 September (New York)

12 September to 16 September (London)

17 September to 23 September (Milan)

23 September to 1 October (Paris)

That is four weeks of shows without a day's break, and with journeys between cities, one of them transatlantic. The February 2014 edition of *Vogue* questioned the *fashion circus*:

Buyers and press on a four-week, biannual tour, from New York to London to Milan to Paris, shuttling between locations, herded in and out of obscure venues – some icy cold, others unbearably hot, all a tight squeeze – squashed on benches before being pushed and shoved back out, and on to the next. Repeat 10 times in 12 hours, and that's a day in the life of a professional show-goer come ready-to-wear time. (Harris, 2014)

'The changes we are making will allow us to build a closer connection between the experience that we create with our runway shows and the moment when people can physically explore the collections for themselves,' said Christopher Bailey, chief creative and CEO. 'Our shows have been evolving to close this gap for some time,' he said. 'From livestreams, to ordering straight from the runway to live social media campaigns, this is the latest step in a creative process that will continue to evolve.' Luxury Daily, 2016

Figure 2.10 Fashion week schedule and other information.
(© Gill Stark)

The fashion week schedule

Each fashion week has a schedule of events, created by the organization that manages the fashion week. Schedules and other information can be viewed by looking on fashion week websites. Most fashion weeks have one central venue where some fashion shows are produced while others are produced elsewhere. Some fashion shows and events will be *on schedule* and others will be *off schedule*. Those designers and brands *on schedule* will have been recognized as worthy of inclusion. Entry to shows is strictly by invitation, making live fashion week shows accessible only to the elite. Emerging designers show *off schedule* and their shows often have a more *alternative* feel.

Figure 2.11 The Missoni runway show at Milan Fashion Week in February 2017. (Victor Virgile/Contributor via Getty Images)

Who organizes fashion weeks?

Paris In Paris the *Fédération Française de la Couture, du Prêt-à-Porter des Couturiers et des Créateurs de Mode*, established in 1973, has trade associations which control the haute couture and ready-to-wear shows. The *Chambre Syndicale de la Haute Couture* governs which fashion companies can show at the Paris haute couture shows, a status granted by the French Ministry of Industry. The *Chambre Syndicale du Prêt-à-Porter des Couturiers et des Créateurs de Mode* controls the ready-to-wear shows.

Milan In Italy an equivalent system started in 1958 when the *Camera Sindacale della Moda Italiana* was set up. This was the forerunner of the body which subsequently became the *Camera Nazionale della Moda Italiana*. The association coordinates Italian fashion companies and fashion weeks, publishing fashion week schedules. During fashion weeks in the heart of Milan, there are different venues for journalists and bloggers, photographers, art and photography exhibitions, and a hall for press conferences.

Figure 2.12 The designer Ly Qui Khanh with a model on the runway during Fashion Week Fall 2015 in New York City, United States. (Kommersant Photo/Contributor via Getty Images)

New York The Council of Fashion Designers of America manages the New York shows. *New York Fashion Week*, as it is known today, was centralized in 1993 to bring together the designers who had previously shown in different venues, often in unusual spaces. Fern Mallis, who was then executive director of the Council of Fashion Designers, has talked about how, after ceiling plaster fell onto the runway and front row of a Michael Kors show, and other near disasters, it was decided to bring everyone together in one show space.

London London Fashion Week began in 1984 when the British Fashion Council brought together disparate designer shows and exhibitions under one event. Its first show was in a west London car park and while some of its shows represent classic British fashion, it has a reputation for innovative shows presenting creative London fashion. Supported by the British Government's UK Trade and Investment, sponsors have included Mercedes-Benz, Cannon, MAC and Swatch.

Figure 2.13 One of the official fashion week cars sponsored by Mercedes-Benz. (© Regent's University London; Photographer Jason Pittock)

Industry Insight
Rosie O'Reilly

Figure 2.14 Rosie O'Reilly. (© Rosie O'Reilly)

Rosie O'Reilly, womenswear designer, shares her experience of showing a new collection at London Fashion Week.

How did you take part in London Fashion Week (LFW)?

We had already been shortlisted for New Gen [New Generation]. We wanted to focus on the UK market that year and we saw it as an event in the UK that we could use for publicity and for meeting buyers. It was also partially funded by the Year of Irish Design so financially we could take part in a show in London. Also, I took part because Aisling Farinella was curating the show. She brought together a two-room space with eight brands: three jewellery and five fashion.

What was the physical set up of the show?

We showed the Spring/Summer 2016 collection. I had two rails and a full collection with press images. It was a similar set up to a trade show. Because we couldn't afford a runway show, we did an installation. Aisling got a company in London to create a terrarium-style installation in the middle of the two rooms which was based on landscape from the west of Ireland. I was impressed, it was subtle but it was powerful. When your budget is tight you still want to do something creative.

What did you get out of it?

There was no expectation that people would get sales. Knowing that most of the sales are in Paris, it was going to be an investment in marketing and brand awareness. From the beginning the brand was trans-seasonal and would do a strong Autumn/Winter with filler items for Spring/Summer. Because we were chosen for LFW we did two full collections that year, which in the third year of trading put a lot of pressure on the brand. For the press call, over a period of one hour, models came out in different collections and were installed in the middle of the landscape. This was a nice example of what you can do it you can't have a show. We could use it as leverage for meetings with Irish and other press at London Fashion Week.

Figure 2.15 Rosie O'Reilly's static exhibition at London Fashion Week. (© Rosie O'Reilly)

Figure 2.16 London Fashion Week when it was held at the historic London building Somerset House. Runway shows took place inside a temporary building erected in a central courtyard and were shown on huge screens outside. Static exhibitions and other activities took place in Somerset House. (© Gill Stark)

Globally, fashion weeks differ in character

Fashion weeks naturally vary from one another and reflect the nature of their industries. New York is known for its pragmatic sportswear, Paris for its elitist but exquisite luxury collections, and London for its innovative and experimental fashion. The British designer Gareth Pugh used to show in London where his collections and shows were typical of the experimental element of the city's fashion week. As he matured, he moved on to Paris where his shows retain the humour of London fashion but have become more polished and sophisticated as befits Paris Fashion Week. Some cities specialize in a specific kind of fashion, such as Miami where swimwear is shown. Emerging fashion cities likewise establish their character. Singapore is likely to become known for luxury, while São Paulo and Beijing are gaining a reputation for middle market fashion. Indian fashion weeks are respected for the superb traditional craftsmanship of the clothing. Fashion is still a young industry in India, and the market for bridal wear still dominates India's fashion shows with luxurious, ornate sets and models that move in the manner of brides. The other influence on Indian fashion weeks is Bollywood, with celebrity red-carpet coming a close second to bridal wear.

In addition to runway shows, fashion weeks include static exhibitions where designers and brands sell to buyers and attract press attention, dinners, launches and presentations; increasingly, they also include presentations of fashion films as an alternative to fashion shows. The most prominent fashion weeks are big events. For example, the British Fashion Council website stated in advance of London Fashion Week February 2014 that:

> over 5,000 visitors attend: buyers, TV & radio crews, journalists and photographers. Media coverage equals or exceeds most major news and international sporting events. There are 60 runway shows on the official schedule . . . 45 show off schedule and more than 30 on-schedule presentations and salon shows . . . it is estimated that orders of over £100m are placed during LFW each season – the International Guest Programme alone generates over £50m of orders. (British Fashion Council, 2014)

Figure 2.17 Models on the runway during the Andrea Incontri show, Pitti Immagine Uomo 87, Florence, Italy, January 2015. Incontri trained as an architect and won the competition for young designers 'Who Is On Next?' organized by Vogue Italia. The show took place in the Palazzo Corsini and was a salon style show, with models walking through rooms in the Palazzo and others standing on plinths. The show can be viewed at https://www.youtube.com /watch?v=OrlmjA-08JU. (Vittorio Zunino Celotto/ Staff via Getty Images)

The changed fashion calendar

Fashion weeks now take place all over the world, having developed through different impetuses: established fashion businesses choosing to show their collections together, government initiatives, industry associations or business organizations seeing a business opportunity. Holding a fashion week communicates that a country or city has enough designers and fashion companies of status (a fashion industry) to warrant the event. Cities such as Dubai have set out to establish themselves as centres of fashion. Sadly, some have struggled to sustain their fashion weeks, often due to a lack of financial backing. As Stefan Behmer has said:

> *Sponsors need to commit on a long-term basis and not just for one season. Just as designers grow and develop their work, the structure around them should remain sustainable. . . . every city on the planet had an art fair, and a car show and a design fair. Slowly but surely, the relevant ones survive and the rest will disappear, as sponsors pull out once they realize they are not getting their projected return on investment.* (Interview with Stefan Behmer, 2014)

A global perspective

The pattern of fashion weeks around the world constantly evolves in response to changing cultural, economic and political developments: in the same way that Paris was the fashion capital in the 1800s, and there are four prominent fashion capitals today, the pattern of fashion capitals is likely to be different in the future. Some of the current mature fashion capitals, including Paris, Milan, New York, Tokyo, London and Los Angeles, are likely to remain strong while others are likely to decline in prominence and new capitals will arise within emerged or emerging markets. The pattern of who is based where and who shows where and when is complex. Designers often move to different countries to establish their businesses and brands frequently show in different cities to gain greater international exposure, to show in more prestigious fashion weeks or to enter lucrative new markets.

The runway has also seen a shift towards glocalization (adapting globally marketed products to local markets) as designers and brands use the show to infiltrate new markets with product carefully targeted to the local consumer. In developing markets, a desire for products carrying big brand names has been fuelled by theatrical runway shows with associated powerful Internet marketing and sophisticated advertising. Reminiscent of the 1800s when the *Made in Paris* label carried associations of quality, affluence and style, the wearing of international fashion brands today carries associations of an international lifestyle, affluence and cool not previously attainable in some parts of the world.

While big brands use the show as part of sophisticated marketing campaigns, to enter emerging markets, designers in those developing industries, often supported by their governments, reach out into the international marketplace, producing shows elsewhere that reference their historic and cultural heritage. It has long been the case that designers outside the Big Four have needed to show outside their own countries to gain international recognition. Japanese designers, who started to show in Paris in the 1970s, did so to gain recognition at home and internationally. Yohji Yamamoto was quoted as saying in *The Talks* in 2011: 'Paris is the place for establishing your brand as an international one'. Manish Arora is one of India's most popular and successful designers. The creative styling of his shows expresses his wonderful cultural heritage, while drawing influences from both East and West. In India, there is a high demand for products by domestic designers and for many years Arora has shown his collections nationally and internationally, giving him access to an international audience, while also gaining him the international recognition that makes him worth more at home. Selling garments with traditional, handmade embellishments made in his native India, in Delhi, he stages more spectacular shows, showing different collections from those in the comparative restraint of Paris. By staging different kinds of shows in India and in Paris, he skilfully appeals to both international and domestic markets.

Figures 2.18 and 2.19 Danish fashion designer Henrik Vibskov shows in Copenhagen and in Paris. He and his team create thought-provoking show sets that can be built and rebuilt in different locations. (© Henrik Vibskov, AW2015 Alastair Philip Wiper and AW2016 Helle Moos)

Figure 2.20 The Manish Arora runway show at India Couture Week in New Delhi, July 2014. (The India Today Group/Contributor via Getty Images)

A striking number of designers are based in cities far from their origins. Some work for brands and others have their own labels, choosing to base their businesses in cities far from home because it is beneficial to do so. Young designers who have studied abroad in the mature fashion cities of the world often stay to establish their businesses. Sindiso Khumalo is one of South Africa's newer stars. Her business is based in London despite having won the Elle Magazine (South Africa) Rising Star Competition and being nominated for 'Most Beautiful Object in South Africa' by the Design Indaba Cape Town. Her links with her homeland and her ethical motives are strong: her textiles are a wonderful combination of South African influences and contemporary graphic designs based on collaborations with local crafts people. She is one of a growing number of designers who believe that fashion can be used to empower people economically by purchasing craft-based textiles for a fair sum.

Supporting fashion in emerging markets

Initially, there was much concern about the need to nurture homegrown Chinese fashion design. China has strong production capacities and its focus turned to design and design education. Beijing held its first international fashion event, Chic 93, in 1993 at the China World Trade Centre. The collections were a mixture of traditional and modern Chinese clothing with collections by foreign designers such as Gianfranco Ferré. Since then, Chinese fashion retail has become increasingly sophisticated and China Fashion Week actively supports young Chinese designers, many of whom study in mature fashion capitals such as New York and London. Young designers, such as Simon Gao, who is based in Beijing, were supported to show at China Fashion Week. Having won the Mercedes-Benz China Young Fashion Award, he has shown at Paris Fashion Week, and is stocked in stores in China.

One of the most successful couturiers to establish a couture business outside Paris is the Lebanese designer Elie Saab. Saab has a close relationship with his wealthy clients and this has ensured his success. While Saab's business is not based in Paris, he shows there as part of the Chambre Syndicale de la Couture Parisienne's couture week. Several other Lebanese designers, such as Zuhair Murad, also show in Paris. They enjoy the prestige of showing as part of the chic Parisian couture event, while selling primarily to a Middle Eastern market. Saab has imported a different aesthetic to Paris, but with the same handmade, high-quality products.

Figure 2.21 Simon Gao showing at Mercedes-Benz China Fashion Week AW2013 in Beijing, China. Having won the Mercedes-Benz China Young Fashion Award in 2013, his AW2014 show ended London Fashion Week. (VCG/Contributor via Getty Images)

Figure 2.22 A model on the runway at Singapore Fashion Week October 2013, wearing an outfit designed by Guo Pei. (Suhaimi Abdullah/Stringer via Getty Images)

Figure 2.23 Elie Saab, Haute Couture, Paris, 2004. (Tony Barson Archive/Contributor)

Beijing designer Guo Pei shows at Asian Couture Week. One of China's first couturiers, her garments are made by hand, often taking thousands of hours to create. In contrast to the fast-paced couture shows in Paris, Guo Pei's are extremely slow and highly theatrical. Models walk loftily along the runway, striking dramatic poses so that the audience (and the cameras) can view the highly decorative garments. Models can take fifteen minutes to walk the runway in incredibly high shoes, some of which are meant to make the models feet look bound.

Meanwhile, Michael Cinco was born in the Philippines, and educated in fashion both there and in London. He created his couture house in Dubai in 2003, and sells to celebrities for red carpet events and to royalty in the Middle East and elsewhere. He won the Breakthrough Designer Award at the New York WGSN Global Fashion Awards 2011, Best Designer at the Grazia Style Awards 2011 and the People's Choice Award at Dubai Fashion Week 2010. While based in Dubai, Cinco has shown his collections abroad, for instance in Miami and Los Angeles as well as in the Philippines and New York.

In the same way that European and American clients travelled to Paris couture houses a century ago for the Openings, clients from the Middle East and the Far East now travel to the couture shows in Paris. Recently in decline, couture now enjoys a new younger client, possibly educated in the United States or Europe, and who is fashion-savvy, extremely wealthy and travels to Paris from India, Saudi Arabia, Qatar or China. There are other rich Middle Eastern clients who do not attend the shows, but who spend vast amounts of money on fashion, including couture. Like those who wore couture in Europe in the 1800s and 1900s, they attend social events for which they need many different outfits. Middle Eastern consumers' acquisition of luxury fashion is significant. In complete contrast to the public spectacle of the international shows are the discrete private shows, held for rich clients, which are interestingly close in nature to the origins of the fashion show in the salons of the first couturiers.

Haute couture outside Paris

Paris claims that haute couture only takes place in Paris, but this is hotly debated. Countries that have equally rich traditions of making beautiful, handcrafted clothing, using the most luxurious of materials, challenge Paris' claim. In Singapore the Asian Couture Federation, launched in October 2013, represents couture designers working in Asia. With the support of large sponsors and other organizations, including the Chambre Syndicale de la Couture in Paris and the Council of Fashion Designers of America, Asian Couture Week has shown the work of well-known western couturiers, such as Alexis Mabille, alongside Asian couture designers who are well known within domestic markets, but less so internationally. Now independent of some of its initial collaborators, it shows primarily the work of Asian couturiers, while a few western designers continue to promote their collections there.

Industry Insight
Rhonda P. Hill

Figure 2.24 Rhonda P. Hill at De Marcos Fashion Academy Santa Barbara Fashion Week 2016. (© Rhonda P. Hill)

Rhonda P. Hill started in fashion as a buyer for Macy's in New York and has also worked with Levi Strauss & Co., adidas, and as vice president of merchandising with The Walt Disney Co. Rhonda's current project is EDGE (EDGExpo.com), a fashion intelligence platform which exposes emerging designers through its global network of industry professionals, educators and the arts, promoting design excellence, cultural significance and sustainability.

You've had some significant jobs in fashion. Why did you stop and set up EDGE?

I am doing something that I feel is missing. When I was a buyer, I bought the established brands. I travelled back and forth from LA to New York looking for up-and-coming brands and when I bought them they sold out. There is so much mass merchandising, the voice of emerging designers is not heard, so I started EDGE. I give exposure to emerging brands. I interview emerging designers and publish articles about them on the EDGE website with links from my website to theirs.

How does EDGE work?

When I was a buyer I didn't go to shows. I saw the collections in advance of fashion week. When I got into EDGE I saw the value of shows. A lot of graduates feel they need to be in a show but the designers are saying it is a mixed blessing because there is a cost factor. I usually go to shows specific to emerging designers. LA fashion week lasts for three or four days and the last day is for emerging designers, so that's the one I go to, and I am looking for the designers that are not on a radar. Sometimes I send interns to the shows or photographers. Sometimes I go through the designer lists and go to designers' websites. Then I interview in advance and put the interview on the EDGE website on the day of their show.

A lot of media won't report on the shows. The big media will but the bloggers don't do much. The fashion weeks know that I will do something for the designers. There might be eight emerging designers showing and I may only interview one but I may put three into the look book. I also use Facebook, Instagram, Twitter. Whatever I publish on the site, it feeds into those portals. LinkedIn serves me well; when I publish on LinkedIn, there are hundreds of views.

I notice that you feature designers from developing fashion industries?

I did a series on Africa to see how they are building their infrastructure and supporting their designers. What I learned is that you have women who are based in Africa who are very educated and they are supporting communities, training them to sew, leveraging the resources there. Other Africans who have moved away from the continent reach back and source from there, like Koko Nanga.

Mena Lombard has been supported by Rhonda P. Hill and EDGE to build her business.

How did you get involved in fashion?

It was later in life. I was born in Uruguay in South America and it didn't seem realistic to study fashion so I worked in business. When my daughter was born, I decided to start over. I have always known how to sew: my grandmother does, my mother does. I studied in Florida, then in Milan. When I launched my brand two years ago at LA Fashion Week, it was in the Union Station building and there was a super-long runway. Every brand had their own slot. Magazines, media, press were there. Before the show we had fittings and walk sessions to choose models.

We are probably going to show at Miami Fashion Week. People show at different fashion weeks. The press is usually the same but not the buyers. It's good to spread your brand in different markets.

How often do you show?

My goal is once a year. It's almost impossible because it's so expensive. The first time I took out a loan. You want your name out, you want people to know what you stand for, the collection comes to life on the runway. You're telling a story and it's so powerful. It's very meaningful for a designer to show in a big fashion show. Those minutes of show make everything worthwhile.

To read the full interview with Mena Lombard please visit http://www.bloomsbury.com/stark-the-fashion-show.

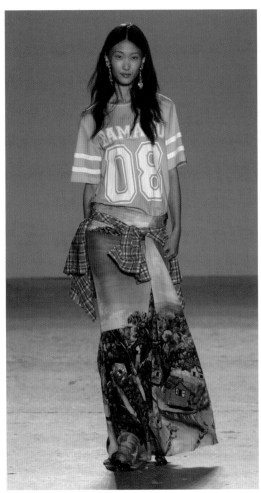

Figure 2.25 Stella Jean's SS2015 collection, Milan Fashion Week, Italy. (Antonio de Moraes Barros Filho/Contributor via Getty Images)

Preserving local culture while promoting global awareness

Africa, with some of the fastest growing nations in the world, a growing affluent middle class and a thirst for western products, is experiencing two large initiatives: the first to preserve the continent's traditional crafts whilst enabling its populations to earn a good wage, and the second to promote African fashion as a globally relevant industry with a distinctive aesthetic. Start-up funds have been made available to support young designers to develop their businesses and there is huge motivation to create an ethical and sustainable fashion industry in Africa that is evident in its fashion week events. Fashion Week Africa is young in fashion week terms and its development is interesting. It developed first in other countries before taking place in Africa. It was created to encourage partnerships with Africa through fashion, while showing the work of African and Africa-inspired designers. Africa Fashion Week New York was staged in 2009, and this was followed by Africa Fashion Week London in 2011. It was not until 2012, and sponsored by Mercedes-Benz, that Africa Fashion Week started on African soil with four days of shows in Johannesburg. Designers from across the continent, including South Africa, Morocco, Ghana, Cameroon, Cote D'Ivoire, Mozambique, Rwanda, Nigeria and Angola, have shown collections at the event.

Various designers from outside Africa have contributed, through international fashion shows, to the appetite for the wonderful vitality and visual exuberance of African fashion design. Stella Jean is a half-Italian, half-Haitian designer whose business is founded on the use of traditional crafts and fabrics that are ethically produced in Africa. She shows her collections at AltaRomAltaModa in Rome, where the International Trade Centre Ethical Fashion Initiative, working with AltaRoma, supports the 'Beat of Africa' fashion show. Having initially struggled to get her business off the ground, Stella Jean won the support of Italian Vogue and AltaRoma, having won 'Who's On Next', a fashion talent competition, in 2011. Funded through a United Nations project, she was introduced to craft weavers and embroiderers who now produce some of the materials in her collections. Her business took off when Giorgio Armani invited her to show her SS2014 collection at his Armani Teatro in Milan, finally catching the attention of the world's fashion press. Stella Jean uses fabrics, jewellery and other accessories produced by hand in countries such as Haiti and Kenya.

Political, ethical and environmental contexts

Fashion weeks and climate change

In 2012 it was estimated that, in the UK alone, 350 tonnes of used clothing went into landfill every year (WRAP, 2012). Given international concern about environmental issues and the need for social responsibility and ethical trading, the fashion industry has made relatively little progress in addressing such matters. The fashion industry perpetuates a constant and unrelenting desire for something 'new'. The fashion calendar is filled with fashion weeks, each of them designed to stimulate desire for more product. The designer Stella McCartney has said of her designs:

I want the clothes to be modern and cool and relevant. And at the same time, they have got to be perfectly constructed in the most beautiful fabric, because I want them to last not just your lifetime but your daughter's lifetime and her daughter's lifetime. And that's just scratching the surface, because inside of that I am trying to source those beautiful fabrics in a responsible way . . . This industry is supposed to be about change, but it's not changing much. But it's complicated, because there's an argument that better-made, better-quality clothing is itself more sustainable. Buying a dress for a fiver and throwing it away after a couple of weeks is not environmentally friendly, whatever the fabric. (Cartner-Morley, 2014)

Figure 2.26 The Stella McCartney runway show at Paris Fashion Week AW2015 in Paris, France. (Pascal Le Segretain/Staff via Getty Images)

Attracting the international press to shows is intrinsic to successful fashion weeks, and for much of the year the media, buyers, models, stylists, production teams, photographers, designers, interns and others increase our carbon footprint by flying around the world to fashion events. While brands may wish to attract international press and buyers, working with as many local models, stylists, photographers and production teams would surely be better for the environment? Given our ability to communicate so effectively through digital media, why don't we fly less and have more digital shows? While local economies benefit hugely from the industry's use of hotels, restaurants and other service industries during fashion weeks, how long will it be before environmental matters are so serious that fashion weeks become events that promote locally designed product through digital media to the rest of the world?

Promoting recycling on the runway

Designers have played with the concept of reusing garments since the early 1990s when there was a backlash against the consumerism of the 1980s. Martin Margiela is a designer who has contributed much to our thinking about second-hand clothing and who communicated his ideas through provocative shows in the 1990s. Margiela and other more avant-garde designers expressed this ethos through the style of the events they produced as well as through their collections, staging shows in old warehouses, car parks and in Margiela's case, as Suzy Menkes observed in the New York Times in March 1993, 'fashion's founding father of recycling . . . has staged runway shows on a squatters' site, in an abandoned garage and in a Salvation Army furniture thrift shop.'

Buy less. Choose well. Make it last. Quality, not quantity. Everybody's buying far too many clothes . . . Instead of buying six things, buy one thing that you really like. Don't keep buying just for the sake of it . . . I just think people should invest in the world. Don't invest in fashion, but invest in the world.
Vivienne Westwood, quoted in Grant, 2013

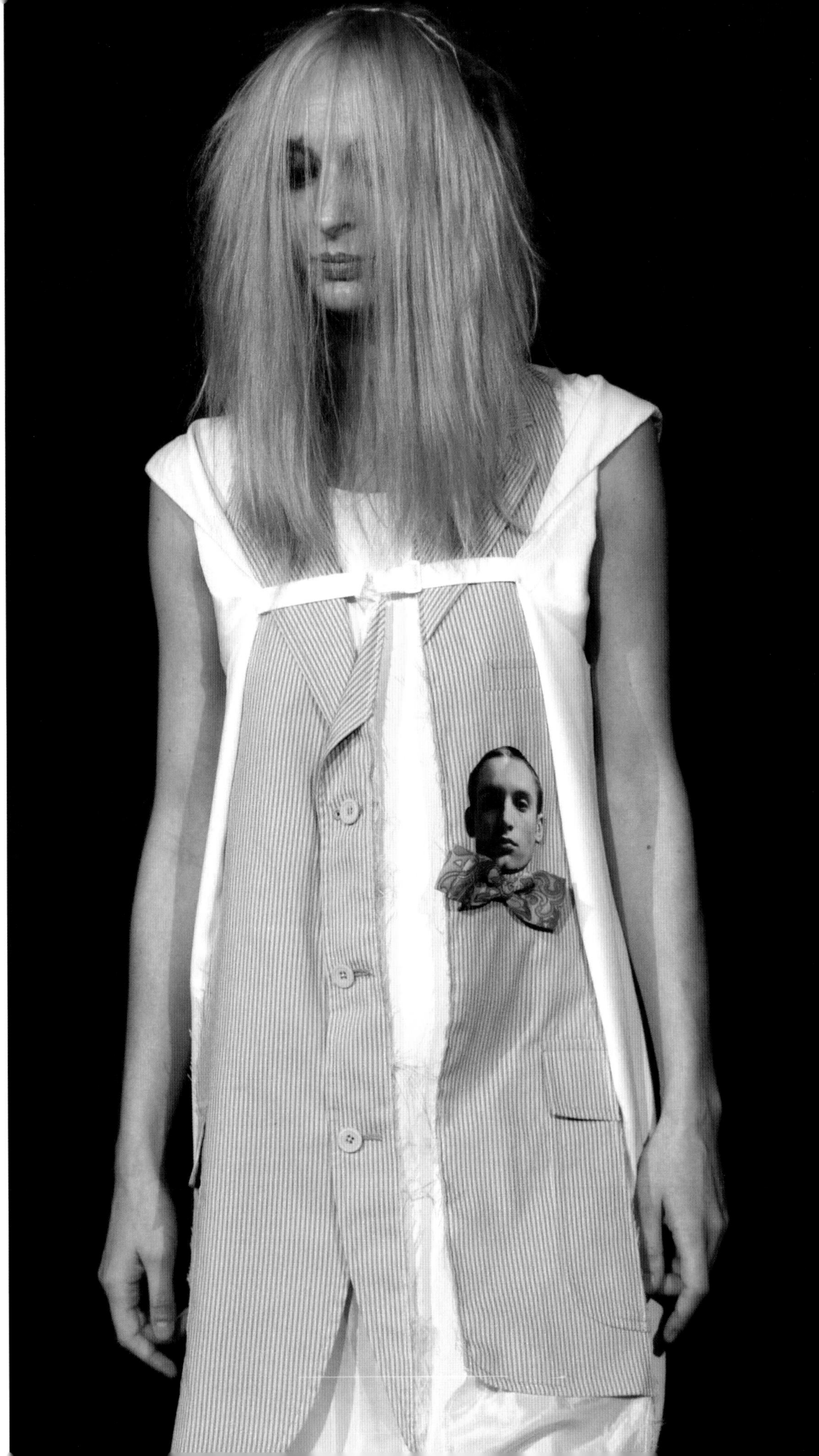

Figure 2.27 The SS2004 Maison Martin Margiela Collection, shown in Paris, France. (Pierre Verdy/Staff via Getty Images)

Figure 2.28 Vivienne Westwood on the runway in September 2012 at the end of her SS2013 Red Label show. (Gareth Cattermole/Staff via Getty Images)

Highlighting environmental matters

In 2013, as Vivienne Westwood showed her collection at London Fashion Week, the Telegraph reported in an article entitled 'Vivienne Westwood: Everyone buys too many clothes' that 'Dame Vivienne Westwood has made a plea to the public, especially "poor people", to buy fewer and better quality clothes'. Working with organizations such as Environmental Justice Foundation and Greenpeace, and with the courage to live by her beliefs, Westwood has used her ability to draw an international press to her runway shows to promote awareness about environmental and other issues. While other designers have used gimmicks to attract the press, Westwood has demonstrated a genuine commitment which has earned her much respect, donating business profits and even having her hair cut off.

The runway as a tool to promote fashion that is ethical and sustainable

The runway is used by ethical fashion organizations such as The Ethical Fashion Initiative to promote the work of designers who are establishing exciting, sustainable and environmentally sound fair trade businesses. Collaborations are forged between designers and artisans in poor nations, thereby supporting craftspeople to be part of the global fashion supply chain, in a manner that does not exploit them, and which enables them to earn a fair wage producing high-quality luxury products. Many of the artisans use their wages to support families and to pay for schooling for their children.

Villa Eugénie

The event company Villa Eugénie produces some of the world's most impressive fashion shows. It demonstrates its concern about environmental issues by working with its clients to limit the waste from its events by using recycled materials in the runway sets it designs.

Lisa Folawiyo is a designer who studied law in Nigeria and who started her business there in 2005, without any training in fashion. She has been supported to present her work at international fashion shows including New York, Paris, Milan and London, while also showing on the runway at Lagos Fashion and Design Week (LFDW) in Nigeria. The brand has a strong focus on design integrity. African prints are combined with beautiful hand beadwork and are produced in Nigeria. Garments can take over 200 hours to complete. The result is stunning modern garments with their roots in the traditions of her native culture.

The myth of exclusive luxury fashion

It is through the shows of designers such as Westwood and Lisa Folawiyo that the power of the runway is being used to promote fashion that is sustainable, that empowers those who would otherwise be in poverty, while safeguarding the traditional crafts of developing nations. True luxury is not about buying a mass-produced but expensive item, with an apparently exclusive brand label; it is about purchasing something that is individually made, using traditional methods, by highly skilled craftspeople. The luxury fashion industry has jumped on the convenient promotional message that buying luxury means buying something sustainable because it may be used for years. This is, of course at odds with persistent aggressive promotion by those same companies through runway and advertising that seduces consumers to purchase new product.

Media attention at fashion weeks

Organizations concerned with the environment have used the presence of the media at fashion weeks to communicate about ethical and environment matters. In February 2014 Greenpeace protested at Milan Fashion Week with a campaign called 'Beautiful Fashion, Ugly Lies? The King is Naked', alleging that products manufactured by companies such as Giorgio Armani, Dolce & Gabbana and Versace released hazardous chemicals, toxic for the environment and dangerous to health. Chiara Campione, Greenpeace campaigner, said of the demonstration that it was set up 'to ask Italian brands . . . to publicly commit to eliminate harmful substances from the various stages of production. Milan's fashion week is just beginning, and probably there will be other protests in these days and also maybe during Paris' fashion week ' (Alessia, 2014).

The extremes of runway spectacle and cheap production

The Ethical Fashion Forum defines ethical fashion as follows: 'ethical fashion represents an approach to the design, sourcing and manufacture of clothing which maximises benefits to people and communities while minimising impact on the environment.' Within this context, the spectacle of runway is highly questionable. Behind the spectacle is the hidden human cost of our obsession to own something new. The worst garment industry disaster to date was in April 2013, when the multi-storey Rana Plaza factory building in Bangladesh collapsed, killing over 1,000 people and injuring over 2,000. It was reported that people working in the factory worked unhealthily long hours and earned very little. There was shock and outrage internationally, and protests by thousands of factory workers on the streets. The factories housed there produced cheap garments for companies in Canada, the United States and the UK.

Highlighting sustainable fashion at fashion weeks

Sustainable fashion has a growing presence at fashion weeks. Australian Fashion Week in April 2014 included the Clean Cut Designer Showcase, showing the work of international, ethically inclined designers. In New York, The GreenShows is an organization dedicated to the luxury sustainable fashion movement, which produces many fashion shows. Fashion Week Stockholm focuses on sustainable development in Sweden through the Global Leadership Award in Sustainable Fashion supported by the Sustainable Fashion Academy. New Zealand has a fashion week devoted entirely to eco fashion called NZ Eco Fashion Exposed, and in London, the British Fashion Council established Estethica in 2006 to promote sustainable fashion through London Fashion Week.

Ethical issues and the modelling industry

Issues surrounding the modelling industry, including underage models and racism, repeatedly hit the news and then fade from the forefront of public attention. There was debate about heroin chic in the 1990s, followed by size-zero models in the 2000s, particularly after the death of model Luisel Ramos in 2006. Ramos died, at just 22, of heart failure after leaving the runway. Excessively thin, she starved herself before fashion weeks and had an extremely low body mass index. Her death shocked the fashion world. Madrid and Milan Fashion Weeks immediately banned models with low body mass indexes, but other cities – shockingly – hesitated to do so. In spring 2017, Balenciaga fired two casting directors for mistreatment of models after 150 women waited for a casting for three hours in a cramped, dark stairwell with no food or water. The matter of underage models surfaces from time to time, but the link between this and thin models is rarely discussed. It is clear from photographs of models up to the mid-1990s that until that time there were models whose beauty was partly due to the healthiness of their look. During the 1990s the fashion aesthetic changed and young models were employed who were naturally thinner, not having yet fully developed as women. Today there are still shockingly thin models on the runway who are clearly far from healthy.

Model size isn't just about runway

The issue of model size doesn't start with the runway; the whole industry works to standard sizes, fitting garments onto agency models or *fit* models (models employed to fit garments onto in designers' studios) during the design process. However, runway images evidence the fact that unusually thin models walk our global runways. Some starve themselves before fashion weeks and a high proportion have eating disorders. We are bombarded by runway images of people who are abnormal in comparison with the rest of the earth's population. Not only are some runway models already unhealthily thin, but in addition, images of models are distorted by digital retouching so that, for instance, already long legs are lengthened and slim hips are thinned. No wonder many young people who want to look like models fail to do so without understanding that what they aspire to is physically impossible. The influence of idealized images of thin models on the development of anorexia nervosa in girls, and a growing number of boys, is hotly debated.

Guidelines

Following outcry about the age and weight of models, the British Fashion Council put up notices backstage at shows to set out guidelines for brands and show producers. This included a ban on the use of underage models with backstage audits taking place to check that models were at least sixteen years old. The second guideline was about the provision of healthy food backstage and again audits were carried out to check that appropriate amounts of healthy food and refreshments were provided.

Models and race

There is also debate about the ethnicity of models that we see on the runways. While a few designers, such as Riccardo Tisci, work with a diverse range of models, most runways are still predominantly white, and Asian models are still rare. In July 2008, Italian *Vogue* exclusively used black models and it caused a huge furore, selling out and having to be reprinted. In February 2008 at London Fashion Week, Storm model Jourdan Dunn was widely reported to have said 'London's not a white city . . . why should our runways be so white?' (Fisher, 2008). Dunn, interviewed for an article in the *Observer*, talked about starting a modelling agency to promote different races. 'I'm really ambitious. When I go back into education, I'm going to do business studies . . . I'd do an agency for black girls – and Asian and Spanish, because there aren't enough of them on the runway either' (Fisher, 2008).

Gender

For an industry that reflects contemporary culture, it was surprisingly slow to employ transgender models on the runway. Some well-known designers used shows to highlight issues around gender. Working within the Parisian traditions of beautiful, hand-crafted clothing, and its chic fashion, Jean Paul Gaultier frequently challenged preconceptions about dress and identity, showing men in skirts and, in his AW2011 show, putting transgender model Andreja Pejic on the runway. Pejic became known for her androgyny when she modelled both menswear and womenswear, working for some of the world's most influential designers, including Gaultier, DKNY and Marc Jacobs. As recently as 2012, Casey Legler was reported to be the first female model to be signed by an agency to work as a male model, and when Laith Ashley modelled in New York Fashion Week, he quickly became a role model with a considerable following. Transgender models now enhance our runways and transgender agencies include SLAY in Los Angeles and Trans Models in New York, while Apple Model Management in Thailand has a transgender division.

The show as fashion activism

In 1984 eco-designer Katharine Hamnett hit the news headlines when she met British Prime Minister Margaret Thatcher wearing a T-shirt with the prominent wording '58% Don't Want Pershing' [a missile system]. Hamnett repeatedly used the runway to communicate messages about environmental issues and became famous for big, bold statements printed on the classic T-shirt. More recently, Angela Missoni used her February 2017 show at Milan Fashion Week to make a political statement, dressing forty models in pink beanie hats in the finale, showing support for protests against US President Donald Trump:

> I wanted to have a regular show, but at the same time I thought that when I have a show my voice is louder, so I can use it for a good cause . . . to support the women [sic] march and movement, and for everybody who believes that we need to raise a voice for human rights. (Segreti, 2017)

Figure 2.29 Andreja Pejic as Gaultier's couture bride. (Tony Barson/Contributor via Getty Images)

Figure 2.30 Katharine Hamnett's AW2003 collection. (Scott Barbour/Staff via Getty Images)

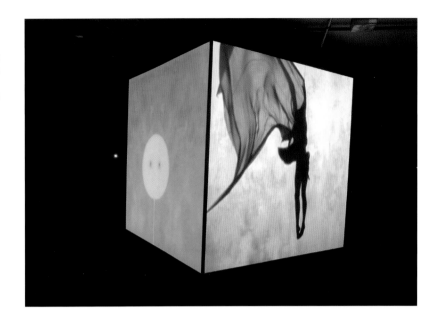

Fashion film

Fashion designers and brands are harnessing film for both creative expression and to sell fashion. Live streaming is increasingly being used to market fashion and 'see-now-buy-now' directly from the runway is a powerful method of selling fashion while the consumer is at their most excited. More interesting is the use of film within a live runway show, or the use of film as creative expression instead of runway. With its roots in the 1990s, fashion film has become an important medium of communication. In the 1980s a few brands, including Armani, produced films instead of runway shows and then returned to the runway. They were quite probably ahead of the trend, and film as an alternative to live runway evolved largely in the 2000s. It is now being used in multiple ways to explore and express ideas about fashion as well as to market it. Tom Ford's SS2016 collection was launched in a fashion film, directed by Nick Knight and starring Lady Gaga:

> Instead of having a traditional show this season, I decided to try something new. Having a runway show has become so much about the creation of imagery for online and social media and watching a filmed fashion show can be like watching a filmed play [which is never very satisfying]. I wanted to think about how to present a collection in a cinematic way that was designed from its inception to be presented online. (Amed, 2015)

Film enables a designer to build a very different kind of experience, one that can be a richer expression of the creative inspiration and meaning of a collection. This is beautifully illustrated by Gareth Pugh's SS2015 immersive fashion film experience. Pugh chose to show in New York instead of Paris and his fashion film opened New York Fashion Week. Breaking many runway traditions, the audience stood to watch the show in a large empty room. Pugh wanted the audience to connect with the emotion that went into the creation of the collection. The resulting presentation, directed by artist-filmmaker Andrew Thomas Huang, was three films shown on huge LED screens, with performances by models, both on screen and live, choreographed by Wayne McGregor. Pugh has presented several fashion films that can be viewed on SHOWstudio or on YouTube. Here is one example to watch: https://www.youtube.com/watch?v=tQhDt_PHqVk.

Figure 2.32 The finale of the KTZ show at London Fashion Week, January 2015, where much of the audience are photographing, Tweeting and Instagramming. (© Gill Stark)

New technologies

So great is the impact of digital technology that it has changed the very nature of the fashion show, and as technology advances, it continues to do so, resulting in radical changes to the industry, partly played out on the runways of the world. One of the biggest changes that new technology has brought to the show is the immediacy of communication. Peter Robinson, head of press and events for the White Company in the U.K., spoke about the speed of communication now:

Because of the immediacy of communication there is almost no exclusivity. Previously after a show, things would be released in a timely fashion, whereas now everyone releases information at the same time. The print media is the same as it was, while the bloggers will send things out immediately internationally. When I look through Instagram and all of the online media, there will be people saying about this show 'this is the finale' or 'we have just arrived and look at the staging at . . .' Everyone now has to create something. They will do that and also have to create something for the print version. They will Tweet live, Instagram, write something for the blog on the magazine site, something for the print version of the magazine: it is multi-faceted. It is the same information, but you have to create four stories. With Twitter it is small, Instagram is just pictorial, the blog nobody reads more than two paragraphs really, and the print version will still be the longest if someone does a large précis of what has been seen at a fashion show, whether it's in a newspaper or in a magazine. (Interview with Peter Robinson, 2014)

Volume of information

The sheer volume of information being pumped out by the industry is astounding, as is the complexity of its mass – and uncontrolled – communication, but have we sacrificed quality for quantity? In February 2014, Sarah Harris reported from the Grand Palais in Paris about Chanel's AW2014/15 ready-to-wear show:

In fact, half the audience – 2,520 guests comprising editors, buyers, bloggers, stylists, celebrities, and a jubilant handful of Chanel's most important shoppers – were still fixated on their iPhones, desperately trying to get a signal (the server at Grand Palais may well have gone into some kind of cardiac arrest from such feverish Instagramming); so much so that no one really noticed that an actual fashion show was going on in front of them until midway through. (Harris, 2014)

Figure 2.33 Topshop's new collection was live streamed to make the viewer feel part of the audience. The consumer could purchase the products on the runway as the show took place. (Eamonn M. McCormack/Stringer via Getty Images)

See-now-buy-now

In September 2014 Topshop's new collection was live streamed on the Internet with the promise of being able to interact digitally. Pre-show, the company built anticipation in what has become familiar as a prelude to live-streamed runway. This includes assurances of front row, celebrity and backstage shots, short teaser videos and the feeling that the consumer can take part in the occasion online. The online viewer watched the audience coming in to the show, saw backstage shots and felt like a live observer. While the show played on computer screens, viewers could click on items and be taken to a page on the company's website where they could place orders for the product. The promised interactive element was that of being able to purchase product.

Figure 2.34 Ralph Lauren's 4-dimensional fashion show video projection in November 2010. (Dave M. Benett/Contributor via Getty Images)

The democratization of the fashion show

Shows are no longer just for the elite. Brands can promote their entire collections directly to the public, controlling the creative presentation of their work, using mass communication to invite their consumers to join them at what had previously been an event for a privileged industry audience. They use short films of their shows for social media and YouTube, and use a longer film format to show runway on their websites. Consumers can revisit and view runway stills and film on the Internet repeatedly, and in response some fashion companies have built websites that are more interesting and entertaining than the collections themselves. Other organizations have based whole companies or websites on showing runway. FirstView.com and Vogue.com are two of the most prominent that make runway shots available to the public.

Virtual runway

On 10 November 2010 Ralph Lauren showed what they claimed to be the world's first 4-dimensional fashion show experience. The company used architectural mapping to present a 4D video projection onto the façades of its flagship stores in London and New York. In Spring 2014, Ralph Lauren used holograms in New York to debut the womenswear Polo Ralph Lauren collection. The show was presented on the Lake in Central Park and holograms of famous New York landmarks hovered over the Lake as holograms of models walked through those cityscapes, appearing to walk on water. The finale was, of course, a hologram of Ralph Lauren. While details of the garments were not easy to see, the spectacle was impressive.

Live runway meets virtual runway

Using floor-to-ceiling video walls and a real runway, virtual image technology was used in a magical spectacle that was one of the most hypnotic fashion shows ever. The production by Burberry was held at a party in Beijing to celebrate the launch of its flagship store there. Fashion and music have a long tradition of cross-fertilization and the production merged that tradition with the utmost in high technology. Hologram models, beautifully choreographed, shattered into a sprinkling of magical dust as they walked the runway. Live fashion and virtual image technology combined with live models, digital models and live music by the band Keane.

Figure 2.35 Model Cara Delevinge flies down the runway during the 'Burberry Brings London to Shanghai' event in April 2014. (Getty Images/Staff)

Burberry

One of the challenges of new technology is the need for brands to ensure that real and virtual worlds communicate the same brand messages. Burberry, which debuted its SS2016 show on Snapchat, is more advanced than most, using sophisticated digital technology in its stores as well as to create runway experiences. Burberry also has a presence in the minds of the Chinese consumer, who love the Britishness of the brand and all that it stands for in terms of tradition. As Burberry acknowledged, they planned a launch party that was intended to expand the brand in the Chinese luxury market, and the use of digital technology to promote to a culture that loves high tech was a clever approach. Its holographic models strutting along the runway were astutely live streamed on the Internet so that wherever you were in the world, you could feel that you were also part of the party.

Activities

01. Fashion week
Choose a city that holds a fashion week, for example, Berlin Fashion Week, Cape Town Fashion Week or Shanghai Fashion Week. Choose a fashion week that you do not know anything about. Imagine that you are working for a designer who is considering showing at the fashion week you have chosen. Research the fashion week and compile a report to include:
A. Who organizes the fashion week
B. Last season's schedule
C. Show venues: on-schedule and off-schedule
D. Who else shows at the fashion week: runway and static exhibitions
E. Costs involved in showing
F. What the organizers offer in addition to runway or stand (e.g., press events)
G. Press information (who attended and what coverage was achieved)

02. Fashion film as runway
Research and review the shows that have been presented as film instead of live runway. Create a presentation to include:
A. Images or footage from the films
B. Discussion about why fashion film was used instead of live runway
C. Press reports about the films and how well, or otherwise, they were received
D. A comparison of fashion film and live runway
E. An exploration of the role of fashion film instead of runway in the contexts of contemporary and future fashion

03. Pitti Uomo
Research Pitti Uomo in Florence. Write an essay of a minimum of 2,000 words to present your analysis of how it developed and why it has evolved into one of the most important menswear fashion weeks in the world.

04. Runway and sustainability
Research the relationship between runway and sustainability. How has the powerful promotional medium of the runway been used to communicate messages about sustainability, and how are fashion weeks promoting issues around sustainability?

05. Each fashion capital has its own character
Using only visual materials and keywords, research and present the different character of ten fashion weeks from different parts of the world, to include Milan, Paris, New York and London and one of the Indian fashion weeks.

06. Ethical issues and runway
Research ethical issues pertaining to modelling such as underage models, size-zero models or racism. Debate whether these issues are the result of show production practices or whether they are the result of wider industry practices. Present evidence to support your argument.

3

Marketing and communications

The fashion show is such a powerful marketing tool that Chapter Three focuses on the role that the fashion show plays in the promotion of fashion. It investigates the psychological lure of shows and how brands use runway as a vehicle for the communication of powerful brand messages, persuading the consumer to engage with the brand and to buy more fashion. Chapter Three examines the impact on runway of digital technology and explores how traditional journalism, social media and celebrity endorsement operate within the context of the fashion show in times of digital multi-channel media.

LUXURY
Haute couture
and couture

HIGH END
Designer ready-to-wear

PREMIUM
Ready-to-wear

MIDDLE MARKET
Middle market

MASS MARKET
High street

VALUE MARKET
Economy / discount

Figure 3.1 Fashion market Levels. Runway has not been widely adopted in the middle market, the mass market or the value market.

The fashion market

Runway and market levels

Fashion shows are such a powerful marketing tool, one might assume that all designers and brands hold shows. However, having evolved within the elite haute couture world of the Parisian ateliers, runway is primarily used around the globe to promote luxury fashion. When mass-manufactured clothing developed, the fashion show was adopted by some retailers to promote merchandise in stores, but runway is little used within the mass market. The fashion show has become associated with luxury fashion and with clothing that is at the forefront of what is new. In recent years, a few mass-market brands have produced runway shows as part of fashion weeks. H&M, Topshop and Jigsaw are three examples. Victoria's Secret is unusual in producing shows with the budget of a large luxury brand while selling mass-market products. The branding expert Kapferer presented luxury brand markets in the pyramid brand model, positioning the most expensive and unique products, hand-made by designers, that would be shown at couture shows, at the top.

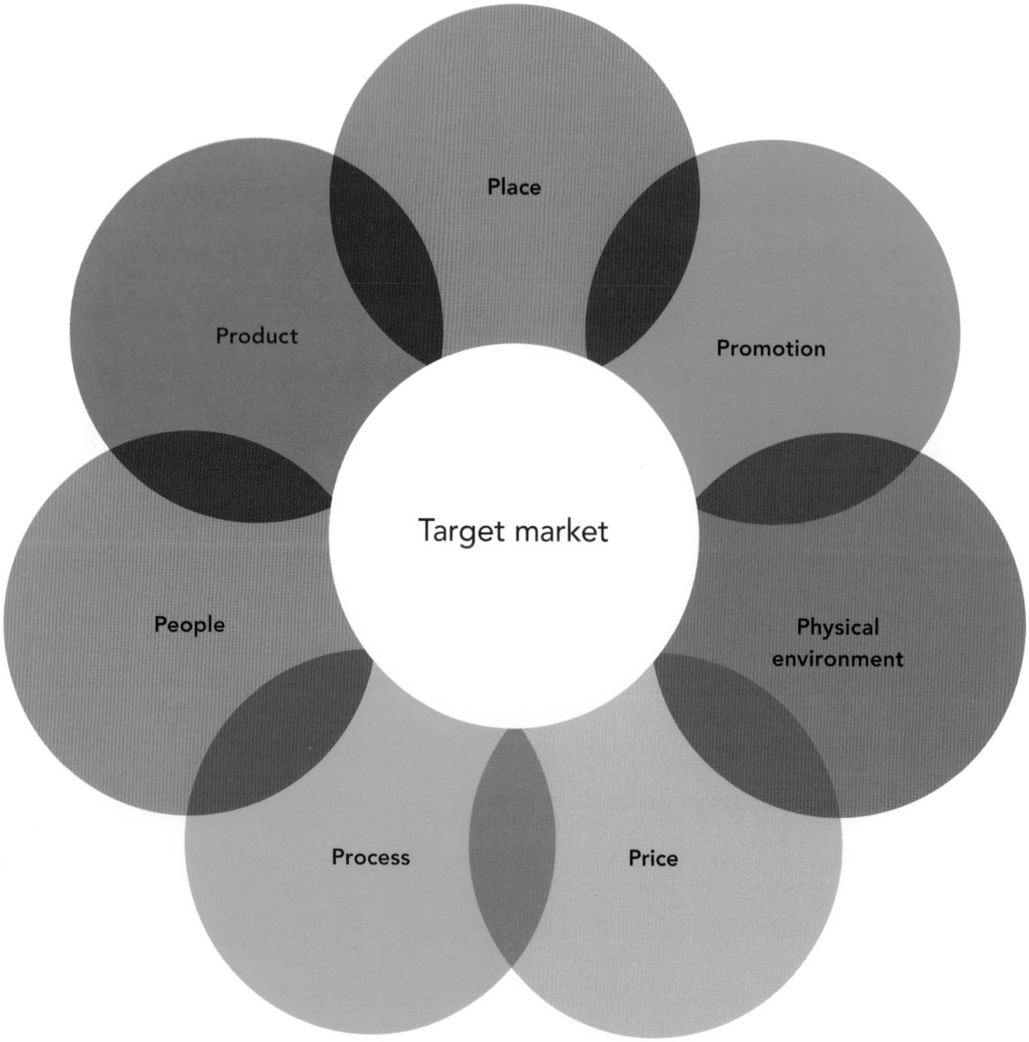

Place

Product

Promotion

Target market

People

Physical environment

Process

Price

Figure 3.2 The fashion show is found within promotion in the marketing mix.

The fashion show and the marketing mix

Kotler and Keller wrote in 2016: 'we see marketing management as the art and science of choosing target markets and getting, keeping and growing customers through creating, delivering and communicating superior customer value.' To plan and manage marketing activities, marketers use the framework of the *marketing mix*. The marketing mix consists of the seven Ps. The first four Ps in the marketing mix are about putting the right *product* in the right *place*, at the right *price* and with the best combination of *promotional* activities. The last three of the seven Ps are about *people*, the target market and people who work with the brand, having the right *processes* in place to deliver great service and business efficiencies and finally *physical evidence* (environments, packaging and so on). The fashion show is found within promotion in the marketing mix. Brands use every element of the marketing mix that is appropriate to their target market to successfully get, keep and grow customers. Marketing plans ensure that every activity they engage in, including shows, is part of a cohesive marketing strategy.

Competing for attention

Monsieur de Betak of Bureau Betak, who produces shows for Isabel Marant, Roberto Cavalli, Dior, Peter Pilotto and Rodarte amongst others, has talked about events that can cost from £100,000 ($135,000 USD) to several million. As the number of shows produced globally has increased, brands and show producers have been challenged to produce shows that are more attention-grabbing and generally also more expensive (Smith, 2014).

The fashion show within the promotional mix

The fourth P is *promotion*. Promotional activities are about communicating value so that customers will choose that brand over all others. There is a *promotional mix*, which is the range of promotional activities available to a designer or brand to communicate brand personality, including advertising, branding, corporate identity, direct marketing, events, personal selling, public relations, sales, social media outreach and special offers. The show is a promotional event which, together with public relations and media outreach activities is used for what Kotler and Keller call 'getting, keeping and growing customers through creating, delivering and communicating superior customer value.'

Some industries develop specialist promotional activities, and runway is one of those. The fashion show

- Reinforces the importance of the brand
- Strengthens brand identity and communicates important brand messages
- Gives designers and brands essential PR
- Creates considerable media outreach
- Generates material (images and film) for other promotional activities

Figure 3.4 From strong make-up to backstage to the audience/
performer dynamic, the fashion show has much in common with
the theatre and its dramatic effects are the result of many common
features. (© Regent's University London, Photographer Tony Rogers)

Runway as communication

Promotion is essential in a competitive market environment

Fashion companies vie for attention to sustain their positions in an unrelentingly competitive environment. Brands spend huge amounts on promoting fashion every year: the fashion brand Chanel spent $362 million on advertising in America alone in 2012. Tweets, blogs, Instagrams, webpages, advertisements, shopping environments, magazines, newspapers, Facebook, Pinterest, YouTube . . . the onslaught of visual information is enormous, all aimed at seducing consumers to buy more. To compete, brands use the most powerful promotional tools they can. Since the dramatic shows of the 1980s, the theatrical potential of the show has been optimized through 'art directed' spectacles to build anticipation and expectation and to communicate powerful messages about brands, perpetuating the excitement that helps to maintain brand identity and drive sales.

Digital technology and social media channels have enhanced the power of runway as a promotional tool. The consumer perceives runway as hugely exciting and technology has turned fashion weeks from industry events into powerful marketing opportunities. Long before the fashion week schedule is released companies control every promotional opportunity to maximize the potential of the event. Announcements and sneak peaks are released as the process of stimulating excitement with spectacular events begins.

Figures 3.5 and 3.6 Lights over the runway at a Topshop show read 'Topshop Unique' and even the umbrellas used by ushers are used to reinforce branding messages. (© Regent's University London, Photographer Jason Pittock)

Communication through branding

The fashion show and brand identity

Branding is about communicating the personality of a brand and stimulating an emotional connection between the consumer and the brand. The richer the positive emotional responses a consumer has in response to a brand, the greater affinity and loyalty they feel and the greater their emotional desire to purchase the brand. Because of the powerful emotional response that a fashion show can stimulate, used well, the show is a very powerful tool. Regular positive communication about a brand is key to its survival and every fashion show is an opportunity for the brand to positively reinforce its unique identity: its essence, values and personality. Every show is likewise an opportunity to communicate the brand proposition, what the brand offers its customers and to strengthen their emotional investment in the brand.

Figure 3.7 The Chanel AW2008/2009, ready-to-wear shown in Paris, where Chanel iconography was wittily and blatantly used to brand the show. (Francois Guillot/Staff via Getty Images)

Chanel

Chanel too reaffirms the significance and uniqueness of the brand every season. Loyal customers enjoy the fashion content of the shows, while being reassured by the overt use of iconic symbols that the house still offers its traditional products, albeit with a modern take. Chanel shows are very heavily branded with globally recognized iconic symbols; the blatancy excused by the supremely confident and witty sophistication of their presentation. Chanel uses these symbols across all promotional activities; consistent use of the symbols ensures the continued success of the brand. Chanel's brand equity is embodied in these *heritage* symbols, chosen long ago by Coco Chanel, one of the most astute marketing minds of the 1900s. Lagerfeld, Chanel's creative director, combines heritage with references to contemporary culture, repeatedly using the iconic symbols: the interlocking C, the no. 5, the chains, the lion, the jacket and the pearls that consumers associate with the brand. While the consumer engages in the hedonistic spectacle of the latest show, they consume repeated messages reinforcing brand personality.

Stimulating an emotional connection between the brand and the consumer

While developing economies use the runway to promote their growing fashion industries, those same economies are targeted by influential brands from mature fashion centres. The runway has been used to huge effect to gain market share in China, with extravagant high-tech shows, independent of fashion weeks, harnessing digital technology to reach vast tech-savvy audiences. In 2013, Valentino held a mid-season show to open a new Shanghai flagship store. Valentino's signature red, a colour popular within Chinese culture, was used to style the show, creating a strong visual association between the brand and its new market. The garments and accessories were red and some of the products were only available in China. Others were released in the Shanghai store before they were available in New York, Paris and London, thereby shrewdly turning on its head the situation where Chinese consumers have had to travel to the United States or Europe to purchase designer fashion. In advance of the show, excitement was generated through social media, including the use of the hash tag: #Valentino上侮# (Valentino Shanghai). The show was live streamed on the Internet. Short video clips and a countdown, both on the web and through social media, were skilfully used to build anticipation in advance of the show and ensure that the show reached an audience far in excess of those actually present.

The fashion show and brand loyalty

Brand loyalty relies on the brand repeatedly meeting customer expectations. As it designs each show a designer or company must consider those expectations. Marketers talk in terms of brand touchpoints. These are the times when the consumer interacts with the brand. The fashion show offers multiple touchpoints, not just during a show, but in advance and afterwards as visual imagery and film are communicated through multiple media channels. Consumers become loyal to a brand when they connect with its values. The designer Vivienne Westwood frequently uses her shows to highlight issues around gender and climate change (Westwood's AW2017 collection entitled 'Ecotricity' did both). Loyal customers buy because of what a brand stands for as well as because they associate with the product. Events such as fashion shows reassure consumers that the money they spend on the brand is well spent. While runway is expensive, each show reaffirms their belief that the brand is delivering its promise.

Branding messages and runway production

A brand is a valuable business asset. Companies leverage brand identity to ensure that all activities, including its shows, communicate messages consistent with its overarching brand strategy. This often leads to repeated elements or formats, such as the use of digital technology by fashion company Burberry in China, or Margaret Howell's use of the same set design. The experimental nature of early Alexander McQueen shows echoed the experimental personality of the brand. The show is sometimes the only opportunity for young designers to communicate about their collections and communicate brand messages, so it is imperative to get the message right. The extravagance of super-brand shows reaffirms the importance and exclusivity of the brand within the fashion marketplace. Get a feel for this by watching the time-lapse video of the build for Dior's AW2016 show in Paris, designed by the legendary Bureau Betak. It took eighteen days to build and eleven days to strike (Israel, 2016).

The extravagance of super-brand shows reaffirms the importance and exclusivity of the brand ... Get a feel for this by watching the time-lapse video of the build for Dior's AW2016 show in Paris, designed by the legendary Bureau Betak. It took eighteen days to build and eleven days to strike. Israel, 2016

Industry Insight

Lucy Williams, fashion designer and fashion blogger

You were one of the first people to shoot street style.

When I first started doing street style for the reports, London Fashion Week was at the National History Museum and there was a little space at the entry to the shows and it would just be me and a couple of other photographers. Of course, people like Bill Cunningham had been doing it for years, but it was me and a few press photographers who had been employed to go down and shoot people and the guys said to me, 'we'll take photos of who you take photos of because we're not fashion and we have no idea'.

People were just wearing what they were wearing and they looked beautiful but step forward to today and people are dressing to have their photograph taken and are walking by in one outfit, then changing and putting on something else; it doesn't reflect the industry, it doesn't reflect street style because it is not natural street style, it is staged. There are amazing people who are part of the industry who do always look amazing and they are style icons, but they are genuinely part of the industry, part of the fashion journalism industry. The people that are seen at shows as fashion industry are fashion journalists, or stylists or photographers. They are the fashion communicators.

Figure 3.8 Lucy Williams. (© Lucy Williams)

It's interesting to explore the emotional experience of the show that consumers can now engage in through social media.

Yes, the way that they are streamed now, so that you are not just seeing stills after the event, you can actually experience the event and a very diluted part of the atmosphere (you feel something). Otherwise, it is a closed room and a limited audience. That is also important because you get that sense of exclusivity and significance. For example, the resort shows are popping up now, and it was Vuitton last night from Japan, and on Instagram a lot of people had posted videos of the final run, their favourite look . . . I found that coverage much more engaging and stimulating than when Vogue runway had posted all the stills up. It was also lovely but it wasn't as engaging and it wasn't as moving. Now we have an opportunity to experience a little of what the front row is seeing.

Do you see your designs on the catwalk?

My stuff gets shot and it's in campaigns or at a press day but I have never worked with anyone high-end enough to have a catwalk show. It is always a static event, but even a press day is a wonderful thing. I'm working with Oasis and their window displays are always so beautiful, it is the same team that manages their press events, so they are always super creative with the stories that the design team have been working on, they take them that step further. The props and the atmosphere, it is just incredible, so the venue and the way the collection is presented [for a press day] is just . . . it is almost as exciting as going to a show, it is really creative. Even though you are not doing a show, you always do something that you call a press piece, something that pushes the limits and we know people won't buy lots of it, but you do it because it garners excitement and lifts the energy, and the press will feature it and then it will lead people towards the rest of your collection, so in that respect there is something designed with press in mind.

The fashion consumer and the fashion show

The consumer as informed audience

Digital technology has exponentially changed the fashion consumer's engagement with the fashion show. Today's fashion consumer absorbs more information about fashion than any consumer ever before and at greater volume and speed. Relatively recently fashion shows were part of an elitist world which consumers could not access. Now the consumer has unprecedented access to fashion, changing the relationship between designer and consumer as well as the ways in which consumers engage with and consume fashion. Direct contact builds trust between designers and consumers as brands nurture digital relationships. Live streaming means that consumers can gain much greater understanding of brands. Brands can market their products directly to the consumer through shows that generate great excitement. The consumer can commentate about runway and can purchase the products that they see live on the runway.

The power of the consumer

Now that the consumer can see the latest collections as they appear on the runway, an unforeseen shift in consumer demand has occurred. Consumers no longer want to wait for those products to reach the stores, wanting to be able to purchase them immediately. Consumer pressure has prompted the 'see-now-buy-now' trend. This has coincided with disruption in the industry caused by other factors: copying, a proliferation of collections, seasonless clothing, the merging of menswear and womenswear, the lack of synchronization of seasons and stock in stores and a widely held concern that the traditional fashion system is no longer fit for purpose.

The consumer as fashion commentator

Through social media channels the consumer responds to new collections, backstage looks and runway spectacles, and social media builds expectations of consumer involvement through such commentary. When consumers enjoy the spectacle of runway and use social media to commentate about what they experience, they take part in marketing of the brand. Meanwhile, fashion companies gather valuable data, including consumer email addresses. They gauge consumer response and analyze which runway images audiences from different markets share on social media. This data can be used to inform industry decisions on, for example, what merchandise should be stocked in which stores.

Why is the fashion consumer motivated to watch fashion shows?

Maslow's theory of Hierarchy of Needs proposes that we need to feel that we belong socially. Fashion is a vehicle for social connection and style tribes comprise people who choose to dress in a shared style. Consumers with allegiances to specific brands unwittingly form brand communities. By watching the shows of brands they associate with, consumers have a greater sense of shared experience and enjoyment, a sense of connection and belonging within that community. The theatre of the show enhances the strength of a consumer's experience, and creates a stronger sense of belonging as well as greater emotional engagement with the brand and its community, reinforcing their choice to buy that brand's products.

At the highest levels of Maslow's hierarchy are esteem and self-actualization. Consumers often choose brands because of the status this affords them. Investment through watching the runway shows of brands, and comment through

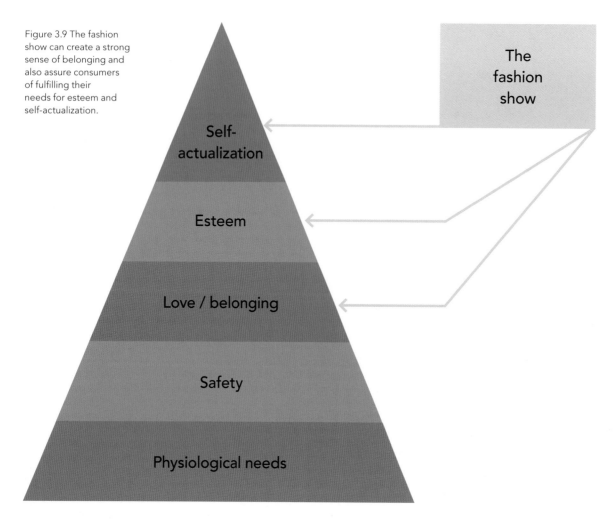

Figure 3.9 The fashion show can create a strong sense of belonging and also assure consumers of fulfilling their needs for esteem and self-actualization.

The fashion show

Self-actualization

Esteem

Love / belonging

Safety

Physiological needs

social media enables the consumer to engage more actively and send messages about their own status. The more exciting a brand's runway show, the higher esteem the brand community enjoys. By watching a brand's hugely impressive and emotionally stimulating show, commenting about it through social media and consuming its products a consumer is assured of fulfilling their needs for esteem and self-actualization.

The psychology of the show and the buying process

The fashion show is a powerful promotional tool because when consumers experience the interest, excitement and pleasure that it stimulates, they want more of those hedonistic feelings. The magical theatre of the show suggests that everything to do with the brand will be equally pleasurable setting up hedonistic ideals in the minds of consumers. Consumer psychologists suggest that consumers engage in a decision-making process which comprises seven stages. Watching the show takes place in the information search phase of the process, but because of the hedonistic ideals, consumers have expectations of similar pleasurable experiences at every stage of the process. Such is the power of the hedonistic drive to purchase from the brand that it reaches beyond the expensive clothing on the runway, stimulating a desire to purchase the peripheral products such as handbags, cosmetics, perfume and even interiors products from which the brand makes its real profits.

Industry Insight

Chantal Durivage, Co-President, Sensation Mode Group

Figure 3.10 Chantal Durivage. (© Louise Savoie)

I understand that the Montreal Fashion & Design Festival takes a more democratic approach to fashion?

The business that I own is called Sensation Mode Group and seventeen years ago the vision that my partner and I had was to bring fashion to the people, so we created a fashion and design festival. It is very different because it is consumer oriented, it is about the democratization of fashion, and it brings 500,000 people to the festival every year.

It is like a jazz or music festival but around fashion and design. It is outdoor and indoor. Fashion is alive on the streets and we bring a conversation between the people and the industry players. We involve all the different players from schools, to students to avant-garde, up-and-coming and established designers, retailers, wholesalers, model agencies . . . We have installations, performances, fashion shows, fashion experiences, designer installations . . . when people come to the festival they can experience everything.

The consumer can create their own identity and style from everything they see at the festival. It is mainly women (76 per cent) and it is different kinds of tribes, some interested in avant-garde, some interested in more commercial brands. They come to see the shows over six days. There are 150 different brands and around 50 shows. We have conferences, speakers, atelier; it is full of different experiences for the consumer. It takes place once a year in the summer and it is one of the main events in Montreal just after the jazz festival. We call it fashion-tainment.

So your fashion event is aimed directly at the consumer?

Yes, seventeen years ago, the big thing was having a website. When we started, the industry didn't understand what we were doing. There was a snobbery and what is funny now is that we are so on target as a concept. In the meantime, we produced the Montreal Fashion Week which was for the buyers and the media, a more traditional way of presenting fashion. We got a lot of feedback and that helped us a lot to grow and to develop the experience. I believe that retail is challenged so now the designers can meet their consumer directly.

We don't do a specific activity for buyers but we believe that . . . if we have a delegation of Canadian influencers coming to Montreal next season, and of course some of them will be buyers,

they won't see the next collection on stage, but we make sure they go to studios and meet the designers in the VIP areas. What is interesting is that the buyers see the reaction of the consumers to the collection. If the consumer (it could be 20,000 or 30,000 people) comes for one show and the buyers see the consumer reaction, getting excited, the buyers get a strong message.

There are two stages for fashion shows. There is the main one and there is the 'MAD' which is for music, art and design. This is about avant-garde, up-and-coming designers, collaborations between designers and painters and musicians. It is pushing the boundaries: new ways that you can present fashion. We find that the consumer is very interested in these shows because they are spectacular and because the consumer is curious to push the barriers. There are a lot of interesting conversations with the consumer around this stage.

On the main stage it is more commercial. There is a big screen and the brands have boxes that they need to stay in. We have to work closely with the brands to propose different artistic ways to present. We cannot just do a 100-piece fashion show for half an hour, people get bored, so that is why we learned to create a story around the show, and that is why we call it fashion-tainment.

We also create our own productions. For example, with the Montreal Opera, we asked a stylist to reinterpret the opera costumes in an interesting way. We had a collaboration with a stylist who redefined the costumes with some fashion pieces mixed in and there was also modern music, and opera and traditional and modern images. We also presented it in New York for TV5 and in LA for the opening of Cirque de Soleil because it was a theatrical story.

Problem recognition	Consumer desire for new fashion
Information search	Consumer watches fashion shows
Evaluation of alternatives	Consumer associates or doesn't associate with the brand messages communicated through the show
Purchase	Consumer purchases through see-now-buy-now or alternative method
Consumption	Consumer uses product
Post-consumption satisfaction or dissatisfaction	Consumer perception of wearing the product affects their brand loyalty and their liklihood of watching further shows and purchasing from the brand
Divestment	Consumer perception of the product and the brand, including satisfaction or dissatisfaction, affects their decision about how to dispose of it

Table 3.1 Stages in the buyer decision-making process

Influencers, style icons and opinion leaders

Rogers' theory of the Diffusion of Innovations groups consumers according to the point in time when they adopt a new trend. There has long been a perception that new trends emerge on the runway. Consumers with a keen interest in fashion are likely to be those who watch streamed shows and they are likely to be *innovators* and *early adopters*. The presence of people at a fashion show who are labelled key *opinion leaders* (KOLs), also known as social influencers, is essential to successful PR. Consumers look to this group of people to endorse their brand choices. Such people are known as influencers, style icons and opinion leaders. Consumers identify with celebrities whose perceived characteristics they associate with, and consumers who are interested in fashion associate with celebrities who have a strong fashion profile. The combination of celebrity and front row is powerful enough to persuade a consumer to buy from a specific designer or brand.

The front row echoes a designer's target markets

A company's intended markets determine its front row guests. If a brand is entering a new market, its PR team will attract high-profile people from that area, seating key celebrities, popular within the market, in the front row. PRs keep up-to-date lists of celebrities and people from the fashion, music, media and design industries as potential front row guests. Established brands successfully target lucrative new markets using the power of local celebrity endorsement. Chinese celebrities, such as actress Zhang Ziyi, star of *Crouching Tiger, Hidden Dragon*, and 'it girl' Zhang Xinyuan (who has over 1 million Weibo followers) now sit front row at the shows of brands for whom China is an important market. Such is the popularity of media stars in China, with their own huge social media followings – their attendance at a fashion show means valuable PR.

Figure 3.11 Actress Zhang Lanxin and dancer Hou Honglan at the Diane von Furstenberg fashion show in New York during Mercedes-Benz Fashion Week, February 2014. (Larry Busacca/Staff via Getty Images)

Industry Insight

Katherine Boivin

Figure 3.12 Katherine Boivin, a project coordinator for the Montreal Fashion & Design Festival. (© Chantal Durivage)

Katherine Boivin grew up in Montreal, Canada and studied administration before moving to London, England in 2013. She received a degree in fashion marketing at Regent's University London. She has worked as volunteer in many sportive events and had many work experiences related to customer service. Katherine aspires to work in the sport fashion industry.

How is Montreal Fashion & Design Festival different from what you saw of traditional fashion weeks?

Having lived in Montreal until I was nineteen, I never really paid attention to how fashion could be seen or treated differently than in any other big city. Once I moved to London, I started to notice certain aspects of the industry such as the unattainability and how fashion was sold to the elite. The proximity to the rest of Europe allowed me to travel a lot during the last four years and helped me realize that not all cities treat consumers equally. In my eye, fashion in London is more focused on the relationship between social groups and brands. Fashion companies tend to focus on the customers wearing their products and creating an elite society around the brand. Compared to London, Montreal is focused on promoting local artisans and brands to a wide audience. Prices will internationally be a deciding factor for a brand's audience, but the general approach in Montreal is aimed to attract an audience that is interested by the art and less about the status behind the product.

Currently working for Montreal Fashion & Design Festival, I notice how brands want to eliminate any feeling of unattainability and division. Brands are looking to be present in the everyday life in a very realistic way. The fashion industry in Montreal is influenced by international trends mixed with the wish of staying unique, refreshing, accessible and avant-gardiste.

To find out more about the Montreal Fashion & Design Festival please visit http://www.festivalmodedesign.com/en.

Show production on a grand scale

One of the most compelling stories to date was that built around the opening of Louis Vuitton's flagship store in Shanghai. The audience at the AW2012 Louis Vuitton show in Paris arrived at the Cour Carrée, a courtyard at the Louvre Museum to find themselves in a set designed to look and feel like a railway station. Just after the Vuitton station clock struck two, the train pulled in. As the station doors opened a full-size locomotive emerged through the steam. Porters accompanied models along the platform, carrying for them the sumptuous Louis Vuitton luggage and handbags from which the company makes its money.

As many brands do, and to maximize sales, Vuitton took the show elsewhere, in this case to China. This was storytelling on an impressive scale. They continued the narrative as Todd Selby, photographer, travelled from Paris to Shanghai, posting images and film of the train journey on a blog. Consumers could look on the Vuitton website to see a map of the route and access images and footage of the journey and events and interviews along the way. Four months later the train steamed into another railway station, set in China. The company had brought its AW2012 collection to Shanghai, as part of a celebration of Vuitton's 20th anniversary in China, the opening of an exhibition of Vuitton products spanning the 20th century and the launch their flagship store in Shanghai. These are positive brand messages communicated on a grand international scale.

Figure 3.13 The AW2012 Louis Vuitton fashion show held in China in July 2012 in advance of the opening of their first store in Shanghai. (Peter Parks/Staff via Getty Images)

Figure 3.14 *Vogue* editor Anna Wintour arrives at a runway show. (© Regent's University London, Photographer Jason Pittock)

The fashion show and PR

What is PR?

The Chartered Institute of Public Relations defines PR as follows:

Public relations is about reputation – the result of what you do, what you say and what others say about you. Public relations is the discipline which looks after reputation, with the aim of earning understanding and support and influencing opinion and behaviour. It is the planned and sustained effort to establish and maintain goodwill and mutual understanding between an organisation and its publics.

Fashion PRs use communication around the fashion show to build and reinforce a brand's reputation. This involves creating a compelling story around the collection and the show to persuade everyone that this will be the most important show (and therefore brand) of the season. PR teams ensure that every element of the show communicates strong positive messages about the brand so that press coverage makes people feel positively towards it. PR involves getting the right VIPs and celebrities into the front row so that the event generates essential third-party endorsements and social media coverage. A good PR works closely with the designer and with the show production team on the concept and presentation. A fashion week show may only last for ten minutes but PRs optimize the opportunities it presents to communicate brand messages before, during and after the event.

Who does PR for a fashion show?

There are PR agencies that specialize in fashion. They have strong relationships with the fashion press, stylists, fashion photographers, show producers and journalists. Larger fashion companies sometimes have an in-house PR team or press office that manages PR activities. When they stage big events, they may buy further help from PR agents or event organizers. Many young designers cannot afford to pay for PR, so they do most of their own PR, and pay for PR for events such as runway shows to ensure press attendance. External PR agents charge their clients a regular 'retainer', or a fee for an individual activity. Activities and fees are set out in legal contracts between PR agents and clients. When a brand shows in another country they may employ a local PR agent who knows and is able to attract the right press to the event. Being in the stable of a good PR agent is expensive but it can be essential in getting a return on the investment of a show. Getting the right people to a show and getting coverage in newspapers and magazines, online publications, and through social media and third-party endorsement is essential to the brand. Having the right people in the front row and maximizing press and social media coverage is everything.

Industry Insight
Peter Robinson, Head of Press, The White Company

What were your first experiences of fashion shows?
My first foray into catwalk was when I worked with Kim Blake and her agency Kim Blake PR. I worked London Fashion Week and later Paris, also for brands such as Michiko Koschino and Robert Cary-Williams who were our retained clients. Often the agency would be engaged only to work on the seasonal shows as these are so time-intensive with the holy grail of the seating plans being the most political thing of all.

Tell me about the seating plans.
Seating is graded, with editors-in-chief, editors and fashion directors front and second row depending on importance of the title they work on. Important freelancers also need to be seated in prime positions with no obstruction to view. The size of the show and your venue also dictate how many junior stylists and assistants you could admit to each show. At Kim Blake PR we did a Boudicca show in a car park in East London – we had limited seating so most people had to stand. Boudicca were interesting designers, maverick non-conformists so the international press came in droves. I was in charge of seating the international buyers who'd come en masse with especial interest from Japan and the US. It is important they have good seats in order to see the collection as the money they can put down can be the lifeblood of emerging talent.

Figure 3.15 Peter Robinson. (© Peter Robinson)

What did you do next?
I went to Marks & Spencer to look after womenswear PR. There I experienced the fashion show in a different context. We decided to exhibit our collection on the catwalk as part of the wider press day – a big production. The press could call in outfits directly from the show. The look book that we gave away featured an edit of the outfits, there was a release and line sheet on each of the chairs; it was almost the way that salon shows work. It looked very beautiful and was applauded within the press. It was not the first high street fashion show, but it was unusual at that point, a gamble that paid off.

Then you went to Harvey Nichols, which is famous for its designer fashion?
I was group PR manager for Harvey Nichols stores internationally. There, my catwalk experience was different because I attended shows; the four main fashion cities and the menswear shows. It was very different from being behind the scenes with the headset on. I would accompany the buyers to the showroom buying appointments afterwards, or the look-sees, to review what we had seen on the catwalk. You realize what an edit the shows are, and how much larger whole collections are once you arrive at the designers' studios often rented especially due to proximity to the shows. What appears on the runway is very much the stylist's point of view of the collection.

Because the show tells the story of a collection?

Yes, the show is still key in terms of publicity even and especially with the advent of online and streaming capabilities. The spectacle of the catwalk show is a PR tool, but it also helps buyers to work out what their edit will be, what the designer's story is, and how it will sit within stores amongst peer brands for their customers. At the buying appointments you realize how much isn't on the catwalk. Every label will do a white shirt, a T-shirt, a piece of denim . . . that will sell more than the outrageous, colourful, expensive catwalk pieces; these pieces are often pure theatre, the pieces that get the PR and keep the brand front of mind in saturated markets.

Why do people travel the world for live catwalk rather than film or online?

You hear what people say, their reactions to the collections, members of press. It's about atmosphere, grandeur, spectacle, some of the big shows with amazing sets can never be captured on social media. If there is an amazing collection, there are still standing ovations . . . when the front row will get up and applaud and the whole auditorium will follow suit because they have witnessed something that will change the industry. That is why those arbiters sit in the front row, and when they applaud, you know that this is a *moment*.

Of all the shows, what do you remember today?

In Paris I saw McQueen collections that really were outstanding – moments in time. Paris fashion week is always about the show, New York is always very slick and well produced. Milan is perhaps the old guard – it is often said the money is spent usually between Milan and New York. London is always very experimental, I think London gets away with more, it is a bit more tongue in cheek, rather than spending a fortune on shows, apart perhaps from Burberry who have been responsible for changing the perception of the London show.

After Harvey Nichols you headed PR at New Look?

We did a number of internal shows with about 1,000 people in the audience: directors, area managers, store managers, marketeers – these were big productions: forty models plus and quite long in terms of time. These shows were educational – about how the clothes could be put together, the trends: engaging the staff and giving them information that they would use with customers in stores. For a lot of people who hadn't been to a fashion show, it was a game changer in terms of getting enthused.

How has social media changed things?

The playing fields have forever been changed – the immediacy of communication, the impossibility of exclusivity. Everyone releases information at the same time whether bloggers or the online versions of the biggest fashion titles globally, celebrity front rows have become editors and arbiters in a way never seen before. Brands are now beginning to see how this can be advantageous with the move by many brands to 'see-now, buy-now' offerings as well as the more traditional season ahead that still builds an anticipation and excitement.

Figure 3.16 Rei Kawakubo's
1997 'Body Meets Dress,
Dress Meets Body'
collection. (Guy Marineau/
Contributor via Getty
Images)

The PR value of shock and surprise

Oscar Wilde said, 'The only thing worse than being talked about is not being talked about'. Sometimes the shows gaining the most media coverage are those that are surprising or shocking. Rei Kawakubo of Comme des Garçons' SS1997 show in Paris was called 'Body Meets Dress, Dress Meets Body'. Some of the press called it the 'bumps and lumps show'. Padding distorted the natural body shape in a way that challenged conventional notions of beauty. The show shocked the audience and caused a huge stir, but in publicity terms it was a success. In 2010 Tom Ford shocked the fashion world when he held his first womenswear show with an audience of only 100 people at his Madison Avenue store during New York Fashion Week. Echoing the early salon shows in Paris, Ford explained each outfit to a select audience, who no doubt felt privileged to be there. One house photographer shot the looks and the elite nature of the event created a media furore. Subsequently he has held intimate shows in Los Angeles and elsewhere, attended by few but reported to many, resulting in increased perception of the brand as exclusive.

Celebrity and the PR role

PRs spend a lot of time populating the world's front rows, so essential has celebrity (third party) endorsement become to runway. It can be lucrative for celebrities to sign contracts with big brands, sitting front row and wearing the brand's products (known as celebrity seeding). Other celebrities who do not have a contract with a brand may be paid (in money or product) to attend a one-off show. For some brands, photographs of celebrities are as important as images from the runway and they work with celebrities their target consumers aspire to emulate, who are appropriate ambassadors for the brand. There has been criticism that celebrities are not interested in the collections, merely in being seen. The relationship is mutually supportive; some celebrities want to be seen at the right shows for their reputations (and their bank accounts). The big shows are glamorous, and part of the celebrity scene. The most valuable celebrities at shows are those who also have a large social media following. The attendance of a celebrity with a following of millions means essential social media coverage and endorsement of the brand as they tweet or Instagram from the front row.

Figures 3.18 to 3.20 The press devotes much coverage to images of celebrities. (© Regent's University London, Photographer Jason Pittock)

Agents and stylists

Most celebrities have an agent who organizes their attendance at shows and negotiates a fee for attending. As well as appearing in the front row, celebrities are photographed arriving at a fashion show and chatting with other celebrities, and may pose in front of what are known as *branding boards* or *step-and-repeat boards* showing designer or brand and sponsor logos. Stylists are also involved, getting celebrities into the most lucrative brands: 'It is about getting the celebrities in an expensive brand, but then it is about moving the celebrities up . . . It is all about the celebs being paid to go to the shows wearing a brand's clothes . . . . they must know that they are paid to wear it' (Interview with Julia Robson, 2016).

Celebrities and the media

Steven Rogers works with celebrities in the media, and here he talks about the relationship between celebrities and the runway.

Celebrities either get paid to sit front row or they get loads of clothes. They will be flown out on a private jet, have a nice place to stay, presents . . . treated like royalty. The PR team for the fashion house will look after them. It's about publicity. Making sure a car is booked, making sure they arrive, making sure the 'paps' are there taking the picture. There was the Versace show [Haute Couture, January 2016] and the main picture of Rita Ora in that dress, she was probably paid. Most stars look good now because they have stylists. If Rita is at a Versace show in a Versace dress, there will be a Versace stylist. Monica [Bellucci] dressed in Chanel at the Chanel show, she will have been paid. That is a day's work for her. And there are Kendall Jenner and Gigi Hadid on the catwalk [Chanel Haute Couture, January 2016].

And now to be a famous model, you've got to have a big social media following so they're becoming celebrities again. I think social media has changed things. It is a way of speaking to audiences. You can't just be a model, you have to be a model with a following. That brings more to the brand. Gigi Hadid is everywhere. Over 12 million followers. That is one of the reasons Versace will have employed her. It will be part of the deal that she uses social media.

For the full interview with Steven Rogers, please visit http://www.bloomsbury.com/the -fashion-show-9781472568489.

Figure 3.21 Goody bags on front row seats at a fashion show, with products sponsored by Shu Uemura. (© Regent's University London, Photographer Tony Rogers)

PRs and sponsoring fashion

Sometimes PRs will be involved in attracting sponsors and they must keep sponsors happy by ensuring that their company names and logos (and sometimes product) are used repeatedly to reflect their investment in the event. Considerable sponsorship comes from hair and beauty brands but also from outside fashion. Non-fashion companies exploit the power of fashion to excite by sponsoring fashion shows which are heavily branded with their logos. A prime example is Mercedes-Benz, which sponsors many of the high-profile fashion events around the world. Likewise, Swarovski has a prominent section on its website called 'Sponsorship and Events', filled with photographs of fashion celebrities, parties and other events. By association, non-fashion products look exciting if they are photographed at fashion events and if they are perceived as popular with fashion insiders.

Figure 3.22 Photographers in the press pit. (© Gill Stark)

Runway imagery

Digital technology has increased the importance of photography and film for PR because persuasive runway images carrying powerful messages about a brand can be pushed out at speed around the world. Brands create sophisticated media communications strategies around runway events which rely upon visual imagery to realize the promotional opportunities that runway offers. One of the most iconic fashion show images is the photographers banked up at the end of the runway, black lenses poised. The *house photographer* and the *house videographer* shoot from prime position in the centre front of the press pit, employed by the fashion house to shoot images for the brand. That position gives a view straight down the centre of the runway at the right height, ensuring the best shots. PRs also confirm the presence of other photographers at a show: agency photographers and those shooting for instance for photo galleries, including sites such as firstVIEW. Publications get images from PRs or from agencies. 'Such is the ease and convenience of transmitting imagery that newspapers and magazines rarely run their own images anymore' (Cope and Maloney, 2016).

Film and the consumer

For some time, short film clips have been posted on sites such as YouTube and footage has been used on company and other websites. While film of the runway has long been used as a record of collections and shows, fashion film is developing as a genre in its own right. Some of the most interesting fashion shows over the past few years have been, or have included, fashion film such as Ralph Lauren's 4D show in November 2010.

With the advent of live streaming, and the opportunity for fashion companies to invite online audiences to join them for a stream of their fashion shows, new promotional opportunities have arisen that are being exploited to the fullest. Now the consumer can experience the excitement and anticipation in the build-up to a show, they can watch the audience arrive, see the photographers and the models, they can see and hear the drama and the spectacle, and just as a new collection is presented to the world, the consumer can be in the privileged position of being one of the first to see and order it.

Sponsorship

Mercedes-Benz' sponsorship of so many fashion weeks ensures that its cars appeal to a consumer group that would otherwise not consider its product. Sponsorship, either as *title-sponsor* or *co-sponsor*, includes providing cars that transport fashion influencers from show to show, associating the company with exciting luxury global events. The number of fashion weeks that it sponsors is evidence of the success of this association.

Figure 3.23 A Dior fashion show in Paris in August 1955. (John Chillingworth/ Stringer via Getty Images)

The fashion show and media outreach

The fashion press

The wonderful photograph in Figure 3.23, from a Dior show in 1955, shows Marie Louise Bousquet, the Paris editor of *Harper's Bazaar*, and Carmel Snow, editor in chief of *Harper's Bazaar*, in the centre front with Alexander Liberman, the art director of American *Vogue*. In 1955 and until comparatively recently, this was the tradition: select journalists attended the shows and the public read in a relatively small number of newspapers their articles about the latest collections, accompanied by a few photographs. Items from collections might be seen later in editorials in magazines, styled around a specific story. The public would rarely see a whole collection.

Since the 1990s the role of the journalist has been changing, largely due to digital technologies. Now that we can all see collections ourselves, the role of the journalist has become to contextualize and comment upon a collection, exploring its meaning and its contexts, and explaining its relevance to contemporary fashion, society and culture. So much comment is generated now in relation to runway that those with a deep historical and contextual knowledge of fashion and the ability to assimilate collections quickly (sometimes ten a day) and with authority have become revered.

Those in the front row have huge power to influence, so people talk about the power front row: journalists, buyers, bloggers, celebrities and other influencers.

Industry Insight

Julia Robson

Figures 3.24 and 3.25 Julia Robson, British fashion journalist. (© Julia Robson)

Julia Robson is a British fashion journalist who has been deputy fashion editor of *The Daily Telegraph*, fashion editor of *The Sunday Mirror* and columnist on international fashion for *The National*, the influential English national newspaper of the United Arab Emirates. A fashion journalism graduate of Central St Martins, she has written fashion features for glossy magazines including *Elle* and *Instyle*, and reported on international runways – both pret-a-porter and haute couture – across global fashion capitals for many British and international publications over several decades. Julia worked on the concept and launch of several retail online sites including British giant Next, and continues to be involved as a fashion consultant/lecturer in media. She is also a regular 'frockwatching' guest on Sky News (during the Oscars) and BBC Radio 4 *(Woman's Hour)*.

What is the process of runway journalism?

The zeitgeist! Going into a show season, you are aware of talking points. This season [2017] there were a lot of talking points about Demna Gvasalia; what was he going to do to Balenciaga? They [talking points] might also come up during the shows. You have to be aware of the bigger picture. I always say 'before, during and after'. Before you go to a show, you have to think about the brand, the context, what they are good at, what they are known for, who is designing. Then you get to the venue and think about all the decisions that went into choosing that venue, and look at the show notes on the seat. Get any information you can: talk to the PR, find out about the designer, what was he inspired by?

What do you think about during the show?

Today we are quite spoiled because you can watch again online, but the way I was trained, you have to be writing all the time: about silhouette, proportion, usually there are sections [to the show] like chapters of a book. You have to think about the bigger picture, and then there are highlights: 'there was a jacket which had sparkles on it'. And you are thinking 'where does this fit into the history of the brand, is this a good example? Is it typical? Has it shocked me or is it just same old?' And after the show it is all about analyzing and thinking why was I disappointed or . . .? Why was that a moment? As a journalist, I am thinking about words that come into my head that can best describe what I am seeing.

So you are already writing in your head?

Definitely, but there have been shows where the next thing you think is: what just happened? You have lost yourself in the moment. There is something about being very focused: you know you've got to write something. Often my deadlines were ten minutes, twenty minutes, to put together a piece. There are lots of points you can put in but you have to work out which is the most important . . . and someone like Suzy Menkes makes it sound so easy. You can go with a hundred angles, but what is the right angle? You have to make a decision very quickly. It is quite a competitive sport watching a fashion show. The fashion editors are all poker-faced, not giving the game away, even at a fantastic show. The only show where I ever saw people go 'wow' was Versace in the 1980s/90s and McQueen and Galliano.

How much do you use the show notes?

A lot because until recently they were a link to the designer. It's what the designer is telling you is in his or her head. Now they get journalists to write the show notes. In London, Mary Katrantzou gets Alex Fury from *The Independent* to write hers so they are press ready. Show notes used to be very esoteric, they are not now. The designers want to control what the bloggers will say. This week at London Fashion Week, Erdem, who is a real fanatic about detail, had listed the 6 inspirations in a little white package . . . with a velvet ribbon. It was very well done. I went backstage to speak to him. A student there had spent the entire night folding the show notes. They were little works of art.

Figure 3.26 Social media from the front row. (© Julia Robson)

What about the show invitations?

Usually the show invite hints at what the show will be about. You arrive in your hotel and all of the invites are there. They are all beautiful. You have to work out which show you are going to review for the newspaper, and some of them, you think 'wow' that looks interesting. So, the invitation is also to tempt you.

Have bloggers changed fashion journalism?

When I started, the front row was real rank and file. Bloggers have changed things, particularly in relation to the fashion show. You could see it coming. I was going to the haute couture shows when the bloggers started to arrive. There was a real us and them. You could see that there were some fashion editors who were put out by the bloggers. Even Anna Wintour who has now succumbed to it all was very cross. It was the fact that they had a twelve-year-old Tavi Gevinson next to Anna Wintour, a young girl with a different perspective and it did feel quite right for the time, but they didn't have that huge knowledge of fashion.

How have bloggers changed fashion journalism?

I have had to change my style slightly to make it chattier, more subjective. As a journalist, you are taught to be objective and balanced, unless you are writing a column. Bloggers can be quite outspoken. I think it has had an impact on critical vocabulary. We had to say 'this was an interesting show' . . . but suddenly they could say 'I really liked the show'. I think now there is another renaissance because some of the bloggers are also good writers. Susie Lau and Leandra Medine, they have a perspective, so that is like a journalist.

So, fashion journalism has changed and is still changing?

There is a whole audience out there that doesn't want to read intellectual fashion, that is the world we live in now. It has been bad news in terms of brands getting greedy and being able to control things. There is the fact that the bloggers have not quite earned their position and yet they are allowed in. The critical has gone. Fashion used to be an industry but now it is for everyone and it is accessible and it is democratic. When you do it online it is about doing it in three lines and getting the interest of the consumer before an advert comes up. It is a different way of consuming news. Fashion shows are changing, it is about bringing in the followers and the consumers, rather than 'the designer'.

A new kind of commentator

A relatively new commentator about fashion exists in the form of bloggers and other influencers, communicating through social media from the front row. Social media has transformed the fashion show. As with traditional journalists, bloggers such as Scott Schuman, whose blog *The Sartorialist* is one of the longest established and best known, are revered for their knowledge of fashion and their feel for what is relevant within contemporary fashion. PRs work hard to get the right mix in the front row so that there are enough bloggers and social-media savvy celebrities to generate influential social media activity that will flood Instagram feeds from the runway once a show starts. There has, however, been criticism that audiences are more interested in their iPhones than in the collections on the runways. Ironically, some of the people who have invitations to sit front row and watch a show live choose to view the runway largely through the eye of a lens.

Social media is so influential that PRs also look at the social media activities of people who are employed to work on shows. Models, especially those who are famous, may be chosen for their followings on social media. A good number of models are now scouted on social media, receiving messages via Facebook and Instagram to ask how tall they are and whether they are interested in modelling. Likewise, hair artists, make-up artists, backstage teams, stylists, music designers and show producers all use social media as part of their work if they want to attract more business. Meanwhile designers such as Alber Elbaz have been said to create collections with social media in mind, ensuring that the looks on the runway will be great on Instagram. Many designers cannot afford the high cost of advertising and would not survive without the ability to expand their businesses using social media, benefitting from immediacy and from direct contact with consumers. An example is the London designer Henry Holland of House of Holland, whose background is in PR.

'It's about total immediacy now. We are in an age of more, faster, bigger.' Alexandre de Betak.
Anaya, 2013

Figure 3.28 Fashion Scout (a London-based organization that supports young designers) encourages the use of social media at its shows. (© Gill Stark)

Susannah Lau

Susannah Lau, whose blog is called *StyleBubble*, has built a reputation based on her knowledge of fashion and her eye for the contemporary. She has over 200,000 Twitter followers, is respected by the traditional press and by the fashion industry and she has become a fashion celebrity in her own right: she sits front row at shows internationally and is invited to work as a guest stylist, fashion journalist and commentator as an acknowledged influential fashion blogger. Established and respected bloggers such as Susannah Lau follow ethical codes and declare financial relationships with brands. While traditional journalists may be paid a wage or a fee for their writing, bloggers often rely on advertisers paying to appear on their websites, or other forms of income such as freelance work or financial collaborations with brands.

The important role of social media

Millions of blog posts, tweets, Instagram images, Facebook posts and YouTube videos are posted every year, but only a small percentage are ever looked at again. Fuzzy photographs, tweets that mean nothing in serious fashion terms and aspirational but un-revisited blogs fill cyberspace. There are many thousands of aspiring fashion bloggers, but only a few become influential fashion authorities, with a reputation recognized by the industry and millions of followers. Social media in the form of blogging is so popular that organizations like the British Fashion Council (BFC) have dedicated areas on their websites with information for bloggers and the BFC has created a 'blogger strategy' to deal with the large number of applications for accreditation each season. British style journalist Sasha Wilkins is quoted on the BFC website saying:

> As both journalist and blogger it's been an extraordinary experience to watch the exponential growth of blogging from both sides since I started blogging in 2006. With that growth has come many unforeseen logistical challenges for the entire industry at London Fashion Week, and I'm very pleased to be working with the British Fashion Council as they start to implement a continuing programme of measures to help bloggers and editors alike navigate London Fashion Week in the digital age. (British Fashion Council, 2017)

Figure 3.29 Style-spotting
at London Fashion Week.
(© Gill Stark)

Data science

Because social media has become such a powerful form of communication, data science is used to collect information about the use of media channels such as Twitter, Facebook and Instagram. Data is analyzed to determine the effectiveness of different practices and approaches to digital media. This enables companies to make decisions about their use of social media: the size of headlines, the length of posts, content strategy and what to post where and when. It gives them information about the reproduction rate and how they performed on different platforms. Ironically, social media, which started as consumer-to-consumer comment about fashion, has become another sophisticated method of promoting fashion to that same consumer.

Style and trend spotting

Runway is only part of what happens at fashion weeks. What goes on off the runway is almost more reported and this includes *street-style*, *trendspotting* or *cool-hunting*. Visitors to shows are photographed outside events such as Pitti Uomo in Florence and London Fashion Week. Some street-style stars are paid by brands to wear their garments, and many street-style stars borrow garments from brands or from the young designers they support. Street-style stars know that if they wear specific brands they are more likely to be photographed. A whole industry has grown up around style-spotting and while it looks spontaneous, it is orchestrated, so that stars arrive at or exit shows at the most opportune times, and fake phone calls to stay in front of photographers longer. Because street-style in cities like London and New York reflects fashion trends, businesses have evolved selling photographs of street-style stars. The legendary photographer Bill Cunningham, who was fascinated by personal style and the way that people chose to wear clothes, was often to be seen around fashion week in New York photographing people of all kinds and became known as the original street fashion photographer.

Instagram

There are over 300 million Instagram users internationally, and Instagram is used to communicate photographs quickly, giving the fashion industry the ability to send images of runway out to millions in one press of a button. Instagram can be used to build a collection of images, and it can be linked to other platforms such as Flickr and Facebook, further perpetuating the use of the image. The advent of Instagram video means that film of shows can also be communicated at speed around the world.

Figure 3.30 Chanel Haute
Couture AW2014 with Suzy
Menkes, Carine Roitfeld,
Grace Coddington, Mario
Testino, Anna Wintour,
Catherine Martin, Korean
K-pop singer CL, guest,
Jung Ryeo-won, Swai
Lun-Mei and Angelica
Cheung in the front
row. (Rindoff/Dufour/
Contributor via Getty
Images)

When the commentators become the celebrities

Our culture's assigning of celebrity status to those who are considered arbiters
of style means that respected fashion journalists, bloggers and those who excel
at social media have themselves become celebrities. Susan Lau is one example.
Anna Wintour, one of the best-known journalists in the world, and Suzy Menkes,
probably the most highly respected fashion journalist internationally, are also
excellent examples of commentators assigned celebrity status.

The fashion show and integrated communications strategies

Runway is part of an integrated promotional strategy

Fashion brands with sophisticated marketing strategies create *integrated*
communications strategies, which set out how all of their promotional activities
will work together, ensuring that consistent messages are communicated to the
consumer. For these big companies, runway shows are not created in isolation,
but are part of their integrated promotional strategies. Promotional strategies
contain clearly defined promotional objectives. The fashion show is designed to
communicate messages, which are part of how the company builds, maintains
and constantly reminds the consumer about the personality of the brand. The aim
is to ensure that the brand is the first that comes into consumers' minds when they
consider buying new products. An example of a company that very successfully
uses the fashion show as part of an integrated promotional strategy is the US
underwear giant Victoria's Secret.

Figure 3.31 Singer Taylor Swift and a model in wings on the runway at a Victoria's Secret fashion show. (Kevin Kane/ Contributor via Getty Images)

Victoria's Secret

Victoria's Secret shows are promotional exercises and PR events that are heavily reported in the press and followed a week later by televising to an audience of millions; such is their reputation for exciting entertainment. During the 'countdown', PR is used to generate excitement and to build anticipation. With celebrity models on the runway, wearing lingerie that is designed to result in highly sexualized images, styling is dramatic and the productions are famous for the angels' wings worn by celebrity 'Angel' models. Models interact on the runway with equally famous musicians – Taylor Swift in 2014 – all designed for press attention and consumer sales. The power of runway to generate brand excitement is exploited to the full in these shows. Its messages are very sophisticated. The tremendous cost of producing a Victoria's Secret show, reputedly $12 million in 2014, is evidence itself of the power of runway to sell the company's products.

Video packages about the models on the company's website give them a 'girl next door' feel mixed with celebrity sparkle. Footage of the run-up to the event, backstage video and further documentary add a reality TV feel as anticipation is built. When the consumer is most seduced by the glamour of runway and backstage, they can buy into the lifestyle of the Angels by making a purchase. The ordinariness of the company's low-priced products, and the fact that it also sells cosy slippers and pyjamas, is forgotten.

As part of its integrated promotional strategy, the company uses strong iconography to perpetuate the excitement of the shows. Visual imagery, such as the angels' wings, is repeated in advertising, on the website and in myriad other ways. Backstage shots show models wearing the same backstage wrap that is for sale on the website alongside runway-inspired looks and references to angels and wings. In this way, the show contributes to the story that determines how the consumer perceives the brand, ensuring that this is the brand uppermost in the mind of the consumer, who is seduced into buying more Victoria's Secret products.

Activities

01. Branding the runway

Choose a brand that produces spectacular shows. Research the brand and review its various communications (including websites, YouTube, advertising, in-store promotions and packaging) to ascertain how it uses branding to communicate its messages.

A. Analyze how it reinforces its branding messages through the medium of the runway.

B. Ascertain how images and footage from its shows are used to promote the brand: stills, short film clips and longer film formats.

02. PR agents

Imagine that you are employed by one of the PR agencies that you have researched and that you are working on the show for one of their clients. Put together a press release to be sent out in advance of the designer or brand's next show.

03. Influencers

Choose a well-reported runway show. Research who attended the show, who sat in the front row and what media coverage the show achieved.

A. Identify which influential bloggers, journalists and other influencers sat front row and what media communications resulted from their attendance: press articles, editorials and what they sent out through Twitter, Instagram and other social media channels.

B. What celebrity endorsement did the show achieve and was there any celebrity seeding?

04. Style-spotting

Choose a runway look from a very directional show. Look at images of it on the runway and read reports in the media. Then track the look as it is worn by celebrities, appears in further media communications and as it appears in stores and on consumers in the street. Use images to present this information with a timeline. Alternatively, style-spot a particular look on the street and track it back through to the runway.

05. Runway as part of an integrated communication strategy

Select a fashion brand that uses runway shows as one method of communication. Research, analyze and present the brand's integrated communications strategy, setting its fashion shows within the context of its overall communications strategy. Explain how the show relates to the other elements of the strategy and how integral or otherwise it is to the strategy.

4

Creating a spectacle:
Planning a fashion show

Chapter Four takes the reader through the different elements of pre-show work, exploring how creative vision and practical project management combine in successful show planning. The chapter explores practical matters such as venue hire and how to select and book models. It sets out show teams and responsibilities, explains set design and how hair and make-up is designed, and it covers budgets, sponsorship and the role of PR in pre-show work. It takes the reader through all of the preparatory work for successful fashion show production.

Figure 4.1 Alexander
McQueen's AW1999
show called 'The Outlook'
was a winter wonderland
fantastical presentation
with models ice skating
through a birch forest.
(Alexis Duclos/Contributor
via Getty Images)

When you see an Alexander McQueen fashion show, you are taken on a journey. It's surreal.
de La Baume, n.d.

The vision

The starting point for a show is an idea; a vision of what the show will be like. It may be the vision of one person or the shared vision of a group of people. It will be partly determined by the purpose of the show and the target audience: is it a high-profile fashion week event, a charity show to raise money, a college show or a retail event to generate sales? From this initial vision comes the *concept*, which is the starting point for producing a show. The *brief* can be a full, formal and detailed written brief, setting out the goals and including elements such as the budget, number of outfits, the size of the audience, the look of the show and the model-look. Sometimes the brief is more informal and could be as simple as a verbal discussion, a few words, sketches, pictures or mood boards to communicate what kind of experience a designer or creative director has in mind.

Not everyone wants a spectacle

The recent trend for immersive experiences might include a powerful set, moving images, dramatic lighting and even fragrance. But while there is an element of drama to every show, a spectacular production is not for everyone. Many prefer to present a simple, more traditional event, designed to present clothing in a way that allows it to speak for itself. As Etienne Russo of Villa Eugénie said in *Dazed Digital*, 'Some people want to whisper it and some want to shout it out loud. Spectacle is not right for everybody. It's about doing the right thing, finding the right balance and doing things the right way' (Woo, 2013).

Industry Insight
John Walford, fashion show producer

How did you become a fashion show producer?

I have a background in theatre. I was working at Stratford and my contract ended. Trevor Sorbie was doing a hair show and he needed someone to produce it. We had a meeting, he showed me the ideas, and so I did it. We were at Wembly Conference Centre with about 5,000 people, so no pressure! That was my first show. We had punk girls doing free-form machine gunning and dancers from the Royal Ballet doing a routine to 'War of the Worlds'. It was very much a dramatic presentation.

You've created some spectacular shows.

Yes, for people like Hussein. We spent ages hunting for places where we could run streams down the catwalk or project lasers. The big spectacle-type shows have been people like Mugler, Chanel with Lagerfeld, and Victoria's Secret. They are big money productions. Mugler had been a dancer before being a costume designer: a girl going down the catwalk with a dress like a motorbike with the handlebars built in, that was all inspired by dance.

Why aren't there more innovative shows?

There are three issues. One is the investment; designers are very worried that, having spent all this money . . . if a shoe breaks, or there's a wardrobe malfunction, that is what they're remembered for, not for the beautiful collection. Secondly a lot of the stylists have a huge amount of say and a lot of the stylists look at flat images, very few go to the theatre or the ballet, they are not aware of what you can do with sets and lighting . . . and the third thing is that the main focus for the fashion show is the Internet, people see one still image after another.

How do you work on a more innovative show?

I always try to do an intro. One designer's collection was based on black and white and chiaroscuro. I showed her things like *Dr. Caligari*, that huge shadow of him on the wall. We created the shadow and the first model came out and posed and we had lights that kept changing as she walked. At the back, where people weren't photographing we had the shadow, and at the front we had the girl being shot completely white. At the end of the finale I got all the models to come out and make a triangle, we had blondes and redheads in black and white clothes: it looked beautiful.

Figure 4.2 John Walford. (© Regent's University London, Photographer Simon Armstrong)

There is a strong correlation between the fashion show and the theatre.

Yes, I did several shows for Robert Carey Williams and often the starting point was Pina Bausch's ballets. Robert liked the images and was keen to do interesting things, but he had little budget. One season we did a *Jack the Ripper* show. We wanted a cobbled catwalk and a Victorian type gas lamp . . . there was a film and a prop place that I knew . . . and the season after that we did the show where we laid doors to make a catwalk. When I work with the models, I often give them an idea – an *intention* it is called in acting – of what to do on the catwalk. With Margaret Howell once, the girls were all wearing gumboots and asked how to walk, and I said imagine you are in a country lane and you are walking to the gate at the end of the catwalk.

Is it easy to get sponsorship? How do young designers produce shows?

There used to be a lot of sponsorship in terms of putting money in, but companies don't have the money now. That's why we started Vauxhall Fashion Scout. We split the show costs between the four designers who had graduated in our 'Ones to Watch' show and we also had our Designer Award where they got their show fully paid for in the first season, the second season was 50 per cent, third season 25 per cent. We did the PR for them. But it has been getting harder for anybody to get any monetary sponsorship. Some designers still get help from shoe companies but not like they used to. One of the Chinese designers I worked with at LFW [London Fashion Week] said they were showing a film about tea before the show, so I said let's do something with tea leaves. I rang a tea supplier and asked if they would sponsor two kilos of tea. We scattered it down the catwalk. It looked like calligraphy and because it was an orange pekoe, it had an orange scent.

With some creativity, you don't need a huge budget?

Elspeth Gibson had a starting point of a beautiful picture by Cecil Beaton of girls standing in a garden by a bush. I got set people to do a three-dimensional paper cut-out of the bush at the entrance of the catwalk and that was very beautiful. Bora was influenced by Brothers Grimm. He couldn't afford set people so we made distinctive Brothers Grimm trees with scaled grids. We got scalpels and cut it out, and we fixed the end to a batten and took it into London Fashion Week. It took seconds to put up, and it looked very beautiful.

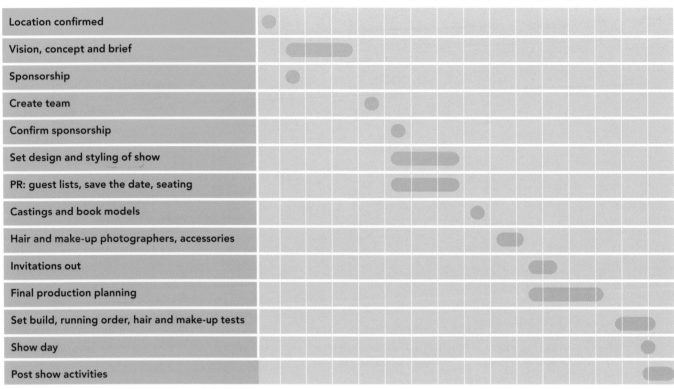

Figure 4.3 Simple Gantt chart example. (© Gill Stark)

Planning

The show production process

Planning for a runway show starts up to a year in advance even though many shows last for about ten minutes. Within those few minutes, a collection will be observed, analyzed and judged. It is a transient experience. Expectations are high because investment is high. Runway is now accessible to the consumer and the industry, so the messages being communicated must be cohesive and every detail must be perfect:

> the people who pull the strings now are the consumers, and they can be part of it. Today the person who wants to buy the fashion gets the information. They can get educated. That means more pressure on us because the message has to be crystal clear and every single detail has to be right. (Etienne Russo, quoted in Woo, 2013)

Project management

Planning usually starts with the creative concept, which is swiftly followed by practical considerations such as the budget and the venue. Shows are complex to plan and organize; nothing can be left to chance and everything must be planned down to the smallest detail. Show production has much in common with other kinds of projects and effective project management is essential. A Gantt chart is a popular project management tool that can be used to plan the activities involved in producing a fashion show: the timing and duration of each activity, who will do what, and the deadlines involved. Gantt charts are useful for tracking the progress of multiple activities and are particularly useful for larger, more complex events.

'Typically we'll have an early sit down with a designer, talk through what their goals are for the season, what direction the collection is taking shape in, what they're looking to accomplish, then a series of meetings as the collection evolves'. Keith Baptista, Managing Partner of PRODJECT who produce shows for Balenciaga, Fendi, Chanel, Chloé, Kenzo, Joseph and many more.
Smith, 2014

'You're under incredible time restraints sometimes; it's a very
intense process and you're so invested in the project. With
Marc sometimes we'll be changing things until the last minute.
If he's getting another idea and the collection's really coming
together he'll be like, "Oh, it'd be great if we could try this
other detail in the set." There are a lot of last minute changes.'
Stefan Beckman on working with Marc Jacobs. Skidmore, 2015

Organization

Meetings are held to communicate information, plan and coordinate. For instance,
the show producer, sound team, lighting team, photographers, film crew and live-
stream videographers hold production meetings. Using plans of the venue and
of the set design, they will look at the layout and at everyone's requirements in
terms of, for example, access and egress, power supplies, broadband connection,
cabling and positioning of cameras. Regular communication, coordination and
progress checks are essential. Shows can change right up to the last minute.
Risk assessments, plans, contracts for venue hire, models, security staff and
contractors all have to be organized. On the day of a show, the crew could run to
hundreds of people, and a show producer has to know who everyone is and what
they are doing. Schedules and crew lists help to organize everyone.

Designer/fashion company	Creative vision Collection Accessories Running order
Show producer	Source and manage whole team Liaison with designer/brand and others Show planning, preparation and performance Health and safety Insurance Security
Creative Director	Creative vision and concept Venue Set design Styling, set, make-up, hair, accessories Refreshments Choreography
Public Relations team	Communications Promotion Sponsors Seating Guest list
Set and technical team	Set build and strike Sound design Lighting design Sound and lighting tech Filming
Backstage team	Models Dressers Backstage organisation Backstage charts Model welfare

Table 4.1 Roles can be divided in many ways. The above chart lists some examples.

The team

Teamwork

Show production is about teamwork, and those who work on shows are natural collaborators. Members of the team are known as the crew. The size of the crew depends upon the size of the show. Every show involves the same specialist activities. A smaller fashion show may mean that people are responsible for several different activities; a show producer may have overall responsibility for the event and may also do the model castings and backstage organization. Larger shows may have a separate creative director, show producer, casting director, backstage manager, head of lighting and head of sound, with whole teams working under each. Show production becomes more complex if the event is more than a simple runway presentation, for instance, if it involves live musicians or projections. More complicated events require more detailed planning, are more time-consuming, involve more people and necessitate greater communication. Some common responsibilities and teams are as follows:

- Show producer
- PR team
- Creative director
- Stylist(s)
- Set builders
- Lighting designer
- Music designer
- Photographer(s)
- Film crew(s)
- Casting director
- Choreographer
- Backstage director
- Models
- Dressers
- Hair stylists
- Make-up artists

Show production

Have you ever wondered how ambitious runway events such as McQueen's final show 'Platos Atlantis' are created? The answer is that designers work with producers whose creative vision echoes their own. The success of an event will depend upon the leadership of someone who can communicate the vision of the show, lead a team and manage the project to realize that vision. With many diverse activities to coordinate, it is a challenging role. The producer usually manages the budget and often books the venue, puts a team together and hires sound and lighting companies and other contractors. They may do castings and book models and liaise with hair and make-up artists. They constantly check everyone's progress so that deadlines are met. Their role may involve creative work as well as management responsibility for the project. A fashion show producer needs both a creative vision and a head for business.

Creative direction

The creative director (or art director) works on the concept for a show. Creative direction may be the role of a show producer or of a brand's creative director. Alasdhair Willis, creative director of Hunter, is responsible for the design of collections and for shows. He said of the SS2016 show, 'The concept is reflective of the new collection, which is based on the festival . . . festivals have become much more significant to the business over recent years, so we wanted to do a collection that reflected that' (Creative Review, 2015). Designers such as Willis have reputations as innovators, but fashion has many creatives. People who conceive, plan and work on shows are also creatives: show producers, lighting designers, stylists, hair and make-up artists, set designers, choreographers and music designers.

International show production companies

The designers behind Rodarte have a strong vision for their shows and work with creative show producer Alexandre de Betak of Bureau Betak, and his team, to realize that vision. Brands with big marketing budgets work with creative production companies and huge organizations have developed that produce spectacular entertainment events around the globe. Many have international offices. Bureau Betak has offices in Paris, New York and Shanghai and works with Dior, Chanel, Isabel Marant, Jacquemus and Sies Marjan. Look at YO, OBO and PRODJECT, doll and INCA. IMG (part of a global entertainment agency) owns some fashion weeks and sponsors others, having been instrumental in launching new fashion weeks around the world as well as repositioning others, most notably New York Fashion Week.

The budget

The budget determines many factors, for example, what venue can be hired, how many (and which) models can be booked and what kind of set can be built. Runway can be produced for very little and some of the most inspiring shows have had tight budgets, but a professional show generally means considerable expense. Some brands and designers have financial managers who control the budget. Most young designers control their own budgets. Whoever controls the budget specifies how much there is to spend on what. Producers must work to the budget. If they go over, that comes out of their fee.

The cost of producing a show is broken down into different elements, for example:

- Venue hire
- Sound and lighting
- Set build
- Models
- Music design
- Lighting design
- Choreographer
- Hair and make-up
- Accessories
- Refreshments
- Security
- Cleaning

Each of the above may be broken down further and contractors (companies supplying services such as lighting) provide quotations. Sound and lighting, for example, might include building a rig, installing sound and lighting equipment and operating the sound and lighting equipment during the show. The quotation would be broken down into the build, operating the sound and lighting equipment during rehearsals and the show, dismantling the build at the end of the event and transport. Each element of this would include costs for technicians' time and hire of the equipment.

PR activities are often a separate cost, and can include:

- PR fee
- Invitations
- Presents or goodie bags before or during the show
- Refreshments
- Paying influencers to attend or giving free clothing
- Cars
- PR team

Young designers

The big brands have the promotional budgets to spend millions on advertising and further millions on runway. For young designers, the expense of shows is very problematic. Runway is a tradition, to show is to be recognized as part of the industry, and a new designer usually shows for at least two seasons before being acknowledged. Alexander McQueen's American Express Black show in 2004 was significant for his reputation as a designer, but it was phenomenally expensive and swallowed the whole of the year's promotional budget. Runway footage can be viewed on YouTube, re-edited by SHOWstudio: https://www.youtube.com /watch?v=PEmfJtyNGH4 (Knight, 2015). Unless a young designer has money or sponsorship, they have to produce a show that costs very little. They do this by calling in favours and persuading people to work for nothing in exchange for clothes or the promise of being there from the beginning with the next big name. There are famous examples of such shows. John Galliano's AW1994 collection comprised eighteen black silk outfits, produced in just weeks and shown on supermodels who worked for nothing, presented in a mansion in Paris borrowed from Sao Schlumberger. Galliano had no money and was sleeping on a friend's floor but the show was a turning point. Some of the most spectacular of shows historically cost very little but of necessity were innovative. Watch the show at https:// www.youtube.com/watch?v=l6ysNYAC5h0 (Videofashion, 2013).

Figure 4.5 Charlie Manns of Electric Hairdressing London, which sponsors the hair styling at various prestigious shows, creating directional looks. (© Regent's University London, Photographer Simon Armstrong)

Simon Costin, who works with Gareth Pugh and produced many of the celebrated Alexander McQueen shows: 'You find yourself working in a more fluid and spontaneous way, free to suggest mad ideas . . . like an inflatable runway, which many a designer would recoil at in case it didn't work or models fell over . . . You end up being creative in ways you might not have expected, like blocking the entrance to the runway with a giant weather balloon which gets burst by the first model to appear!' Woo, 2013

Sponsorship

For years, young designers have found funds through sponsorship, but this has become more difficult to obtain. In the 1980s and 1990s some young designers managed to attract considerable funds, but it was a precarious way to work, with some sponsors pulling out at the last minute, forcing designers to cancel shows or find new funds quickly. There are two primary forms of sponsorship: money and sponsorship *in kind*. The first can pay for one element of the show, or for the whole event. The second is for goods or services such as hair or make-up, drinks or accessories. The later is more common but both have become difficult to attract because of the financial pressure on sponsors themselves and the fact that there are now many more competing designers and shows.

Working with a sponsor

A designer and a sponsor reach agreement about what the sponsor will provide and what the designer will do in return. Sponsor packs (there are good examples of these on the Internet) set out the costs and benefits of being sponsors, which often include brand exposure and media coverage. Sponsorship packages in the form of money set out sliding scales of different levels. For example, gold sponsorship for a show may cost US$50,000, with benefits: the logo being used in all printed materials, four VIP seats at the show and mention in all press packs. More expensive diamond sponsorship might additionally include heavy use of logo, including branding boards for TV and other media and more VIP seats. Sponsorship packs can include runway images from previous shows and list previous sponsors. It is easier to get sponsorship once you have one or two companies on board because you can use their involvement to generate further commitment.

Figure 4.6 Sponsors can receive coverage from fashion shows if their logos are on branding boards/step-and-repeat boards, in front of which celebrities are photographed before and after a show. (© Regent's University London)

Figure 4.7 Goodie bags await the press at a Regent's University London BA Fashion Design graduate collections. (© Regent's University London)

Goodie bags are a tradition in fashion although their contents have changed: 'Goodie bags on your seat at fashion shows used to be highly personal (containing the music to the show on a tape for instance at Versace) or a gift that would only be for that show. Shows were so exclusive. Now it's just L'Oreal or Max Factor because they sponsored a fashion show. It is more about sponsors than the brand itself.' Robson, 2017

Getting sponsorship

A good way to get sponsorship is to search for brands that are introducing new products into the market. Soft drinks are an example of a product frequently provided free for shows in exchange for photographs. Sponsors know that images of aspirational characters like models using the product backstage has considerable promotional worth. When Vitamin Water was introduced into the U.K., the company happily delivered thousands of bottles for backstage use, knowing that the exposure would be valuable. Likewise, popchips and a drink called Neuro found their way into goodie bags and backstage areas by the hundreds. As sponsorship has become rarer, so has the goodie bag. Lined up on seats or benches as people arrive at a show, they make powerful visual branding. Sometimes only on the front row, they are aimed at those with influence. The PR team's interns will often spend time in the run up to the show, making up and filling the goodie bags.

Public relations

The use of the show as a marketing and PR tool is fully explored in Chapter Three. Because PR and show production are closely integrated promotional activities and it is not surprising that some companies now offer both PR and show production services. KDC has offices in New York, London and Paris and offers both fashion public relations and show production services. A good PR will work closely with the designer and the show production team from initial concept through to presentation. Below is a list of some pre-show PR activities:

- Creating stories
- Writing press releases and creating media packs
- Engaging producers and stylists
- Liaising with sponsors
- Organizing guest lists
- Liaising with the press
- Sending out invitations
- Encouraging significant press and buyers to attend
- Organizing seating plans
- Arranging backstage interviews
- Securing attendance of celebrities and other influencers
- Gathering logos and ordering branding (step and repeat) boards for interviews and photographs
- Liaising with photographers and film crews
- Booking cars to bring important guests to the venue
- Myriad other PR and front-of-house activities

Pre-production PR

An essential PR activity is to develop a compelling *story* around each collection and its presentation on the runway. In the highly competitive fashion marketplace, storytelling has become essential to differentiating a brand and reinforcing brand personality. The story must be newsworthy with an interesting angle. A good press release has a killer headline and contains information for the press that is easily digestible and written in such a way that it can easily be transferred into their publications. Stories are released in the form of media packs, press notes or press releases and teasers go out to generate anticipation amongst consumers. In advance of shows, PRs organize previews of the collections for key journalists. They record advance requests to attend, and they categorize guests in order of importance so that A-list guests can be seated in prime position.

Every PR's job is to keep their mailing list up to speed. It is so much easier now because you just email a 'save the date' out, you don't even need a venue at that point, at least you can say 'venue to be confirmed' or something like that. So, it is BFC first, get the date, then sort out a venue.
Interview with Kim Blake, 2014

While some writers are employed by specific publications, others work freelance and some of those are equally influential. The most important job of a PR is to know who is who and why they are important. While many invitations are electronic, many brands and designers still create real invitations, as imaginative and as interesting as their collections, which go to important press and VIP guests, hand delivered or couriered. For the SS2015 menswear collections in London, Dries van Noten sent out invitations with a red wax seal on the envelope. Inside was a beautiful dye-cut card 'R' in red. The invitation referenced Rudolf Nureyev, the Soviet ballet dancer, who had inspired the collection. Meanwhile Kenzo sent invitations with Eiffel Tower tourist trinkets threaded onto giant key rings, a reference to the inspiration of his collection: tourists discovering a new city.

Audiences

For on-schedule shows at fashion weeks, PRs know who is going to attend. For lesser-known designers, as an event draws closer, PR teams spend increasing amounts of time on the phone generating interest with tempting information and lists of who is attending and getting agreement from press and influencers to attend the show, sending out little goodies or presents or booking cars. PRs use seating plans (based on set design plans) or seating charts to plot who will sit where, and increasingly shows are being designed with the longest possible front rows so that press, bloggers, celebrities, important buyers and other VIPs are all FROW. As responses come in, PRs shuffle people around to ensure that the guests are seated according to their importance. Invitations are often coded with stickers to show the importance of the guest and whether they will be seated or standing. Labels are used on press invites stating who the guest is and what publication they represent.

Figure 4.9 Part of a
press pack for London
Collections: Men AW15.
(© Gill Stark)

The concept for each show is developed together, starting with research and evolving into something that for Prada is about surprising the audience and challenging preconceived ideas.

Developing the concept

The initial concept or creative vision must be developed into practical, detailed plans. The development of the concept happens in different ways for different designers and brands. Some designers are very specific about what they want, others are happy to discuss a concept and let the show producer develop ideas.

Concepts are often developed in parallel with a collection

Miuccia Prada has a long-established collaboration with the Dutch architect Rem Koolhaas of Studio AMO. Once a designer and a producer find they have a rapport, they will often continue to collaborate. The concept for each show is developed together, starting with research and evolving into something that for Prada is about surprising the audience and challenging preconceived ideas. The collection is developed alongside ideas for the show, so that Prada and Koolhaas present shows in the Fondazione Prada in Milan that are surprising. Watch the Prada SS2017 menswear show, where Koolhaas designed a metal environment with mesh ramp runways, mesh for audience seating and psychedelic lighting, reflecting the collection's inspiration, which was outdoor pursuits.

Industry Insight

Henrik Vibskov

The show concept sometimes evolves as part of a designer or design team's broad concept for a collection so that clothing, and the way that it is presented, are part of one creative vision. Danish designer Henrik Vibskov and his team work in this way.

Your creative expression is much broader than fashion. Do you see yourself as a fashion designer?

That's a good question, I am educated in menswear but I could have ended up being an architect or doing film. I ended up in fashion, and what I actually try to do is to use the sources I have to do what I feel passionate about . . . if you only focus on products and on product placement . . . I need something more, I need a bigger perspective, conceptual . . . all other senses: this space around it, the smell, the audio, all of the different aspects of creativity that surround the clothing.

    I have been playing music since I was ten; concerts and a lot of different music. It's very important for me to say, let's have some students there and some friends, get this mixture, and the same thing with fashion: let's work on the space, let's work on a stronger concept . . . to work on all different aspects.

So, you develop a concept that is about clothing and show?

That is what we are aiming for. You need to keep the passion and the energy for what you are doing. We do everything internally, so I work with my team, maybe with friends . . .

Do you work with a production company?

Sound is mostly in house. We have a production company but the more creative side, we do everything in our studio. We are around twelve to fifteen people. It's a very good size, we are extremely fast and mobile. With that size we can still move mountains. Sometimes we have workshops where we have whoever wants to help us . . . maybe 2,000 paper cuts. For our Paris show there are maybe twenty to twenty-five people backstage. Compared to the show an hour before where there are maybe 200 to 250 people. Money, of course . . . economy speaks.

Would you call your shows performances?

It's close to something like performance. You have a social gathering. For me, as an artistic experiment, it's a great moment, when you have 1,000 people sitting there and you can trigger their senses with mood, light, audio, you can play some really dark music, you can play some happy music, it is kind of like a human experiment. At some point my whole team was German, and I had German interns and a German press office so we decided that everyone should speak German for the show, and some should go in before the show and go round and do notes in lab coats, speaking German. That was an example of how to shake it up.

Figure 4.10 Henrik Vibskov is a musician as well as a designer and has been playing music since he was ten years old. (© Henrik Vibskov, Lange Per)

Figure 4.11 Henrik Vibskov and team work on a concept that encompasses collection and show. (© Henrik Vibskov)

Figure 4.12 'The Mint Institute', 2008, shown in Paris, Copenhagen and Scotland. (© Henrik Vibskov, Alastair Philip Wiper)

Figure 4.13 'The Last Pier Pandemonium', SS2011. (© Henrik Vibskov, Shoji Fujii)

Figure 4.14 Henrik Vibskov's SS2017 collection. (© Henrik Vibskov, Victor Jones)

Can you tell me about your creative process?

It's a bit random. An idea can be triggered by a dream . . . you cannot really turn creativity off, but suddenly there is an idea and that can give something to start developing concepts. Fashion is one of the fastest creative fields compared to furniture, architecture, music. It is a massively quick reflection of society or the community and how people are communicating. We start with 5 random researches, or questions. It can be weird things happening under water, a dance ceremony in a special tribe in Africa, cinema rituals in Guatemala . . . and so on. And we try to do five smaller concepts under the main concept.

Sometimes one or two questions that we started out with doesn't give anything, but it could be that suddenly . . . whoa! . . . that kite thing in Guatemala with a funeral, they are sending beautiful kites up, maybe that is something that we can work with . . . We made a whole installation with bird's necks hanging down and there were bits inspired from kite systems from Guatemala where the overall idea and concept was researched from death; can death be beautiful as well? Are there dance movements connected to death in special tribes somewhere? Are there special ceremonies somewhere? . . . and on and on . . . That is how our creative process is.

Is it different showing in Copenhagen and Paris?

We do the same show two to three times: firstly, Paris Men's, then Copenhagen where we add the womenswear and then sometimes we do a third and a fourth. But, the two or three same shows . . . it's very different; the reaction in the different markets, the different cultures. Sometimes I have been doing crazy things in Paris and people are just standing there not saying much, or the opposite; people are clapping in Paris and silent in Copenhagen.

Industry Insight

Erin Habes

Interview with Erin Habes, Lecturer at Buffalo State University, USA

How did you start teaching fashion show production?

I used to produce shows in college as a student. I am a big collaborator: I like to bring people together. I worked for three years in New York. I went to shows during Fashion Week. I came back to Buffalo and opened a store. Then I had the opportunity to teach the fashion show production class. I love theatre, I love the production side of fashion shows.

Do you have sponsorship for the shows?

Sponsorship is from local companies and goes directly into scholarships. A Buffalo company sponsors $15,000. At the show we present the scholarships and the runway winners. The local connections are important. The sponsors sit front row in VIP seats. We had sponsors who came to the show and donated $15,000 in my honour. They were overwhelmed by the student effort. I use $1,000 each year to help students to buy accessories.

Figure 4.15 Erin Habes. (© Erin Habes)

How did you develop the university's shows?

I collaborated with the Albright-Knox Museum to do their first runway. We worked with our senior designers, local boutiques and designers. We had a red-carpet VIP area. 2,500 people showed up and it could only hold 500: Buffalo State was thirsty for a fashion show! Later we moved to a big warehouse space and we had the show there for several years. It was wonderful having the show out in the community.

How do you teach the students show production?

I have job descriptions for the different groups. I send this to students in advance. I have a waiting list for the class. I sit down with everyone and I treat it like an interview. I decide who should do what. They all want to be show producer but I am flexible, I relate their roles to what they want to do as a career.

What do you do about models and hair and make-up?

We have model castings on campus. We use students and local modelling agencies. We get the word out, using social media (I have a big following). That's been a wonderful tool to get more models, hair and make-up ... local freelance stylists work with us. Fashion shows are about fantasy and everyone wants to be involved in the fantasy.

Figure 4.16 John Walford choreographing models. (© Regent's University London, Photographer Simon Armstrong)

Under Lee's direction, the Alexander McQueen show was always the highlight of any fashion week, more a dramatic performance than a runway display.

Akeroyd, 2015, p.8

Show concept developed in response to a collection

The concept for some shows is developed once a collection is almost complete, collaborating with a creative director or show producer whose own design process may be like that used to design a collection. Starting with research, they may develop ideas which evolve into creative concepts that are sometimes surprising. John Walford is a show producer who has worked creatively with many designers internationally in just this way and who worked on many of Westwood's early shows:

> With Vivienne Westwood we would do 'tableaux' such as Sarah Stockbridge being carried down the runway on the shoulders of a very handsome man dressed as a sailor, pouring vodka down his throat. Vivienne would come up with ideas, would say things like 'I see this' or 'I sort of see Sarah being carried, but it has got to be sexy' and we would work from there. In Paris, we did Café Society, we had Saffron Burroughs, Kate [Moss] and Jasmin le Bon in bikinis and little French coquette hats eating ice creams and giving each other ice creams to lick. That's how the show developed: Vivienne would get the ice creams and would say 'I want them eating ice-creams' and I would develop the ideas and work with the models.

The show can be watched on YouTube at https://www.youtube.com/watch?v=W2Rb9-aeizw (Vivienne Westwood, 2010)

Fashion and art collaborate to create runway

Artists, architects and designers from outside fashion conceive ideas for the production of spectacular shows. Rich collaborations have included Danish artist Thomas Poulsen working with Phoebe Philo to create sets for Celine, architectural artist Maya Lin with Phillip Lim in New York and artist Mahmoud Saleh Mohammadi with Antonio Marras in Milan. Set design has much in common with architecture, so some designers work with architects. The womenswear designer Erdem Morahoglu's sets are designed by architects, sometimes Philip Joseph. His AW2015 show was featured in *Architectural Digest*, testimony indeed to the collaboration between show production and architecture (Desimone, 2015). Miuccia Prada, who uses every show to turn preconceptions on their heads, working with Dutch architect Rem Koolhaas of AMO. Rodarte, working with Alexandre de Betak, stated: 'Alex brings an ingenuity to our shows, utilizing space and light in an innovative and creative way . . . and uses his knowledge of art and visual cultures to bring our vision to life every season' (Woo, 2013).

At one extreme are the innovative shows that evolve from the creative vision of designers and producers, and at the other is straightforward runway. The spectacles attract attention and are memorable. For the *fashion pack*, watching days of back-to-back shows, a dramatic production alleviates the boredom. One of the dangers of producing a spectacular show is that the show may overshadow a collection. Some designers have been accused of designing costume and presenting it as theatre. The most successful shows are those where collection and show work together to express a designer's creative vision. Alexander McQueen, who conceived some of the world's most spectacular shows, said 'Balance is the main thing. The show shouldn't overshadow the clothes and vice versa' (SHOWstudio, 2003).

The location and the venue

The location and venue are determined by the purpose of the show, brand image, show concept, cost and importantly how convenient it will be to travel to, for unless you are a very big name, audiences will not travel far. Venues are one of the first considerations because they are booked well in advance and they determine many other factors. The big entertainment companies employ people to constantly search for new and interesting spaces and in some cities, such as New York and London, it is difficult to find new venues. If a show is part of a fashion week, the location will either be the official venue, or a space that is close enough to give the fashion pack time to travel between shows.

Big names may be able to attract the press to one-off shows in unusual locations and sometimes transport is arranged for guests to travel to far-away places. There has been a trend for holding shows in unusual locations to which brands transport whole audiences: in 2016 Gucci showed in Westminster, Dior showed at Blenheim Palace in Oxfordshire, Chanel in Cuba and Vuitton in Rio. Occasionally an interesting location is not well received, as happened with Alexander Wang's AW2014 show entitled 'Extreme Conditions and Survival'. Held in the New York Naval Shipyard, the fashion press was not impressed by a trek through snow to the venue, resulting in some bad press.

Practical considerations
There are some very practical considerations to consider when choosing a venue:
- Is the venue in the right location to attract your target audience?
- Is the venue the right size to hold your audience?
- Will the venue work for the experience you envisage creating?
- Is there a sound and lighting system installed? It is very expensive to build a whole sound and lighting rig from scratch.
- What broadband capacity is there? If you want to live stream a show, you will need the capacity to do so. Is there enough capacity for all of the Instagram, Twitter and other social media messages that you hope will be transmitted during the event?

The perfect venue

Some brands find a natural home for their shows. For some years, Dolce & Gabbana showed in nightclub-style venues: perfect for their collections and their target audience. Some brands have created their own spaces, including Teatro Armani in the Armani headquarters in Milan, designed by Japanese architect Tadao Ando. Armani also supports young designers to show there, including Christian Pellizzari and Stella Jean. Burberry sometimes builds temporary buildings. The AW2012 womenswear show for Burberry Prorsum was held in a temporary transparent building in Hyde Park, London. The finale started with a loud roll of thunder and a downpour of rain on the roof and walls, while on the runway models walked with umbrellas under artificial rain. Bailey wanted a show with some British humour. Watching the show on YouTube you can see first surprise and then how amused and enchanted the audience was.

Figure 4.17 Karl Lagerfeld's supermarket show for Dior in Paris. (Patrick Kovarik/ Staff via Getty Images)

- What is the access to the building? Will set build and strike be affected?
- Will it be easy to get the audience in and out of the venue quickly?
- Are there practical things such as toilets, a backstage area, a kitchen area, a cloakroom?
- If part of a fashion week, can people get to the venue within the fashion week schedule?

Legendary locations

There are shows that have become legendary for their locations. The most legendary to date is probably Fendi's 2007 show on the Great Wall of China, but Lagerfeld is also responsible for events in an Austrian castle, the Palace of Versailles and numerous exotic locations around the world including an island off the coast of Dubai and Zaha Hadid's Dongdaemun Design Plaza in Seoul. It is, however, possible to transform an ordinary venue into an experience to remember. Season after season Karl Lagerfeld has shown in the Grand Palais in Paris, transforming it into a private jet, a Parisian street, a supermarket, an iceberg and an art gallery. Other designers and show producers continue to transform venues and transport audiences: Dries van Noten with his 'A Midsummer Night's Dream Garden' for his SS2015 collection and Raf Simon's 'Garden of Delights' for Dior in 2013, all viewable on YouTube.

Figure 4.18 A model, centre, attends a fitting at Nautica Studio for New York fashion company Nautica during preparations for a fashion show. In the background, boards show the outfits and running order for the event. (Chelsea Lauren/Stringer via Getty Images)

Clothing

Decisions must be made about what looks to show. For an industry show, the selection is an important commercial decision. For a charity show, it may be about entertainment. The number of looks multiplied by the time that each model is out on the runway determines the length of the show. For example, if thirty models are on the runway for one minute each, the show will be thirty minutes long. Add a three-minute finale and the show will last for thirty-three minutes. Industry shows are fast, others tend to be longer. Most fashion week shows tend to be short and the audience moves on to the next event as soon as it finishes. For other events, the show may only be part of the experience. Arriving at a venue, having a drink, finding your seat and watching others are all part of the build-up to the spectacle.

Putting together looks

Garments are put together and accessorized for the runway, and hair and make-up completes each look. The looks must all work together as a cohesive collection. Sometimes a whole collection is shown on the runway. More often brands show an *edit*: an edited selection rather than the full collection, leaving more wearable but less interesting pieces for the showroom. Sometimes showpieces are created to lift the collection for the runway and to obtain publicity. Fashion is not just about individual garments; the look of a specific time is about how pieces are worn together and how they are accessorized to create a look that is relevant to contemporary fashion. All of this is important when creating the edit for a runway show. Whether pure showpieces, a full saleable collection, or a combination of the two, while a show is being planned a full *line up* will be put together. This is usually represented visually through photographs or drawings on a board, showing the order in which the looks will go onto the runway. This is known as the *running order*.

The running order

The *flow* of the running order affects the audience experience and tells the story of the collection. It is used to create a strong audio-visual performance and to control audience emotion. It is always best to organize the running order so that a show starts and ends with strong pieces. More theatrical shows tend to finish with *showstoppers*. The last piece onto the runway is sometimes what everyone remembers. There is a tradition in runway for fashion houses to show a wedding dress as the finale, and while few designers follow that tradition today, some have used it to great effect. Fashion is often about pushing social boundaries, and Jean Paul Gaultier is a designer who has used runway to push boundaries about sexuality and gender over many years, deliberately subverting conventional expectations. He has frequently ended his runway shows with a bride in a bridal gown, and with a witty twist on this tradition, he has used transgender brides.

Figure 4.19 To complete
an outfit for the runway
it must be appropriately
accessorized. Design by
Flaminia Mechoulam.
(© Regent's University
London, Photographer
Tony Rogers)

Accessories

To complete an outfit for the runway, it must be accessorized; an outfit that is not accessorized looks unfinished. Companies such as Louis Vuitton and Mulberry make huge profits from their sales of accessories, so they get as many great accessories onto the runway as possible. Accessories perform other roles on the runway. If a collection is quite diverse, accessories can be used to make it more cohesive. If a collection needs to be lifted, accessories can be used to do that. If models are to wear several different outfits, accessories must be carefully planned: complicated accessories and quick changes do not work well together. Accessories must be carefully organized backstage so that they are worn with the right outfit, which will be covered further in Chapter Five.

Models

Selecting models

The choice of models is critical to the look of a show and successful models have a look that is *of the moment*. Professional models know how to stand, move and pose. There are many controversies around models and these are explored elsewhere in this book. To plan a show, a team must decide how many models to book and what kind of models will achieve the desired look. For some of the big budget shows, there is one model per outfit, making the finale impressive while enabling a brand to show the whole collection together. The optimum number of models will depend upon different factors: the budget, how many outfits there are, how long each look will be on the runway and how much space there is backstage. Models who wear more than one outfit need enough time to leave the runway, get changed and be ready to go back out, looking fabulous and composed.

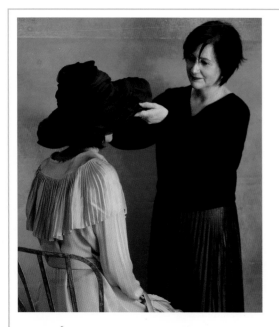

Figure 4.20 The couture milliner Prudence designs her own line and also designs millinery for others. (Prudence for Lock & Co. Hatters/Photo by Sandrine Dulermo and Michael Labica)

Figure 4.21 One of Prudence's pieces for Lock & Co. Hatters, London. (Prudence for Lock & Co. Hatters/Photo by Sandrine Dulermo and Michael Labica)

Collaborations

Some designers collaborate with milliners, footwear designers and jewellery designers to commission pieces for their shows. Sometimes the collaborations extend beyond the runway as accessories are also sold in the designer's stores. Menswear designer Joshua Kane has cleverly set up collaborations with accessories manufacturers and both his shows and his store benefit from the broader and more comprehensive product ranges. The couture milliner Prudence and the millinery designer Stephen Jones work with clothing designers to create millinery that will complete the looks that are presented on the runways of the fashion capitals. Couture milliner Prudence points out that accessories don't just complete an outfit; they also help to tell the story of a collection. Prudence sells her own line and produces one-off commissions for private clients, but it is her work with designers such as Vivienne Westwood that appears on the runway.

> The accessories give the collection direction. It is an exclamation point, it is punctuation. Otherwise it would just be a frock, a woman in a dress. It is not until the hair is done, the make-up is on, it's accessorized, the music and lighting are there, and you get where it's going, it's about telling the story. At a St Laurent show when you see the clothes coming out they have to look precious, there are not a lot of them, but at the same time, it has to sell like Coca Cola. And Tom Ford more than anyone is the best at that: to feel like everyone could have it and it is still exclusive. Like you belonged to a club that had a secret that no-one else knew about. Sometimes I watch the show and sometimes I am backstage. Watching it I think about things that I could have done better. I always wish I had more time. Watching is really serious, it is the first time that you see it with everything together. I am always judging everything.

To read the full interview with Couture Milliner Prudence please visit http://www.bloomsbury.com/stark-the-fashion-show.

Figure 4.22 A model walks in a David Jones casting in Sydney, Australia, in 2013. (Marianna Massey/Stringer via Getty Images)

Sourcing and casting models

To choose and book models, a designer or show producer will contact one or more model agencies and explain what look they need. The agency will select models, put together an electronic portfolio and send a link so that the team can look through and choose models for castings. Models will be booked into castings at a specified time and place. At castings, models will be asked to show their *model card* or portfolio and they may be asked some questions about the work in their portfolio or their experience. They will be asked to *walk*. This is essential for runway because some models look good in editorials or other photographs, but don't have the right walk for the runway. Others will just not have the desired look for a specific show. Castings for fashion shows are not about individual models but about selecting models who will work together on the runway. For big shows a casting director might be employed to source models, and a whole role within the industry has developed around this. Angus Monro is a casting director who works with Elite Premier Model Agency, working closely with designers to understand their collections and putting together visual boards of models that he thinks will achieve their desired look. For big events, casting directors sometimes create a selection panel in front of whom models walk.

Industry Insight
Claudia Cooper, model

Claudia Cooper models with agency Models 1.

How did you start modelling?

I got into modelling through a Topshop and Models 1 competition. There were various rounds; the first round was a test shoot so that they could see what you were like in front of a camera; the second round was a runway show in the Topshop store at Oxford Circus. They had judges like Erin O'Connor. There were ten guys and ten girls in the final. There was a long straight catwalk and they showed you how to walk and how to pose. It was a great experience.

Did you get nervous before your first show?

Yes, and it's this mad rush beforehand with hair and make-up . . . then you forget your nerves when you go on the catwalk. I loved it. I hadn't really considered modelling beforehand. I enjoyed the shoot and the show. It was brilliant and I was hooked!

I understand that you modelled at Graduate Fashion Week?

I modelled at Graduate Fashion Week which was all quite crazy stuff. I wore something that was like a straightjacket and I remember thinking that I hoped I wouldn't fall over! There was very dramatic music. We had to walk in the round. I still do some modelling but I now do more print and commercial modelling rather than catwalk. There are only so many years that you can do as a model, especially catwalk.

Figure 4.23 Claudia Cooper. (© Claudia Cooper)

Figure 4.24 Photographs taken before a show can be used for publicity and for backstage information as per this image from a final collection at Regent's University London. Backstage teams can use the photograph to see how the outfit should look on the model. (© Regent's University London)

Figure 4.25 Photographs taken during fittings are used for information backstage. (Benjamin Lowy/Contributor via Getty Images)

Booking models

Once castings have taken place, models are booked through their agencies. At busy times, producers may request, in advance, a first option on individual models. Once a decision is made to book certain models, there is a discussion with the agency about which of the models chosen are still available, what the model fee is and what the timings are: call time and end of event. This all sounds very straightforward but it is not always so. A model has to be available on particular dates in order to attend fittings and show. It is time-consuming to find a full line-up of models that have the right look, only to find that some may drop out (sometimes on the day) due to more high-profile offers of work. It is always advisable to have a back-up list of other models. Otherwise you will have to accept those that the agency replaces them with and they may not suit the look of the show. A contract will be drawn up by the agency for each model and signed by the producer thereby entering a legal contract. The agency charges a model fee plus 20 per cent agency fee. After the show, the agency sends out invoices which must be paid within a set time.

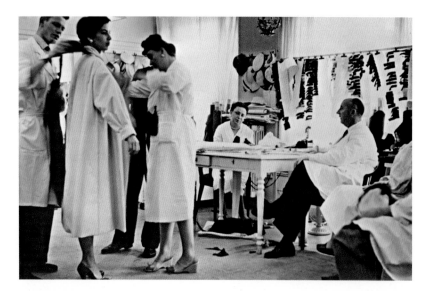

Figure 4.26 Christian Dior in his atelier in Paris in 1956 doing fittings in preparation for a show. (Staff/Staff via Getty Images)

Model fittings and model boards

A model board is often used as a visual record of the models selected and helps the team to plan who will wear what. It is useful for fittings and on show day it is used to identify models as they arrive and backstage when putting outfits on rails. The industry works to standard sizes and samples are all the same size. In advance of a show, models will be called in for fittings. This ensures that outfits fit the models and look their absolute best on them. In the couture and luxury fashion industries, a model may be chosen to wear one outfit, and the outfit will be fitted specifically to them. Some companies will have one or more house models and garments will be fitted on those models during the design development and making stages. Models are photographed during fittings and this gives the company photographs that they will later use on backstage boards.

Figure 4.27 A model chart shows all of the outfits that a model will wear. The number tells the team what number the outfit is in the running order. The photographs show the team what the outfit looks like and how it should be worn.

Model name

5.	17.	32.
57.	79.	

Figure 4.28 Garments for the Cavalera show at São Paulo Fashion Week in April 2015. (Fernanda Calfat/Stringer via Getty Images)

Stylists

It was in the 1980s and 1990s that stylists began to work on fashion shows. As John Walford reflected during an interview:

> When I started doing shows, there were no stylists: the designer and design assistant would do the styling. When magazines such as ID and Dazed started, people like Ian R. Webb and Karylin Frankin, Simon Foxton, and Judy Blame started styling but didn't work on runways straight away. When the first stylists worked on shows, I worked with Bella Freud and Judy Blame. The PRs saw that if you got a Vogue or ID stylist, it would raise the level of your audience; the equivalent of pop stars in the front row. At first, they were working on the clothes; the shoes, the tights, the accessories, and then the role grew.
> (Interview with John Walford, 2013)

Backstage boards

A backstage chart and model charts are created before the show. The backstage chart is a large chart with photographs of all outfits, taken at fittings, and laid out as per the running order. The model charts are smaller versions of the backstage chart and contain photographs from fittings of every outfit each model will wear, laid out as per the running order.

Styling

Stylists tend to be people with an intuitive feeling for the fashion *zeitgeist*: having a feel for the mood and look of a particular moment in time. Styling in relation to runway, at its most basic, is about deciding the running order, how garments should be worn together and accessorized and how the hair and make-up should be styled. However, styling can encompass the whole show. Stylists work closely with designers to do many of the things that a creative director would do: having a vision for the show and selecting appropriate elements to make sure that the vision is realized in such a way that the show powerfully communicates the brand's messages. Vanessa Reid is a stylist who has worked with Missoni, Rag&Bone and Ferretti. She is known for taking designers' collections and presenting them on the runway in a way that emphasizes their texture and colour. Her beautiful layering of textiles and garments was evident in the Kenzo 40th Anniversary fashion event in 2010, which was much praised and can be watched on YouTube.

Industry Insight
Georg Meyer-Wiel, artist and costume designer

Figure 4.29 Georg Meyer-Wiel.

You graduated from the Royal College of Art (RCA) having studied menswear design. What was the inspiration behind your graduate collection and how did that relate to its styling for the catwalk?

When I was young I trained in taxidermy. My work now, in any medium, is always informed by anatomy; the morphological details in animals, their behaviour, evolution, nature, camouflage, protection mechanisms, exoskeletons, all these things have inspired my drawings, painting, costume designs, fashion, styling, even photography. My final collection at the RCA was all about exoskeletons, animal protection mechanisms, and feathers. Print, the shapes of pleated leather jackets, knit patterns, crochet armour, even taxidermy elements came from this theme. If you have a thorough concept to your collection, and have researched something in depth, it is obvious what to do as styling. Styling should stem from the concept of the collection. A collection may be amazing but if the styling is wrong is goes unrecognized.

Tell me about the styling of your collection.

First I had the concepts and designed the outfits. Once I had the entire collection outlined, I started to think of possible styling. It became obvious to do head-pieces for my final collection because I had all these predatory animal-like warriors represented through menswear with armour that was like exoskeletons. I researched falconry masks; they are beautifully made with pull-string mechanisms, leather in the back and a tassel or feather on the crown; so, every model had a falcon mask. I had to modify the shape of the masks so they were huge leather hats with beaks on them and feather pieces at the back. I introduced entire accessories from taxidermy . . . for instance I had several crows that I stuffed myself hanging down like from a hunter belt. It was menswear but what you see on the catwalk is not what goes into the shops, it's a vision, a story that's told to the people that are there. Designers like Thierry Mugler put all the emphasis into the creation of a single moment that just blows you away and if you are one of the few privileged people who can witness the show . . . later it is toned down and of course you wouldn't wear a bird mask on the street.

Figure 4.30 Georg Meyer-Wiel. Final Collection, Royal College of Art, London. (Photography by RCA/Kerstin Zu Pan)

Did you talk with the models before the show?

As a student, you can't choose your models because it is a collaborative decision. So, the styling has to work regardless. I met the dressers and the models and I briefed them. If you do a styling shoot or a fashion show you must brief the model. If the model does not know how to perform, what expression to have, you will not get the result that you want. In my case it was quite easy because they just had to walk but I wanted them fairly aggressive, I made them think of particular animals. I like to tell models what the story is, give them an idea of a situation that they can put themselves into. Something that they can think about before you go in front of the camera and it really helps with model expressions and poses. Otherwise the work will look casual and not considered.

Did you get feedback after the show?

I had feedback from fashion designers like Mary Quant and Issey Miyake. At first I was disappointed when Issey Miyake said he thought my future was also in costume design. I was hurt . . . but I look back and it was the most wonderful advice. I have been a designer for performance: ballet, film, dance, theatre, opera and I really love it because you must think from the start about an overall look.

'Designing a runway is almost like designing a temporary public space . . . You have to seat 700 people for 12 minutes in an interesting and different way.' Ippolito Pestellini of AMO who creates Prada's sets.
Woo, 2013

The set

Style of show: from the traditional to the immersive

Set design depends upon the purpose and style of a show, the budget and the creative concept and also the target consumer. 3D models, drawings, plans, computer-generated mock-ups, sketches and mood boards are all used to communicate set design ideas and plans. A fashion show set can be a traditional salon-style floor show with chairs along the runway or at the opposite extreme it can be a theatrical build, creating an immersive experience that transports the audience to a fantasy world. The primary aim of set design is to tell the story of the collection while promoting the brand. Simon Costin said, 'Often the designer has had inspirations that aren't apparent in the clothes, so you can play that out in the scenography. It's all about adding layers of meaning' (Skidmore, 2015). Whether a designer chooses salon style, like Prada's AW2015 show, or wants to be hugely ambitious and immersive will depend upon the collection and the style of the designer. Examples of the latter are Yohji Yamamoto's Y3 AW2008 show, which had twelve-foot-high walls of ice and each member of the audience was given a Y3 stadium blanket and foil-wrapped hand warmers because of the cold, and Dior's SS2016 show, where Raf Simons's vision was a mountain covered in live flowers through which guests and models strode. Technology is being incorporated, particularly for communities where digital communication is influential. Burberry has produced spectacular high-tech 'runway' experiences using multiple screens as they have opened flagship stores in locations in China, notably the holographic runway in Beijing in 2011.

Practical considerations for set design

01. Audience view: The set design must enable a live audience to have a good view. Those watching a live stream or video later need a feel for the atmosphere and a good view of the collection, including some detail of the garments.

02. The photographers and film crews must be able to get good shots.

03. The live audience needs to be able to take good shots for social media.

04. The show needs to look good in different formats: on a mobile, in larger scale and so on.

05. It is ideal to have as long a front row as possible. Using tiered seating enables those behind to have a good view.

06. The set must be safe for the models, audience and others. It must meet health and safety requirements such as exit routes in the event of an emergency.

07. The set can't obscure the lighting.

08. The set must integrate sound and lighting equipment.

09. It is advantageous to be able to strike the set quickly.

Figure 4.31 The Boiler House, Truman Brewery, London. (© Regent's University London)

Figure 4.32 The runway is usually made of staging built in sections to standard dimensions. (© Regent's University London, Photographer Tony Rogers)

The build

Events companies employ carpenters, set builders and artists to create the sets for fashion shows. They also employ sound and lighting engineers because lighting and sound systems are integral to the design and construction of a set. All elements of the set are designed to work together, including decoration of the venue, flats or drapes, flooring, runway, seating, projection, sound and lighting. While this sounds simple, coordinating all elements while achieving the desired effect often poses problems. Each show is different and presents its individual challenges. See Marc Jacobs' AW2014 show, where 500 clouds suspended from the ceiling presented considerable lighting challenges.

Runway construction

A runway is a raised structure along which the models walk, like a theatre stage, but stretching out into the audience. It is usually made of wood and/or staging, built in sections to standard dimensions. Cloth, vinyl and a range of other materials can be laid on top or stretched over the staging to create the desired look. While the traditional runway colour is white, fabulous colours can be achieved using vinyl and other materials. A mirrored runway can be stunning but reflects the strong show lights and for this reason, it is not a favourite of the photographers!

Figure 4.33 Material is laid on top and stretched. (© Regent's University London)

Figure 4.34 The legs of the staging are also covered, giving a clean look. (© Regent's University London)

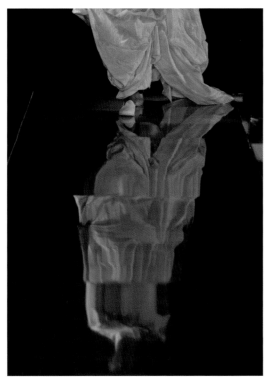

Figure 4.35 Photographers do not like the reflective quality of some runway coverings. (© Regent's University London)

Figure 4.36 Fabulous runway colours can be achieved using vinyl. (© Regent's University London, Photographer Tony Rogers)

Figure 4.37 Building flats to create a backstage area.
(© Regent's University London, Photographer Tony Rogers)

Figure 4.38 Flats and runway being built together.
(© Regent's University London)

Runway shape

Traditional runways are long and straight but there has been a trend towards more varied and interesting designs to attract publicity through differentiation. A more unusual set design might involve models walking through the audience as in Prada's SS2012 show or moving around a central area as in Cavalli's AW2014 event and Wooyoungmi's SS2016 show. A square walk with audience inside and out (see Thom Browne SS2017 and Jil Sander AW2014), a snaking runway (see Givenchy AW2015), a cross shape, a V shape (see Pal Zileri SS2017) or a T shape all add interest. The longer a raised (staged) runway, the costlier it is. If the show is salon-style, also known as a floor show, the cost of building a runway can be avoided and material laid on the floor may be used to define the runway. With enough budget and some creative thinking, runways can be constructed from any number of interesting materials, and a review of shows by well-known brands illustrates this. Paving slabs, foliage, second-hand clothing, carpet, metal, glass, old doors and endless other items and materials have been used to create fashion runways. While the cost of some of these is high, with imagination, and working within the boundaries of what is safe, it is possible to create an interesting set.

The flats

A venue may already have a natural backstage space. If not, flats can be built to create a backstage area. Flats are vertical frames, usually covered in canvas, which screen the backstage area. For a solid screen, plywood can be attached to the frame. Flats are built in sections to standard sizes so that they can be reused and they can quickly be dismantled and reassembled as required. They can be joined together to create walls and they are braced onto the floor using weights. They are designed so that creating and striking the set are quick. Sometimes a softer look is required, and drapes can be hung to create a backstage area with one or more entrances and exits for the models. The drapes can be hung from a frame, wires or poles and must be fire-retardant. Like flats, they must be weighted and can be projected onto.

Figure 4.39 Back-projection onto the flats to show designers' names. (© Regent's University London)

Figure 4.40 Benches are used at many modern shows and can be painted any colour. (© Regent's University London, Photographer Tony Rogers)

Projection

At some shows, films or images are projected to great effect and it is customary with collaborative shows to project the names of designers. Projection onto flats, drapes or a white wall can be very successful and where and how to project must be incorporated into the set design. A projector can be hung from a ceiling or from a lighting rig, however this can be expensive and can interfere with runway lighting. Back-projection onto flats gives a very clean look; alternatively, digital screens can be used for huge visual impact. See Kenzo's SS2013 show on YouTube (Fashion Channel Milano, 2012) or Prada's SS2010 womenswear show which was intersected by a wall onto which were projected scenes from grand old hotels.

Seating

While occasionally an audience may be happy to stand, it is customary to supply seating for a fashion show audience. Historically, the fashion show seat was a gilt chair with a red velvet seat and these are still seen at the Paris haute couture shows (see Jean Paul Gaultier Haute Couture AW2014). More recently, shows have often seated guests on benches and this has become accepted as a more modern look. If there is no raised runway, it is advisable to have raised seating for those in back rows so that they can see the models. Tiered event seating and staging, made from steel, can be hired and show producers have suppliers that they work with regularly. The seating is part of the set design and as such must work with the overall concept. See Givenchy's AW2015 show, which saw a jumble of different chairs, and Tom Ford's AW2014 show, where the whole audience sat on grey sofas. There was also Mark Jacob's AW2014 marshmallow cylinders.

Industry Insight

Dahren Davey, Course Leader, BA Fashion
Design, Regent's University, London

Figure 4.41 Dahren Davey. (© Regent's University London)

Where did the idea for the moving audience come from?

The space limited the size of the audience. I thought, if people stand, what can they do? We do two or more shows a year and that show can be experimental. The theme was sexuality and we wanted a show where the models could be on plinths, doing each other's make-up and hair, taking selfies, posting on Instagram, taking photos of themselves, to get it more interactive. Fashion shows seem to be moving away from straightforward catwalk and anything different tends to get a bit more press.

Did students come up with the idea of the moving audience?

We all worked together. Usually I have a few initial ideas and I say to the fashion show production students 'I am thinking about something like this' and then the students come up with ideas, so it kind of builds. It is never just the lecturers and it is never just the students. Also, fashion show production students communicate with the design students so it's a three-way conversation.

What was the process of designing the show?

We looked at the space and the lights that we had. We put the plinths down and then figured out the choreography. We wanted the audience to move, we wanted them to follow the models or the models to fight through the audience. We tried to have random choreography so that people didn't know where the models were going to come from or where they were going to stand or what they were going to stand on. We were in the audience encouraging people to move around and take photographs.

How did the models know where to go?

It was like a map and each model was told for instance 'go from A to B to C to D'. The next might go from C to A to B to D. Each model knew where they were going and they didn't bump into each other. We had about five different routes. There were three or four entrances and three or four exits.

Did the photographer move as well and what about the sweet spot?

The photographer moved as well. That was difficult. Ideally we should have had four photographers because he was battling through the audience trying to get good shots. The audience got some interesting shots. Every shot they took was different from what they would get at a catwalk show. Some students loved it because it was original; some hated it because they are more classic in their tastes, but if you want to move things forward you can't remain the same.

What effect did it have on the audience?

It was different, deliberately so, and people remember that show because it wasn't a simple catwalk. Everyone came out saying 'that was interesting'. When I look at shows, the ones that I find interesting are the ones where they use a building with models walking throughout, like Yves St Laurent or Aitor [Throup] with puppeteers turning outfits into puppets instead of using models. Those shows are the ones that people talk about and the ones where the photographs online are different. Because people are taking photos at shows: Instagram, videos, Facebook live and so on, it is so instantaneous that a show needs more thought to create a buzz. If it is simple and straightforward there is less of a buzz, less photographs being taken, less live video . . . it is important to step away and do different things.

'We even add light or effects with the audience perspective in mind, instead of focusing solely on where the professional photographers are gathered.' Mr. de Betak of Bureau Betak.
Smith, 2014

Working with a set production company

Set building companies work with show producers and creative directors to build sets, from simple salon shows to jaw-dropping immersive experiences. Some designers and brands know exactly what they want, but others don't, so set building companies also help designers to develop ideas into final concepts. They put together quotes for builds, which usually include building the set, seating and backstage area, the sound and lighting installation, sound and lighting desk(s) and platforms for photographers and film crew. They provide tables and chairs backstage for hair and make-up, mirrors and rails, build refreshments areas and whatever else might be desired! They provide technicians to operate the sound and lighting equipment. If a venue is dry hire, which means that it is an empty venue, they do everything that is needed to transform an empty space into an experience. Diagon built a spiral runway with a tilting roof for the Anya Hindmarch SS2017 London Fashion Week show. Tested in their workshops, it was then built in the show venue. The result was impressive and can be seen here: https://www .youtube.com/watch?v=zlJb7jZuabw (AnyaHindmarchMovies 2016).

The art of lighting

Most people associate bright lights with shows, but this vastly underestimates the role of lighting in set design and does a huge injustice to the creative thinking and technical expertise of lighting designers. Lighting controls the mood of an event. Good lighting is essential to the quality of the film and photographs that brands rely on. Photographers and film crews need the best light in the optimum spots to get good shots of the looks, silhouette, texture and detail for web and print, live streaming and video footage. The lighting must enable the audience to see the clothing clearly and those using social media need enough light to capture great shots from all positions along the runway.

One of the greatest lighting designers is Thierry Dreyfus. Dreyfus started by lighting operas and moved on to runway where he has been influential. He runs a production company in Paris called Eyesight. Dreyfus is responsible for many shows in Paris and New York. An artist who works with light, Thierry has become a legendary lighting designer whose work creates the atmosphere and the mood that is so intangible yet essential to the immersive show experience. In addition to the experience that those at the event enjoy, the lighting creates the mood that those watching online and seeing photographs later *feel* through the purely visual.

> Light doesn't have words or speak intellectually . . . It is reflecting on the girl, the boy, the floor, the back and the set – it has to be a unity. It is about emotion. What you try to express is the way you see the designer. (Thierry Dreyfus, quoted in Woo, 2013)

Figure 4.43 If there is no rig in a show venue, a temporary rig is built. (© Gill Stark)

Figure 4.44 Even in a building with plenty of daylight, considerable extra lighting is needed for the runway. (© Regent's University London)

Figure 4.45 Lighting in the ceiling rig at each end of the runway; uplighters focus large amounts of light onto the runway. It's all intended to create a sense of theatre, show the garments at their best and get the best possible still images and film footage. (© Regent's University London)

The lighting rig

Lighting is usually built into a rig above the runway. Some venues do not have any lighting installed, and this will certainly be the case where a show is being produced in a tent or marquee. In such cases a temporary rig will be built, which can be very expensive. If this isn't possible, lights can be placed on stands at the sides and ends of the runway behind the audience and photographers, but this is far from ideal and should be avoided if possible. It can pose health and safety risks, so it must be carefully designed and monitored. Lighting from a rig generally results in much better runway photographs. A lighting rig is a scaffolding of metal bars which lights are attached to. The lights can be moved along the rig and pointed in different directions so that the optimum lighting effect can be achieved. The lighting has to be designed as part of the set, planned and equipment booked. Lighting is angled so that it lights the full length of each model, because lighting from directly above creates shadows.

Sometimes it is the music, there is a really good fashion journalist called Tim Blanks who was originally a music journalist so his whole thing is music. When you see a show online often it is different music because of copyright. Tim Blanks says things like 'it was the riff of Led Zeppelin' and he sees fashion through sound.

Julia Robson, Fashion Journalist

The power of sound

Sound is one of the most important elements of the live fashion show, yet it is one of the least well considered. Fashion is a visual world and the primary focus is on how a show looks. However, what every successful producer knows is that sound can be used to control the pace of the event and is tremendously powerful in controlling the mood of the audience. The use of sound, mixed or created especially for a show, adds a dimension to the originality of the event. Sound must work perfectly with a collection and with all other elements of a production. Sometimes sound other than music is used at shows. Original recordings, compositions and mixes, live musicians and other interesting and original ways of creating sound as part of runway presentation adds another layer of interest to the fashion show. Sound and lighting work together, contributing hugely to the atmosphere of runway. As Nathan Prince, Silent Studios' creative director, says, 'It can make you feel happy, uneasy, it can make your hair stand on end.' Prince creates sound for Burberry and Anya Hindmarch and is an advocate of working on the audio-visual elements of a show together and early, because runway sound is too often an afterthought.

Figure 4.46 A pianist and a cellist play on the runway as models walk at the SS2014 Erdem show at London Fashion Week. (Victor Virgile/Contributor via Getty Images)

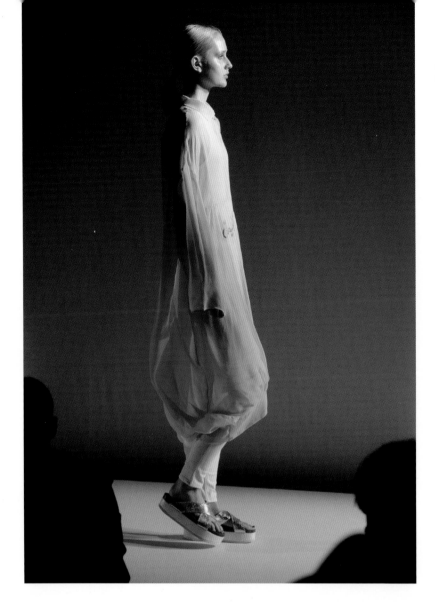

Figure 4.47 Beautifully styled, simple hair. (© Regent's University London)

Hair and make-up

There are trends in hair and make-up styling just as there are trends in clothing. New ideas emerge quickly and directional hair and make-up artists are well-known and respected. Hair and make-up can be highly innovative and can reflect a new look, start a trend, shock an audience or be deliberately simple. Each fashion week, in the build-up to the shows, backstage shots give sneak-peeks of hair and make-up looks. The hair and beauty press attend the shows and new looks are much anticipated and reported. Designers often work with the same hair and make-up artists knowing that they will understand their vision. Employing a highly respected hair or make-up artist means fabulous styling that completes the look for the runway. Beauty brands benefit from association with high-profile designers and the most exciting shows. Brands such as M.A.C., L'Oreal and NARS sponsor runway shows as part of their own promotional strategies. They know the top hair and make-up artists, who sometimes bring the sponsorship with them as they work for different designers and brands.

Rei Kawakubo

The styling of Rei Kawakubo's shows has challenged convention and fashion for over 30 years. In her 1983 show called 'Destroy', the models' features were displaced by the make-up, with lips painted on models' cheeks. So extreme was Kawakubo's creative vision that even the fashion industry, who are used to the new, were shocked. As Fury wrote in Future Beauty, 'Kawakubo's vision was simply too extreme a contrast to digest. It is the stuff of fashion folklore that more than a few critics left the space in tears' (Fury, 2010).

Figure 4.48 Model Ayse Hatun Onal having make up sponsored by M.A.C. applied backstage before the Hakan Akkaya show at Fashion Week Istanbul in March 2015. (Stuart C. Wilson/Stringer via Getty Images)

Hair and make-up tests

One of the final stages of pre-show planning is to do hair and make-up tests. Designers communicate what they have in mind by showing the collection, explaining the look they want and drawing, or more usually creating a mood board with different images on it. Hair and make-up artists create two or more looks on models, based on the designer's vision, so that a final look can be decided. This can be photographed as a record for the day. Hair and make-up tests used to happen well before a show, but fashion moves more quickly now and while it is difficult to change the collection, hair and make-up styling can be determined closer to the show. As revered make-up artist Val Garland has said:

> Back in the day, meetings would happen months before the show but the mood alters so quickly now. In the age of social media and the Internet ideas change like a sixpence. If you decided upon the make-up weeks before the show you'd be bound to change your mind nearer the time. (Niven, 2014)

Final steps

Once a look has been decided, hair and make-up artists book their styling teams. They work out how many stylists they need and how long it will take to create the look. The more complex the hair and make-up, and the more models there are, the longer styling will take. The show producer also needs timings to incorporate hair and make-up into the schedule for the day. From this comes the call time: the time at which stylists arrive. Having done the tests and agreed the look, hair and make-up artists need to arrive at a show with enough product to create the look. They work with product sponsors to make sure that they have the product their teams will need. Meanwhile, the show producer communicates the address and call times and ensures they have a suitable space and furniture in the venue for hair and make-up styling.

Figure 4.49 Hair and make-up tests enable stylists and creative directors to agree on a look. (© Regent's University London, Photographer Simon Armstrong)

Refreshments

Refreshments are not served at all fashion shows. They are less likely to be served at a ten-minute fashion week show and more likely to be served, for example, at a charity show, a university graduation show or a store launch. Refreshments can be expensive without sponsorship. If a team decides to serve food and drink, it is advisable to plan this well in advance and to be aware of all health and safety regulations. It can be fun to design the food and drink and the way that it is served, and this can be part of the overall styling of an event. It is time-consuming to plan and prepare and it can also be time-consuming to clear and tidy afterwards. Good planning and a well-organized team is required to do this effectively; for industry events, catering is typically outsourced.

As show day approaches . . .

Show production is a serious business activity, involving large budgets, health and safety imperatives and serious legal responsibilities. Pre-production speeds up as the event approaches and excellent organization is essential. By the end of the planning period and as show day approaches, all documentation must be in place:

- Agreements with contractors
- Contracts for models and security personnel
- Risk assessments and other health and safety documents
- Insurance cover for people and property
- Plans
- Schedules and crew lists

The nature of show production is such that the process starts slowly and gradually speeds up, so that during the final phase things tend to move very fast. As the day of the event nears, the show producer will send out crew lists, information about the location, contact details and a schedule. The show producer's role in the final stage is to keep all plates spinning so that everyone is on track. They will be at the venue to oversee the set build and they will be in regular contact with everyone involved in the event to sort out any last-minute glitches. If they have several shows during a fashion week, they will move back and forth between them. With every event, there are last minute glitches: a model who falls ill and has to be replaced, a change in the running order or a problem with one of the materials supplied for the set. That is the nature of show production, but careful planning in advance means that glitches don't become nightmares. However well planned, the final days and hours in the run up to a show are always very busy. During fashion weeks, the whole industry buzzes with activity and infectious energy, first in one city and then in the next. After months of planning the collection is ready, the guests are invited and there is huge anticipation as everyone looks forward to presenting another successful show.

Activities

01. Show production

Research a show production company that produces the big international shows. Write a report about the company to include:

A. Who manages the company and who works for it

B. What range of activities the company covers

C. Who its clients are

D. The geographical reach of its activities

E. What its philosophy towards show production is

F. Which elements of fashion shows it spans

G. How its work has been reported in the press

H. An analysis of the style of fashion shows that it produces

02. Working with model agencies and selecting models

Imagine that you are working on a show and that you need to select models. Choose two model agencies and visit their websites. Your client wants a very international look to the show and has specified that 'the models must look as if they have come from all over the globe'. Select models from the two agencies to create a line-up of eighteen models. Present them in the order in which they will go onto the runway. Your client would like the first and last models to have 'striking looks'.

03. Gantt chart

If you are producing a show, create a Gantt chart and list all of the activities that the team needs to complete in order to prepare for and produce the show. Categorize activities under headings. The checklists and charts earlier in this chapter may be helpful.

04. Creating the team

If you are part of a group of people that is working on a show, split the group into different teams to replicate what might happen in industry. Every team is different, and the teams should reflect the activities that need to be completed in order to produce the show, so create the Gantt chart first. Once the responsibilities and teams have been determined, decide what skills each area of responsibility will need. Get everyone to consider what skills they will bring to the show production and where they might like to develop new knowledge. Appoint a leader for every team. Ask everyone who wants to play a major role to do a presentation to explain their experience and skills. The responsibilities and teams could be as follows:

A. Show producer

B. Creative director

C. PR and sponsorship team

D. Backstage and models team

E. Technical (sound and lighting) team

F. Set and styling team

05. Hair and make-up styling

Review directional fashion shows and look at fashion trends to identify cutting-edge ideas for hair and make-up styling. Create a mood board for hair and another mood board for make-up with images to convey the directional looks for the next season. Use these as inspiration to create your own hair and make-up looks. Do three different hair and make-up tests to determine a final look that will work well under the bright lights of the runway. Photograph the three looks to create a third board.

06. Create a sponsorship package

Decide what you have to offer sponsors and also decide what kind of sponsorship you need. Then create a sponsorship pack to clearly and succinctly capture:

A. What you have to offer

B. What you are looking for

C. What sponsorship you have had in the past (use impressive examples)

D. Value to the sponsor (outcomes and marketing value)

E. Details of the agreement

F. Call to action

One of the great advantages of fashion show sponsorship is that you can use fabulous images from previous shows in your sponsorship pack. Include press coverage, audience size and demographics and lists of who you already have sponsorship from and who you have worked with previously.

07. Set design and seating plan

On the Internet, look at show venues and find one that has floor plans of the venue available online. Plan the set design for a show and include the seating plan. Create mood boards to illustrate the look and the atmosphere of the show. Use the floor plans to create a seating plan with as long a front row as possible.

08. Sound and runway

Look at the runway reports of Tim Blanks and analyze how he reports on music at shows:

A. How does the sound created for the show help to tell the story of the collection?

B. How does the sound set the context for understanding the collection?

C. How is the sound used to create the mood of the event?

D. Watch ten shows online to find out when the sound used at a show is the same as the sound that eventually accompanies the show online.

5

Show day

Chapter Five explores what happens on the day of a show, from how to make sure that everything runs smoothly, both backstage and front-of-house, to managing the press and controlling the audience. It explains the order in which to carry out activities on the day and how to schedule and coordinate the different aspects of the production. It covers how to work with photographers, film crews and models and how to open and close a show. It shows you how to project manage an apparently effortless runway.

Figure 5.1 China Fashion Week, AW2016. (VCG/Contributor via Getty Images)

Show day

The day of a fashion show is an exhilarating one: marking the culmination of months of hard work, celebrating creative achievement and offering multiple touchpoints where powerful messages about the designer or brand are communicated to an excited consumer. It is, as Simon Costin said, 'an addictive feeling'. For those producing one show, it is a potentially gruelling process. For those who produce many shows, for instance at fashion weeks, this is a time that demands considerable stamina and a strong constitution. They survive on adrenalin and very little sleep. Other productions – the opera, ballet, the theatre – are usually rehearsed and performed many times. A fashion show is a one-off live event and it has an energy unlike any other.

The schedule

The show producer creates a *schedule* for the day. This is a sheet that tells everyone where to be and when and the times of different activities. This is sometimes called a *call sheet*, a name borrowed from the film industry. The schedule keeps everyone on track and ensures that the show starts on time. The schedule or call sheet may list crew and contact details and the address of the venue. It may include:

01. The time that set-build starts
02. Call times for models, hair and make-up, security guards, house photographer and film crews
03. Times for the tech-rehearsal, choreography and dress rehearsal
04. Times for health and safety meetings
05. When the doors will open
06. When the show will start
07. The time the team expects to strike the set

'Directing live, immersive experiences more than pays off with the audience's reaction. "It's such an addictive feeling. The risk of working in a live environment does heighten certain stresses, but I think the reward of that is that you're an onlooker . . . So it's just so rewarding to see people experience it."' Simon Costin, art director and set designer. Skidmore, 2015

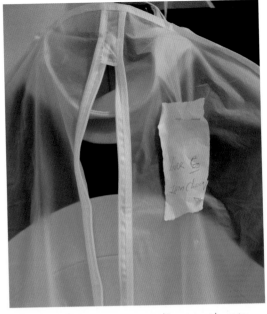

Figure 5.2 Garments are transported in garment bags to keep them pristine for the runway. (© Regent's University London

The director's chart

The show producer might create a director's chart to manage and coordinate the different elements of the show. The director's chart is used by the backstage team, sound technicians, lighting technicians and those live-editing for the live stream to keep them on track during the show. This is a chart with columns for different elements of the show, which tend to be:

01. The running order

02. The number of the look

03. A brief description of the outfit

04. Name of the model

05. Name of the dresser

06. Notes about accessories

07. Notes about difficult changes

08. Information about introductions before the show, finale, speeches after the show or compere

09. Lighting: which lighting state is to be used and when it is brought up or down

10. Sound: what sound or music track is to be played and when it is to be phased in and out

NOTE: An example of a Director's Chart can be found later in this chapter.

Packing and transport

If the venue is a *dry hire*, everything must be transported to the show site: the collection and other items for backstage, the set, the sound and lighting equipment, front-of-house and backstage furniture. If a show is to be built and struck in a day, everything will arrive on lorries early in the day. Deliveries are staggered to avoid clashes with parking spaces and access to the building. The speed with which those who build sets day-in-day-out can unload items and build a set is impressive.

Garments, accessories and other items also have to be safely transported to a show venue. Garments are packed in *garment bags* or *garment covers*, either individually or in bulk garment bags and transported on rails in a lorry or van. Items are usually labelled so that when everything arrives backstage at the venue, it is quick and easy to organize. It is advisable to have a full list of everything that is being transported. Most of the items for fashion shows are transported in vehicles that are hired or rented. A lorry or van can be rented for part of a day so that items can be transported to a venue at the beginning of the day and returned that evening. It is also possible to arrange for transport and overnight storage, so that items can be returned the following day. If a show takes place late in the day or if there is an after party, it can be helpful to have items stored safely overnight.

Figure 5.3 Items for fashion shows are transported in vehicles that are hired or rented. (© Regent's University London, Photographer Tony Rogers)

On the day of a show, the producers are usually backstage with headsets on and stopwatches in hands, timing the show. They cue the lights, the music, the lifting of the protective covering on the runway floor, and the models' walk down the runway – as well as the designer's end-of-show bow.

Smith, 2014

Figure 5.4 Guests, who stayed in hotels nearby, received handwritten invitations and arrived by boat or in a fleet of Mercedes. (Jacopo Raule/Contributor via Getty Images)

Private shows

In contrast to the celebrity-endorsed shows that are available for all to view on the Internet are private affairs for extremely wealthy couture clients. Dolce and Gabbana's July 2015 event for their womenswear and menswear couture collections and their Alta Gioielleria jewellery was a four-day event held in Portofino, inspired by the 1999 film version of *A Midsummer Night's Dream*. It comprised fashion shows, dinners, fireworks and other events including a party in a coastal nightclub with tented pavilions, entered through a grotto and with guests dressed in gold. The event took a year to plan and 'build'. Ninety-four models showed the womenswear, wearing one couture outfit each, many made from rare cloth. Each outfit could be ordered on a first-come-first-served basis. Guests competed to be first to claim outfits by texting their orders from their seats at the show. All next day there were fittings and in the evening the festivities continued with the menswear show.

Figure 5.5 The blue cube seating grid. Prada's SS2012 show. (Olivier Morin/Staff via Getty Images)

Prada disrupts the FROW

One of the most interesting seating designs for a runway event was Prada's SS2012 menswear show. The traditional boundaries between audience and runway were disrupted by the creation of a grid of blue cubes on which the audience sat while the models walked between them. It is fascinating to watch the film of the show and to see the tension in the venue as the audience responded to the non-traditional layout, which of course had no prestigious FROW and no directive regarding which way the audience faced.

Industry Insight
Svend Johannsen of DSA Productions

Figure 5.6 Svend Johannsen. (© Regent's University London, Photographer Simon Armstrong)

Tell me about the build.

The build is interesting. I often think 'wow that's quite amazing'. Between 8am and 2 o'clock, places get transformed. Most of the creativity comes from the show producer or the designer. We are facilitating ideas. Or someone will come up with a hare-brained idea and we will manipulate it to make it doable. Striking the show is not that interesting. One of the beauties of the job is that afterwards, apart from getting paid, you walk away. Unless it's not gone that well and then there is a moratorium but that's rare.

So you work creatively?

We work with [the fashion retailer] Next and they will come up with a two-word concept and they will want catwalk construction designed on that concept. That is the only time we are involved in the creativity. When you are exposed to a lot of creativity, it rubs off on you. You can apply that to other people's ideas. But, what we are really good at is interpreting, facilitating, making it happen.

Huge events: how do those work in terms of production teams?

There are just more people and bigger stuff. There's more pressure, only because there is more money involved. When we build a smaller show, I production manage it and there are people installing and operating the sound and lighting. On bigger shows, you employ set designers and there will be people designing all the different elements of it; you will still have an overall production manager but you will have a sound designer who is managing the sound team and a lighting designer who will manage the lighting team.

Do you have a team that always works with you?

We have a core of people who do set but we also bring in set freelancers. We own no lighting and no sound equipment. We work with two sound companies. We employ those companies and they use freelancers. For lighting, there are three companies we go to: two supply kit and crew, the other supplies kit and we use freelancers. It all depends on the scale of the task and the kind of task. Companies have different kit. We do quite a lot of video projection and that comes from another company.

How does the equipment get to the venue?

We don't have any transport; we hire trucks and drivers. We don't own any equipment. When you own something you are likely to utilize that more than a better thing for the job. We expect our suppliers to have the technology. We are very loyal to our suppliers because you build a relationship. You organize the equipment to turn up at different times: 8am, 8.30am . . .

How do you plan a show?

It's about things arriving in the right place and how long it will take; it is simply experience. There isn't a formula and sometimes I will be calling the lighting company, saying 'how long will it take you to build this?' For the scheduling, we always work from the time we can gain access to the time we need to be ready by and then you develop the schedule and work out how many people we'll need. It's important to know what your time frame is or you can't start planning.

How do you agree the budget?

It is always 'how much will this cost?' I say 'this is how much?', then you will take things out or work out another way of doing it if it's too much.

Do you make the set before a show?

Yes, the flats are pre-fabricated. Standard flats get stored and reused. There is deterioration every time they are used. They get replaced maybe every two years. With one-off stuff, you can't go to another client with someone else's set. Clients wont usually want to use the same set twice. Margaret Howell shows in a studio at Ballet Rambert on the South Bank [London] and she has exactly the same thing, but it's rare that people do that. She has a really fresh identity and if it works why change it. The point of those shows is to get the press and buyers seeing the clothes and to get good photos.

What about the more dramatic sets?

For other designers, it's about the presentation. Burberry shows, which can be pretty much a standard set, take three weeks to build for a ten-minute show. One fashion company spent a month-and-a-half building an outdoor venue in Scotland. They flew 150 people to the space for about twenty minutes. Then there are new designers who can't afford to pay for a show because they need that money for their next collection.

The build

Set-build is the first activity to take place because most other activities depend upon the set being in place. The build for a simple runway can take place on the same day as the show. It is expensive to hire a venue, so unless there is a large budget the set will be built, the show presented and the set struck within a day. Other sets are more complex and take longer to construct or may be used for various shows. Sets are usually prepared in advance so that they can be built as fast as possible at the venue. For events where build and show take place in one day, set-build starts very early in the morning. Large, expensive shows such as those created for Prada or Chanel are a mixture of interior architecture and theatre and can take days or weeks to build. The transformation of whole buildings by set-builders is impressive to watch.

If flats are being used to create a backdrop or backstage area, these are built to integrate with the runway. The order in which the build takes place depends upon the set design. At a floor show (salon style) the models walk on the floor instead of on a raised runway and their route must be marked out by tape, audience seating or material such as vinyl or carpet laid on the floor. The runway is covered with cloth to keep it clean during the day's activities and this is removed just before the show. The runway is usually created before the seating is laid out. Chairs must be arranged in straight lines and modern benches, usually painted in white or black, are repainted in situ for each show.

Technical elements of the build

Lighting

The lighting system is integral to the set and is built at the same time. If a venue doesn't have a rig, a whole rig with lighting is built. Sometimes lights are added to an existing rig to get sufficient light onto the runway. Lighting is also provided backstage and for instance, on backdrops or branding boards. Lighting in the ceiling is installed before the runway is built because the runway would get in the way of the ladders or scaffolding used to access the rig. For safety reasons, other than the technical crew, no-one should be near where lighting is being installed. Up-lighting can be set at ground level along walls or flats and can be used to flood surfaces with colour or pattern. During tech-rehearsals, technicians coordinate with other technical aspects of the show and test that the lighting is working as planned. The lighting technicians and house photographer do tests with a model to ensure perfect lighting along the runway and most importantly on the sweet spot where models pose in front of the press pit. Increasingly lighting technicians must consider the photographs that are taken from the front row and elsewhere for social media.

Projection and film

Projection, back-projection and LED screens are integrated into the build. A trend towards greater use of technology in shows includes film. In the SS2015 Hunter show, Alasdhair Willis, creative director, worked with artist Mat Maitland. Film was shown both behind the models and reflected beneath them in a mirrored runway, making the models look as if they were walking through a swimming pool. The magical finale of Alexander McQueen's show in 2006 in Paris, 'Widows of Culloden', was an optical illusion of Kate Moss in a pyramid to the soundtrack from Schindler's List. The projection was created using a Victorian parlour trick called 'Pepper's ghost'.

Figure 5.7 Runway covered with protective cloth. The benches have letters so that the audience can find their seats. The back three rows of benches are higher, giving those sitting further back a better view. (© Regent's University London)

Figure 5.8 Focusing the lighting. (© Regent's University London)

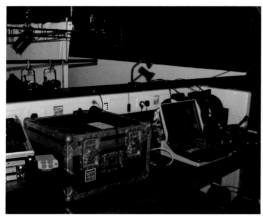

Figure 5.9 The sound and lighting desk is usually tucked away somewhere unobtrusive. (© Regent's University London)

Figure 5.10 The producer calls the show using a monitor backstage which shows the runway area. (© Regent's University London)

Sound

As with lighting, the sound system may be built from scratch or a venue may already have a sound system installed. Sound technicians consider the size of a venue and the acoustics to ensure that the sound is both loud enough and of high enough quality. They monitor levels of noise to meet ideal levels for the location. The sound team provides headsets (also known as the *cans*) for the crew and microphones for speakers, and they coordinate with whoever is operating the lighting, recording the show and live streaming it. Once the set is built and sound and lighting equipment installed, the role of the sound and lighting technicians is key. With the show producer, they control the show. Working to a pre-agreed, rehearsed set of cues, the team coordinates the sound, the lighting and the entrance and exits of the models, fading music in and out and moving between lighting states.

The headsets the crew use operate on a different audio system (either wireless or wired) from that used for the show production. The show producer works backstage wearing a headset. Likewise, at least one person front-of-house, the sound and lighting technicians, the film crew and the live-stream team have headsets. In this way, the team can communicate before, during and after the performance. The sound and lighting team put a monitor backstage at the entrance to the runway which shows a live stream of the runway from a camera set up front-of-house. The show producer can thereby see the runway, enabling him or her to control the show and cue the models.

Backstage

In some venues, there is a natural backstage area; if not, backstage has to be created as part of the set-build. Tables, chairs, mirrors and rails can be part of the contract for the build. A venue with a natural backstage area means that the team can organize backstage during set-build. A team of backstage managers, dressers, runners, hair and make-up artists and designer(s) supports backstage activity. Careful planning means that backstage can be set up quickly. Backstage teams need to be well organized and calm in high-pressure situations. Model fees are expensive, so unless there is a large budget, each model will wear more than one outfit. Shows are more complicated if there are fast changes and if accessories are difficult to put on. The busier the backstage activities, the larger the backstage team should be to support models getting changed and onto the runway in their next look. Runway is simpler when there is one outfit per model, but more models need more space backstage.

Figure 5.11 Running order in a backstage chart at the Rebekka Ruétz AW2013 fashion show at Berlin Fashion Week. (Gareth Cattermole/Staff via Getty Images)

The backstage director

There is generally one person who has overall responsibility for backstage. This can be the show producer or sometimes there is a separate backstage director. Someone must manage the backstage team, setting out clothes and accessories, prepping the dressers, liaising with hair and make-up teams and getting the backstage boards (sometimes called *backstage charts*) in place. The show producer cues the models onto the runway once the show begins, sometimes known as calling the models or *calling the show*. Meanwhile the backstage managers line up the models and make sure that there are always several models ready to go onto the runway.

Organizing the backstage area

Every venue has a different backstage area and every producer or director has their preferred way of organizing backstage. There must be enough space for clothes rails, models and dressers, and to line up the models before they are cued onto the runway. If backstage is large enough, hair and make-up takes place towards the back of the space so that rails are close to the runway. If backstage is small, hair and make-up teams may work elsewhere, possibly front-of-house, their tables and mirrors moved backstage before the show begins so they can touch up models' hair and make-up. Some producers arrange the rails in parallel; others put them around the walls of the backstage area. Given enough space the latter is better because the team can scan the area and see everyone; if there is a problem with a change, it will be spotted quickly. If rails are set out in parallel, it is difficult to see all areas.

Figure 5.12 Outfits grouped per model and ready to go backstage. (© Regent's University London)

Backstage charts

The backstage chart is put up prominently near the entrance to the runway so that everyone can see the running order and how the outfits should look. The chart aids backstage setup and choreography and is used during the show for the line-up. Each outfit in the show has a number in the running order. Backstage, outfits are grouped in the running order for each model, with model charts attached to the rail or onto the wall behind. This means that each model goes back to the same rail and dresser to find their next outfit. Both can see from the model chart which outfit and accessories come next. Difficult changes or instructions for dressing can be put on the model chart. If there is enough space backstage and it is a hectic show, some producers might put any particularly fast or difficult changes onto a rail near to the entrance to the runway so that everyone can help to make sure that those changes go smoothly.

The accessories

Accessories are organized differently by different teams. For instance, if the shoes for a show are used several times, they might be laid out near the entrance to the runway with the sizes written inside so that models can slip on the right size before they go out. Jewellery, hats and other accessories can either kept with an outfit or laid out on tables backstage. It is very easy for shoes and other accessories to become separated from outfits so a good system is essential. Sometimes accessories are stored in bags that hang from hangers or rails, or in boxes under rails. Dressers need to ensure that a model's outfits and accessories are kept together and well organized.

Models and dressers

Models arrive according to their call time on the schedule. During fashion weeks if shows are straightforward, models go from one show to the next. With more complicated collections or shows, models might be booked for longer so that they can learn choreography and rehearse. One team member should have a list of the models, to tick them off as they arrive, chase those who are late and ensure that they rotate through fittings, choreography and hair and make-up. This person can call models for rehearsals and make sure they are all backstage before the doors open. There is always a model who vanishes at the wrong moment – for a cigarette or to use their mobile. If models have several changes, one dresser per model is advisable. Dressers are prepped by the show producer during setup, shown the looks and the accessories and how they must be worn. Some dressers work on a lot of shows and are paid to do so, others work free for the experience. For those new to dressing, they need to learn how to dress, which includes the following steps:

01. Get their model(s) into the first outfit ready for the show to begin.

02. Get the next look ready by taking it off hangers and opening fastenings.

03. When the model comes off the runway, get him or her out of one outfit and into the next quickly.

04. If anything goes wrong (a broken zip, a ripped garment), alert backstage managers.

05. Get the model into the line-up as quickly as possible. If there is a problem, get the model into the line-up and sort out the problem there.

06. While the model is on the runway, put the last look back onto hangers and get the next outfit ready.

Prepping the models

Sometimes mood boards are set up backstage to remind everyone about the look and feel of a show. Suzi Menkes wrote in September 2012 about the Gucci show: 'Frida Giannini sent out her best show yet . . . an orgy of gorgeousness, inspired by the refined elegance of the palazzo principessas . . . with the bloodline of Italy's upper crust, from Marella Agnelli, whose famous long-neck silhouette was pinned on the mood board backstage' (Menkes, 2012). Cue boards are situated where the models line up near the entrance to the runway reminding them what to do. A cue board might show a diagram of the runway if choreography is complicated. It might also contain words to remind models of the mood of the show and how the producer would like them to behave. Alexandre de Betak of Bureau Betak claims to have invented cue boards and the archive on the Bureau Betak website shows some of the cue boards used by de Betak at some of the most innovative shows in the world. Some designers ask models to behave 'in character', so that they act 'in character' while on the runway. Watch https://www.youtube.com/watch?v=kWoQqrRk0ss to see Kate Moss talking about this and about McQueen's 2006 'Widows of Culloden' show (SHOWstudio 2014).

Industry Insight

Charlie Manns, hairstylist

Charlie Manns is a hairstylist at Electric Hairdressing, London, where he is one of the creative directors in the art team that works on fashion shows in London and internationally.

How do you stay ahead of the trends?

We have a monthly art team meeting to review the trends, develop our own ideas and decide what will work. We are constantly educating and updating ourselves. From idea to finished piece it's crucial to have a system. Trends are six months ahead of schedule. Electric Hairdressing source information and inspiration from everywhere but also look at trend predictions like Nelly Rodi.

How do you generate ideas for the hair for a show?

For a photo shoot, we would look at and collect colours, images, materials etc. We might collect one hundred images, for instance. The team works by sourcing materials, sorting different inspirations to narrow the concept and we end up with mood boards. We have eight-foot black-out boards and we put the materials on there. To get materials we might go to the beach, go to the park . . . move out of our usual environment.

Before a show we practice, using the Electric product, doing test runs in the salon. We rehearse and rehearse until its perfect. That's the creative director and the art team plus stylists who want to join the art team. The work is very different from salon work. We work to a very tight time limit. A third of the normal time, finishing hair to photoshoot standard. We have to take a 360-degree view: Is it balanced? Does it work with the neckline? Does it work across twenty, thirty, forty models? Working with detail, it must be absolute perfection.

For fashion week shows, some designers work three months ahead and some change the styling two days or even two hours before a show. Designers usually have a clear concept of the total look and Electric contribute to that. Some designers absolutely know what they want in advance and with other designers I am part of the creative process. We work with different designers. OnIOff at London Fashion Week is brilliant. It's important for our young stylists because they get the opportunity to work in that kind of pressure cooker environment.

Your team generously gives a lot of time to the Regent's fashion shows and fashion shoots.

We like to work with young designers, that raw talent. It's refreshing, we can work together to develop. With Regent's we

Figures 5.13 and 5.14 Charlie Manns and the art team working to a deadline backstage at a show. (© Regent's University London, Photographer Tony Rogers)

have an initial chat and meet with the design students. We come without pre-conceived ideas but we do know what is trending. We work through the creative process with the students, talking about the message the students want. The idea is that the students showcase their work and Electric complement it. We take the students through the creative process. We have to reflect the quality of Electric while also working with students to achieve what they need. It's an important process to work hand in hand.

What is it like to work as a stylist on a fashion show?

As stylists, the team mustn't show stress, must be professional and reflect the brand well. It's easy to get overheated by the lights and the impossible task. Sometimes models are called to do a run-through but you've still got five models to style. It's an amazing, intense situation and you have to channel the adrenalin. High pressure, but that's what is addictive.

After the shows, we clean down the working space so we leave it the same or better. We talk to all models, take out hair pieces, brush through hair and make sure the hair is ok. We always wait to make sure the designers are happy and to do any post-show interviews. Later we do a de-brief to look at the results; this is good reflective practice. We use the images from the show, we are not allowed to take photos pre-show because of confidentiality. We never compromise. They are protecting their brand.

[We] had an architect, who had a set with big blocks that were different sizes staggered all over the stage . . . the idea Gigli gave me was that he wanted it to be like when you walk down the road and see a beautiful girl and she is walking in between cars and you lose her behind something and then you see her again. I set it up with three entrances and three coloured walks. Each girl was told as she went onto the runway which colour arrows she was following. We rehearsed what to do, and where they would pose. The show looked like models walking randomly but they were never going to bump into each other.
John Walford, talking about working in Paris with Romeo Gigli

Figures 5.15 and 5.16 John Walford showing models the choreography before a show. (© Regent's University London)

Hair and make-up

During pre-show planning hair, make-up and nail tests will have been done and photographs taken. Images of these will be backstage at the show so that stylists can refer to them. Sometimes one lead stylist shows the others how to create the look. This is important if artists are working on more than one show a day. On show day, teams of stylists can spend hours creating each look. If it is straightforward, and there are not too many models, the hair and make-up artists may only need a couple of hours to complete their work, but if it is more complicated the process can take longer. During fashion weeks, make-up and hair artists may work for just a few hours per day, but for those working on many shows, fashion weeks are busy times. Unless they have a busy schedule, hair and make-up artists are some of the more relaxed people around on show days. Once all models are finished, one or more stylists go backstage to renew the look before models go back out because hair and make-up get disturbed during outfit changes.

Choreography

There are trends in choreography: the way that models walk and how they pose for the photographers has changed over the decades. Runway looks and behaviours are influenced by the aesthetic of the time as our notions of fashion shift. Choreography is often simple with models walking straight down the runway, posing for the photographers and walking back again. Even simple shows may involve choreography and there will always be designers and producers who do something different. At its most extreme are shows such as Rick Owen's now-famous SS2013, where he used a step team instead of models. The timing of a whole show depends on choreography and a show can be speeded up or slowed down depending upon the length of the walk, the choreography and the number of models on the runway at one time. Choreography is mapped out in advance if it is complicated, and it is timed so that the length of the production is controlled. Producers are often seen with stopwatches, planning when to cue models onto the runway. If choreography is complicated, models need a way of remembering what to do and cue boards backstage and stickers front-of-house direct them.

Figures 5.17 and 5.18 Yohji Yamamoto's beautiful and captivating wedding dress show in 1999. (Guy Marineau/Contributor via Getty Images)

Yohji Yamamoto

Sometimes the models' movements are more akin to theatre. One of the most enchanting shows was Yohji Yamamoto's beautiful, captivating wedding dress show in 1999 that was about the many stories behind a wedding dress. The production saw models walking on a white square floor, putting garments on, taking layers of clothing off, to reveal, sometimes surprisingly, layers beneath. The audience were entranced and some are rumoured to have cried.

Figure 5.19 Timing the show is essential. (© Regent's University London)

Rehearsals

The vision for the show is first realized during rehearsals. Here the team checks that all elements are coordinated and that timings are right, working together on the smallest details until everything is synchronized and the atmosphere, the mood and the energy of the show match the vision. Sometimes a show is well rehearsed but models arrive shortly before the event with just enough time for hair and make-up. Show producers have been known to employ actors to walk the show to rehearse a more complicated production. There are different kinds of rehearsals:

01. The *tech-rehearsal* enables the producer, technical team, photographer and film crew to get the technical details right, for example, the lighting and sound, cues and timings.

02. A *walk-through* is useful as a tech-rehearsal and for inexperienced models and dressers. Models carry the outfits they will be wearing, preparing dressers and models for the speed of the show.

03. A *dress rehearsal* is run as if the show were live. One of the benefits of a dress rehearsal is that outfits can be seen on the models on the runway. If problems become apparent they can be rectified. Someone should sit in the audience, watch the dress rehearsal and note down problems, such as an item that may need different underwear.

The music, light, pace, the models' attitude and the overall timing . . . the way you create tension . . . sad, happy or sexy emotion . . . I can spend hours and hours rehearsing a five second opening of a show. It often is the minimal, last-minute changes that make all the difference. As much as we plan, draw and sometimes even animate beforehand, a show is a live experience and during the technical rehearsal you realise that it could be much better if we extend that introduction, if we change the lighting, or if we make the first model appear 10 seconds earlier or 20 seconds later, if we re-time it . . . because any of these details can completely transform the energy and perception of the show.
Alexandre de Betak, interviewed by Suleman Anaya, 2013

Figures 5.20 and 5.21 Measuring the benches and setting out programmes and reserved notices. (© Regent's University London, Photographer Tony Rogers)

PR activities

Show-day PR activities include:

01. Final communications with the press
02. Finalizing the guest list for the door
03. Finalizing the seating plan and setting out reserved notices
04. Setting out goody bags and other sponsor material
05. Prepping the team that will be seating guests
06. Prepping the team on the doors
07. Checking that all sponsor materials are as agreed
08. Ensuring that branding (step and repeat) boards are in place for interviews and photographs
09. Prepping those giving backstage interviews
10. Liaising with the photographers and the film crews

Seating

Before the show, the PR team labels the rows of seating and puts out reserved seating notices, goody bags and information for the press in the form of line sheets, press notes, programmes and/or acknowledgements. There is a seating hierarchy and if an important guest is not seated appropriately, it can be seriously detrimental to a designer's business. The PR team may have a guest list at the door so that guests can be checked off as they arrive.

Figure 5.22 While the photographers in the pit are prominent at a show, there are others whose presence is less evident. (© Gill Stark)

Figure 5.23 Places marked out in the press pit. (© Gill Stark)

Figure 5.24 The house film crew always has prime position for shooting. (© Regent's University London)

Working with the photographers

The PR team work closely with the photographers and film and TV crews. The house photographer and house film crew usually arrive early for setup and tech-rehearsals. If there is significant sponsorship, PR may have their own photographer to capture images that include sponsor products and logos. This includes images of celebrities arriving and in front of branding boards and every other image that will boost the sponsor's association with fashion runway. On show day, the position of the press pit is marked out with tape or sometimes a raised platform is created. The house photographer and film crew stake out their spots. Those positioned further back stand on boxes and camera cases, lenses pointing over the shoulders of those in front, everyone shuffling to get the best positions. While the photographers in the pit are prominent at a show, there are others whose presence is less evident. With the public's appetite for information about fashion shows, models and celebrities, some photographers work on backstage and front row shots, which are as sought after as runway. Like runway photographers, backstage photographers shoot more than one show per day. Good fashion photographers are very busy during fashion weeks.

Depending upon the importance of a designer or brand, one or more film crews might attend a show. The house film crew might have several cameras around the runway to shoot from different angles. This will vary depending upon budgets, the purpose of the film and the shape of the runway. Edited film is always more interesting if shot from different angles. The film crew comprises camera operators, vision mixer/directors and a production assistant who makes sure that vans can park, arranges access to the building and takes care of permissions and crew food.

Industry Insight
Nick Horrell, videographer

Nick Horrell is a videographer; he works with the team on the day of a show to film the event, and after the event he edits the 'raw footage' to create a final film. Editing includes meetings with the client to agree content and ensure that the edited version is what the client envisages.

Figure 5.25 Nick Horrell. (© Nick Horrell)

What is it like filming a fashion show?

It's a high-energy atmosphere, it's noisy, there's a lot going on. There's a lot of organization. You need to know who is doing what and when. You work with the lighting crew and the stills photographers. It's good to have a tech-rehearsal if you can. One of the most difficult things to get right is the white balance. Because of the colours of the fabrics it is particularly important for fashion. If you are working with several cameras it is better to use the same cameras because of white balances. You can film a fashion show with one camera but to add interest, two or more cameras is good, because then you can capture detail, audience shots . . . it's more interesting.

A fashion show is rarely repeated, so how do you make sure you have the footage you need?

We record a lot. You might have several cameras and some cameras have two recording slots so you record double. The feed from the cameras coming out of the mixing desk is recorded as well. It is a one-shot deal. You have to think beforehand, what shots do I want? There are now high-speed cameras, so you record the model on the runway and when footage is played back in normal time, it comes through in beautiful slow motion so you can see the fall of the fabric, you can see the way the light falls on it . . .

Live streaming has become increasingly popular.

Live streaming is complex. Video feed comes in from each camera to the mixing desk. The feeds are cut live by a vision-mixing director. You need someone incredibly calm, they have to concentrate. They know which cameras are doing what shots: camera one shots of the models coming up the runway, camera two shots of models going away, camera three shots of detail, camera four shots of the audience . . . The director has mini screens and they are choosing, editing live. Once they are in the swing of it, it becomes a flow. The director also liaises with the audio crew who feed the music to go with the live stream through a cable or two into the mixing desk. Permissions have to be sought for the music used in the live stream and the live feed has to be hosted on a website.

It's lovely filming a live fashion show, if you get the opportunity and you're interested in filmography – do it!

Figure 5.26 Popular events that are likely to attract more attention require greater security presence. (© Gill Stark)

Health and safety, and insurance

Health and safety guidelines

It is essential to follow health and safety guidelines. There are potential hazards created by moving people in and out of a venue in a short space of time. Further hazards are presented by the nature of the fashion show. It is essential to meet the legal requirements of the country in which the show is produced, and the event organizer is responsible for the health and safety and welfare of the audience and the crew. Information and advice should be sought to ensure that all requirements are met. Planning for health and safety should start as work on the event begins, and all documents evidencing this should be carefully filed because in the event of something going wrong, these documents will have to be produced.

Show producers are responsible for overseeing this work, including risk assessments. Ensuring that the set is free from hazards and that exit routes are adequate and clearly signposted is serious. Failure to abide by the law can be very serious. Event organizers usually have their own public liability insurance and they seek evidence of public liability insurance from all contractors (from set-builders to make-up artists) and from the venue owners. It is the responsibility of those organizing a fashion show to know the law and to ensure that their own insurance, and that of others, is sufficient to cover any eventuality. How insurance cover works varies in different parts of the world.

Security

Loud music, food and drink and large numbers of people arriving signal that something exciting is happening and people will try to gain access. Security is essential to ensure access for those invited, and to keep others out. Security is also important for reasons of safety. Security personnel are sometimes asked to control the rate at which people enter an event. They often work with the PR team to ensure that VIP guests are given access. Security guards are also available to deal with any difficult incidents. It is advisable to have a security presence on each door into a venue. The total number of security personnel will depend upon the event and the number of entrances. Popular events that are likely to attract more attention require greater security presence. Security guards are usually hired from an agency and work in shifts if overnight cover is necessary and if the event or the build is in place for more than a day.

It's a high-energy atmosphere, it's noisy, there's a lot going on. There's a lot of organization. You need to know who is doing what and when … it's lovely filming a live fashion show …

Before the doors open

Backstage is buzzing just before a show. Dressers are getting models into their first outfits and the first models to go out line up at the entrance to the runway ready for the show to begin. Select journalists and bloggers may be allowed to go backstage and send out sneak-peak tweets and Instagram messages to help build anticipation. There might also be pre-show interviews, providing material for use later or as fillers if a show is being live streamed. Such is consumer intrigue about the hidden world of backstage that sneak peeks and teasers have become another promotional opportunity. Once everyone is ready backstage, there is a pause as everyone waits for the cue for the show to begin.

Figure 5.27 Sometimes film crews do interviews in the run-up to a show. (© Regent's University London)

Meanwhile, front-of-house, pre-show music is cued, the lighting state is changed and anyone who needs to go backstage will do so (particularly in cases where the only route to backstage is across the runway). The protective cover is taken off the runway, unless the audience has to walk across it to get to their seats. The PR team gets ready to identify VIPs, greet guests at the doors and seat people. Part of the trend for a more immersive, multi-sensory experience is the use of fragrances at shows. This is not a new idea and shows have been scented using perfume sprays, flowers on runways and even sprinkled tea leaves: 'modern Bulgarian rose' was the name used to describe the scent used at a recent Prabal Gurung show.

One of the biggest innovations in runway has been the introduction of live streaming. Live video with audio is fed from several cameras to a desk where it is live-edited at the event and fed through to the Internet. Streaming delivers data live in real time and while the consumer cannot download it, it can be uploaded onto a designer or a brand's website. This has created a new dynamic around runway. The transitory nature of shows, the fact that they are one-offs, never to be repeated and on which huge commercial success rests already make them charged events. Live streaming increases this dynamic because the show must start on time, and there is a sense of a huge global audience, waiting to view. Add to this seasonless collections and the ability to purchase directly from the runway through see-now-buy-now, and anticipation is heightened as the fashion show becomes super-charged.

The doors open

The doors remain closed during the set up for a show and it is generally the PR team who officially open the doors, letting the audience into the event. The PR team are at the door to recognize the most prominent media, buyers and other VIP guests. Guests enter in order of importance so that those sitting front row go straight in and others must wait. However, during fashion weeks, the most important influencers (sometimes called the fashion pack) coming from the show before usually arrive last in the official fashion week cars. There are usually several important guests without whom the show cannot start and there is always a tense wait for them to arrive. For those who are new to fashion, mug shots of important guests are printed out and memorized so that everyone recognizes them. One person is usually given the task of counting the number of people entering the building for health and safety purposes. The logistics of getting a

Figure 5.28 Marc Jacobs'
AW2013. (Dimitrios
Kambouris/Staff via Getty
Images)

large audience into and out of a show quickly are considerable. At a ten-minute
fashion week show, the show is usually much shorter than the time it takes to seat
the audience.

Seating is always a juggling act. Except at high-profile shows, there are always
people who promise to attend but don't and others who were not expected and
suddenly appear. A challenging scenario is the important guest who appears
unannounced and expects to sit in an already packed front row and there is the
danger that someone seated further back will think they should be in the front
row. To avoid difficult scenes, PRs have been known to let celebrities and others
know in advance that if they attend there won't be space for them on the front
row. Film and photographs of the event must show a packed front row. People are
identified in advance to fill any gaps in the front row just before the show starts.

Industry Insight
Stefan Hottinger-Behmer, Associate Publisher of *Vogue* Arabia

Stefan Hottinger-Behmer was born in São Paulo, Brazil. After starting his studies (business) at the University of Zurich, he transferred to London, where he graduated with a BA in Fashion Marketing. He always combined subjects in fashion, marketing, business and journalism. This mix has eventually led him to work in trend forecasting agencies with stints in the editorial world, where he eventually came to feel at home.

Figure 5.29 Stefan Behmer. (© Stefan Behmer)

How did you become a fashion journalist?

I have always liked the fast-paced nature of the fashion industry. Fashion journalism aims to bring some coherence and analysis to the ever-changing nature of this diverse industry. Essentially, why should we be buying new clothes every season and what credibility do these designers have, to impose these new visual codes onto us? Fashion journalism is the key to understanding why certain movements become trends. If you look at key figures in the industry, they can make or break global brands. If buyers ask Anna Wintour to speak to a leading brand to change the fabric of a certain catwalk piece to make it more commercially viable, she can make it happen.

If a brand advertises in US *Vogue*, it will be seen by millions and generate measurable increases in sales. When Isabela Blow introduced Alexander McQueen to the Gucci Group (now Kering), she helped mediate that takeover. Fashion journalists often become authors, writing historical books that help us to put fashion in a sociological context or books that become films, eventually becoming part of pop culture, such as *The Devil Wears Prada*. The fashion industry is a colourful one, a fast-paced lab of ideas with an essential global component and it's this mixture that has always attracted me.

How did you get to where you are now?

That was a long journey . . . during my studies I spent summers doing internships, at the Giorgio Armani press office in London, at Alfred Dunhill or at DeBeers. After getting my degree, I joined a start-up trend forecasting agency and through that I fell into journalism, initially blagging my way into shows, for which I was paid $100 per review. The Internet was a new phenomenon and it was very exciting. At the first ever São Paulo Fashion Week, I sat next to another invited journalist, who happened to be the editor-in-chief of *L'OFFICIEL* magazine in Paris. When she realized I was born in São Paulo, she commissioned a thirty-two-page special on Brazilian fashion, which I delivered in just two weeks. With all those pages in my clipping book, I started knocking on the door of every major publishing house in London. I eventually ended up writing for all the major titles: *Elle*, *Wallpaper*, *Harper's Bazaar*, *Collezioni*, *Times* and, of course, *L'OFFICIEL*.

Do you think that digital media will eventually replace live fashion shows?

You can never replace the energy and electrifying buzz of the live presence at a big show. When the lights go down, the celebrities have taken their seats, the music starts and the first top model steps onto the catwalk, there is something magical and very exciting in the air that will never be felt over any digital media outlets. What digital media does, and very well, is democratize fashion. Another side effect is that everything is becoming even more accelerated, so while the shows used to predict next season's trends, companies such as Zara, Mango and Top Shop will already incorporate trends immediately after the shows, just to push sales. Digital media has changed the dynamic of fashion and its seasonality.

What was your last role?

I held the licence for *L'OFFICIEL* in Switzerland and I was the publisher and editorial director. Despite working under such a big global brand, with over thirty licences around the globe, we operated as a start-up, with a small and very dedicated team, so I do a bit of everything. There was a lot of travel involved and I was responsible for the content of all our editions, *L'OFFICIEL*, *Voyage* and *Hommes*.

When did you first go to fashion shows?

I was a student in London and the first show I ever went to was Julien MacDonald. It was held in a hotel ballroom and I entered through the fire exit. It takes years to work your way to the front rows and I have paid my dues. Nowadays every city has ambitions to host its own fashion week. During the past fifteen years, I have been invited and attended quite a few: Australia, New Zealand, Brazil, Russia, India, Switzerland, Germany, Portugal, Spain, South Africa, China and, of course, US, France, UK and Italy.

You watched as São Paulo Fashion Week developed?

São Paulo Fashion Week is a real success story. The Brazilian fashion industry is vibrant and truly relevant in South America. When the industry got organized, they managed to create one of the biggest fashion weeks on the planet. The Brazilian Association of Textile Industries has given big brands and small designers all the support they need to expand their businesses both in the domestic market and abroad.

Which other fashion weeks do you think are currently influential in a global sense?

In a sense, they are all influential because fashion in its very essence has become a truly global business. But to say that any of them is actually changing anything in the grand scheme of things, would be inaccurate. In a world dominated by luxury conglomerates, all that matters is where they are and what their output is. It's a bit like visiting a casino on a Caribbean island for fun, you cannot compare it with the grandeur of Las Vegas or Macau . . . there are always the front runners and those are usually responsible for the direction of any given industry.

Previews

Some brands show important editors their collections before a major show. Karl Lagerfeld, for example, may hold a press preview on the evening before a Chanel runway show at the Grand Palais in Paris. The press often file their reviews just twenty minutes after a show and if editors have seen a collection the evening before they can start to frame a story before the event. Some buyers may have seen the whole collection before the show and planned or placed orders. Runway often presents an edit because the event would be too long and tedious if it showed the entire collection. As explored earlier in the book, showpieces are sometimes made especially for the runway, and are not intended to sell in large numbers, if at all. What buyers see in advance is not necessarily what they see on the runway. Because runway is about generating excitement around the brand, a more wearable collection is often available to buyers. The show enables the media and buyers to see looks on models and to fully understand the mood and the story of the collection, and confirms for buyers that they have chosen the best pieces.

Figure 5.30 Seating is always a juggling act. Film and photographs of the event must show a packed front row. (© Regent's University London)

Controlling the show

Those overseeing front-of-house (usually PR) let the show producer know that important guests have arrived and are seated. From that moment, the show producer steers the show from their position backstage. The producer signals to the audience that the show is about to begin. They might ask the audience to take their seats or there may be a different *lighting state* for those last few minutes pre-show. Alternatively, a different soundtrack might be faded in. The show producer, who is in contact with the PR, and sound and lighting teams via the cans, cues the show to begin, often by sending out the first model, and continues to control the event. This is known as *calling the show*. Once the show has started the most important activity is cueing the models onto the runway, also known as *calling the models*. Having timed the walks on the runway, the producer knows when to cue each model, usually gauged by watching models who are out on the runway, using the monitor backstage. The producer communicates with the sound and lighting technicians and they talk through the show as they work.

Figure 5.31 Waiting for the 'front row' to arrive. (© Gill Stark)

The director's chart

While the backstage chart shows the looks and the running order, the sound and lighting team and others use the director's chart for their elements of the show. The director's chart lists all of the outfits as they will appear on the runway, the model that will wear each outfit and any grouping of looks. Importantly, the chart contains all of the music and lighting information that the technicians will need. It tells them the track titles, the lengths of tracks, lighting states and when sound and lights are to be changed, faded in and faded out. If the show is in sections with different music for each section, the show producer will tell everyone when the last model for a section is on the runway so that everyone is ready to move from one section into the next, with associated changes in lighting and sound. They also cue finale music and comperes and presenters. If there are any problems out on the runway or backstage everyone will be aware and decisions will be communicated quickly.

Designer	Model	Outfit	Accessories	Music
01. Bao	Ali	Ivory jumpsuit with black outerwear		*Now Time* by Balam Acab
02.		Ivory and black dress (centre open) with trousers		
03.		Ivory pleated shirt with black felted jacket and ivory skirt		
04.		Ivory ruffle top with ivory skirt leatherite vest		
05.		Black and ivory dress with slip under		
06.		Back buttoned ivory shirt with black jumpsuit		
07. Sarah	Jordan	Beige jumpsuit with tie "skirt"	Boots	*How To Destroy Angels* by The Believers
08.		Leaf print dress with beige jacket	Gloves, sneakers	
09.		Leaf print shirt, beige trousers and wrap	Gloves, boots	
10.		Cream dress with jailbreak striped coat	Black gloves	
11.		Grey dress with front leaf panel	Black gloves	
12.		Printed chiffon jumpsuit over brown jumpsuit		
13. Karina	Iona	Coat over dress with chain and asymmetric cape	Gold belt, white ostrich feather Jimmy Choo shoes	*Body Language* by Booka Shade
14.		Beige dress over blue hood	Black spiked boots	
15.		Blue low crotch pant, printed top, half sleeve jacket	Doiley visor, black spiked boots	
16.		Printed, hooded top with black hareem pants	Gold laced shoes	
17.		Beige drop-crotch shorts and turquoise cape	Black spiked heels	
18.		Hooded asymmetric dress		
19. Indica	Aba	White button down dress with black ribbon detail cuffs		*Time of Extinction* by Jaubinai
20.		Long red sleeve dress with black leather high-neck front		
21.		High waisted yellow skirt with strong leather collar and shoulder jacket		
22.		Leather underskirt with high waisted yellow skirt an dred ribbon bow	Blue heels	
23.		Long cream ruffle dress with red belt cream wool cropped cross front jacket	Blue heels, silver necklace	
24.		Very small pants leather pants with long red and cream shirt with gold button detail	Blue heels, silver necklace	
25. Johann	Yasmin	Dark green belted coat, yellow/black top, black gloves, trousers		*A New Error* by Moderat
26.		Royal blue and black shirt and matching cut-off trousers, black jacket		
27.		Green and black long sleeve top over black trousers, top		
28.		Black coat over black and yellow top and matching trousers		
29.		Black, green and blue shirt over black rolled-up trousers		
30.		Green and black trousers, black long-sleeved top		

Figure 5.32 An example of a simple director's chart.

Industry Insight
Maria Natalia Rodriguez, Social Media Marketing Manager, TW Toronto Women's Fashion Week

How did you get started in your job?

I work for TW Toronto Women's Fashion Week; the biggest fashion event in Canada. My role is social media marketing manager. Although fashion week happens twice a year, it's a job that never stops. I am only eighteen years old. I knew that I wanted to get into fashion marketing since I was fourteen. After doing a vast amount of research about Toronto's fashion scene, I developed a strategy that would allow me to enter the industry. I knew it would be hard since it is very competitive, but I saw a space in the market for make-up artists, so I decided to go to beauty school to get certified. I knew that as a make-up artist it would be easier to position myself within the industry because it would allow me to network with a lot of different individuals. Soon after I started, I began doing editorial photo shoots and writing for magazines and various publications about beauty and fashion trends. At sixteen, I worked with Toronto Men's Fashion Week doing the makeup for national campaigns, and while doing so, I was able to meet a lot of people who worked in the organization.

I knew that it was the right moment to make the shift from being a makeup artist to fashion marketing, but I didn't feel prepared enough to take a role in marketing. I enrolled myself in a tech-focused school where I learned everything about digital marketing, and I go back to this place every time I want to update my skills. After completing my program, I was able to start working with different fashion organizations, including fashion week. That is how I got into social media marketing. It is quite unconventional, but social media allows younger people to get into the industry more easily than via other areas. It is a space with very few barriers of entry, all you need is to be persistent and have a unique value proposition.

What do you do in advance of fashion week?

Planning and creating a content calendar is super important. We work on establishing our goals, and how we want to build the content around a concept. We spend a lot of time brainstorming and coming up with creative content ideas that will help us attract and engage social media followers. Building a social media presence takes a lot of time and hard work, it is not something you can get in the last minute before an event. Ideally, there are two primary goals, which are to build anticipation and excitement, and establishing thought leadership.

The first goal is all about creativity, breaking through the noise of social media and being able to get to the target viewers. TW Toronto Women's Fashion Week is the most anticipated fashion event in Toronto, so it is essential to keep our followers excited about what is to come in the next season. We keep them engaged by regularly posting updates on what we are working on

Figure 5.33 Maria Natalia Rodriguez. (© Maria Natalia Rodriguez Lopez)

at the moment, whether it is model casting calls, the production of the national campaigns or other activities. These posts are something unique that TW Toronto Women's Fashion Week does, not many other events give access to the production process; it creates a bond with our viewers.

The second goal, establishing thought leadership, what it means is providing value in the form of content. We provide information about what the upcoming beauty and fashion trends are by posting a lot of photos from our runways. People wouldn't have access to this information unless they attended the fashion shows.

What happens during fashion week?

Fashion week is a week full of energy, excitement and a lot of amazing shows, and it is our job to cover them all and make sure we can bring at least a little bit of this magic to Toronto's fashion lovers who couldn't attend the event. We cover the event on all social media platforms to reach all our viewers, but we focus mainly on the most visual platforms such as Instagram, Facebook and Snapchat. We maintain the same relationship with our audiences by granting access to the backstage action, VIP lounge and other exclusive glimpses of the event. We cover live interviews with the designers and other exciting events going on. The power of social media lays in being able to provide coverage in real time, so we make sure that our audiences have access to the best photographs from the runway as fast as possible.

Do you cover the other (non-catwalk) events?

The off-runway events that happen during fashion week are just as important. We hold the TW Talks, which are speaker panels composed of leaders in the industry, and they talk about the major industry trends, events and current discussion topics. We live stream these events and hold live Q&As by encouraging people to ask questions to the panelists through social media. We also cover opening and closing parties, and other relevant events.

After Fashion Week, we recap the fashion shows. TW Toronto Women's Fashion Week aims to promote Canadian fashion and Canadian designers, so we continue posting about the highlights of the shows and the best pieces from the collections.

What advice would you give to someone who wants to work in fashion?

Don't try to follow someone else's career. Career paths in the fashion industry are not set in stone, especially because it is an ever-changing space, it's hard to re-create what someone else did. Find a unique value that you can bring to the industry, find your own path. The best way to get into social media marketing is to stay updated on social media trends and become very comfortable with creating content. To get noticed, build a brand for yourself and keep your network aware of what you are doing. Be active!

During the show

While bloggers and others communicate from the front row, sending out countless fragments of information through Instagram and other social media, the traditional journalists observe and analyze, taking notes or even typing onto laptops from their ringside seats. The legendary Suzy Menkes, formerly of the *International Herald Tribune*, could create an article on her laptop from the front row and finish it in a car on the way to the next show. She has the ability to assimilate a collection and its presentation, analyze its relevance within the context of modern fashion and articulate this with wit and style for an international readership. During the show, the PR team watch the audience reaction, particularly that of the most influential guests. They want to see who photographs what, who is writing and who looks utterly bored. It is often possible to see exactly what the press think of a collection or of individual pieces by their behaviour as they sit front row. Sometimes, when a collection is dull, the look on the face of a member of the press says it all. At the other extreme are the shows where the audience gives a huge round of applause to the designer or even a standing ovation.

Figure 5.34 Part of a finale at a Regent's University London graduate fashion show. (© Regent's University London, Photographer Simon Armstrong)

A show is a live production and because it is usually only produced once, occasionally something goes wrong. When this happens, everyone talks on the walkie-talkies to alert everyone and discuss what to do. For example, if there's a problem with a change backstage, the show producer will let the sound and lighting crew know that they are slowing down the show and they will tell the models going out to walk more slowly to give the backstage team time to sort out the problem; likewise if the producer has to send out the looks in a different order. At front-of-house, the audience should be oblivious to glitches and see a perfect show.

Closing the show

Finishing with a *finale* is one of the traditions of the fashion show: all the models come out and walk the runway while the audience applauds. In shows where there is one model per look, the finale is impressive for the number of models in the finale and because the audience can see the whole collection at once. Another tradition is for a designer to come out and take a bow, cued by the show producer from backstage – another echo of the theatre. Some designers don't feel comfortable in front of an audience and will appear briefly to take a quick bow, while others enjoy the limelight and walk the runway with the models or by themselves. Lagerfeld always walks with the star model of the moment; in the case of the supermarket show, Cara Delevingne. The last outfit onto the runway is often a showstopper, repeated of course in the finale, but sometimes a designer will choose to finish a show differently, as in the famous finale of McQueen's 1999 show where Shalom Harlow wore a white dress and stood on a rotating circle while the dress was sprayed with paint by robots (see Chapter 1).

Activities

01. The schedule

Imagine that you are a show producer, and you are working for a designer who shows at London Fashion Week. Your client is showing off-schedule at a venue in central London at 17:00 on the second day of fashion week. A full set must be built on the day because your client wants an immersive experience that will transport the audience into a different world. The venue is an old industrial building and there is no rig in the building although there are rooms that will suffice as backstage. Create the schedule to send out to the show crew so that everyone has all of the information they need to arrive on time and ready to start work. The schedule should cover the entire event from start of the build to the point at which everyone leaves the venue.

02. Fashion week media communications

Choose a fashion week to study. Before the fashion week starts, research what activities are planned by the fashion week organizers and by different brands. Choose three very different designers or brands and plan to follow their media communications, from pre-show build up through live stream and post-show activities. Analyze their activities, pre-show, during the show and post-show, to understand how they plan integrated communications during fashion weeks and what a consumer would experience. In order to prepare for the research, look at the theory of integrated marketing campaigns and use this to analyze the brands' campaigns. Present your findings in the form of an illustrated report

03. Director's chart

Create a director's chart for a charity show in New Delhi which will show the work of Indian designers. There are sixty outfits in the running order, all of them on loan: six designers have loaned ten outfits each and you plan to show the outfits in sections per designer. Research and select six Indian designers. Complete the director's chart as follows:

A. Include all of the outfits in the correct running order so that the show begins and finishes with striking collections.

B. Details of the transitions between collections and other elements of the show so that sound and lighting technicians know when to bring lights up and down and when to fade music in and out.

C. Make sure that there is a natural flow to the show between one collection and the next.

D. Include a welcome from a compere before the show starts.

E. Include a talk about the charity, with film projected onto the flats behind the speaker.

F. At the end of the show the compere will come back onto the runway, thank those who have worked on the show and invite the audience to move on to an after party.

G. Choose music for the beginning and end of the show while the audience are taking their seats and leaving the venue, for each collection and for a finale. Note on the director's chart.

H. Indicate when the house lights should be up or dimmed and when the runway lights should be dimmed, on full, and when house and runway lights should be faded up and down.

6

After the show

Chapter Six explores what happens after the designer takes their bow at the end of the show. As the promotional campaign continues with post-show interviews and after parties, the chapter explains how the PR teams, photographers and journalists must work late into the night, pushing out promotional materials, selecting images and reporting about the show while it is still fresh in everyone's minds. It discusses how the fashion show is evaluated after the event and how those who produce collections and shows are already thinking about and starting to plan the next runway event. Chapter Six is organized in two sections: *post-show* (immediately after the show finishes) and *after the event* (activities overnight and in the following days and weeks).

Figure 6.1 Backstage interview with Prabal Gurung, September 2016, New York Fashion Week. (Jared Siskin/Contributor via Getty Images)

Post-show

A rousing finale and the designer takes their bow, but the show is far from over. The production team is waiting for the audience to leave so that they can strike the set, the photographers must get images to the PRs, the press need to get their stories out. While the collection and the show are still fresh in everyone's minds, the marketing, PR and communications teams must continue to maximize the promotional opportunities of the event to gain as much positive media coverage as possible. Meanwhile, information about the event and the collection continues to be used to stimulate desire in the fashion-hungry consumer.

Post-show PR

Once the show is over, post-show interviews take place, some of them scheduled in advance. The media, in the form of journalists, TV reporters and bloggers, will want to interview the designer and possibly others who have worked on the show, including influential hair and make-up artists, accessories designers, stylists and the show producer. They will also want to hear what people thought about the collection and the show, including influencers such as industry experts and celebrities. In this way, media involvement and third-party endorsement of the brand continue.

The PR team works with security to control backstage access, ensuring that select media go backstage for pre-agreed interviews. The team will have a schedule of timed interviews to keep everyone on track. For shows that are part of a fashion week, time can be tight as another designer may be showing in the same venue and the media will need to move on to the next event. The PRs of lesser-known designers work hard to get interviews with influential press. While younger designers may give more spontaneous interviews, for others the story they tell is part of a larger communication campaign. As designers talk about the inspiration for a collection and its presentation on the runway, their storytelling is part of a planned set of messages around the show, which in turn is part of a larger sophisticated communications strategy to promote the brand. As the media conducts backstage interviews, celebrities are photographed front-of-house, sometimes against step-and-repeat boards. Post-show is also an opportunity to capture feedback from front row guests as the PRs and the media catch industry professionals and celebrities to seek their opinion. As interviews take place and celebrities pose for more photographs, the marketing and PR teams continue to push material out to the press and to the consumer through different media channels. In this way, the excitement that the show has generated is spun out for as long as possible.

Collective verdict

The team will have measured audience response during the show, noticing the reaction of those front row including influential press taking note of items on the runway. After the show, they will gather as much verbal feedback as possible, talking with influential media and buyers, trying to gauge the collective verdict or judgment about a collection: was it a sound commercial collection, was it a collection that will move fashion forward or was it a disappointment? This judgment by the industry is a long-established tradition and one of the reasons there is so much pressure around runway. However, as increasing numbers of brands sell directly to the consumer the power of the collective verdict is beginning to shift.

Figure 6.2 Model Naomi
Campbell falls on the
runway of the Vivienne
Westwood AW1993 show.
(Photographer Niall
McInerney, © Bloomsbury
Publishing Plc.)

Golden moments in fashion PR

The supermodel Naomi Campbell fell over on the runway of Vivienne
Westwood's show in Paris in 1993, and what looked like a mistake in an
otherwise perfect show performance, was in fact a golden PR opportunity.
Naomi was one of the most famous supermodels of the time; the press could
not get enough information about her to satiate public appetite. Photographs
appeared around the world, a supermodel falling on the runway became an
iconic moment in fashion history and Westwood's show achieved the kind of
publicity that any designer would dream of.

Industry Insight
Courtney Blackman, Founder of Forward PR

What do you do during a show? Do you observe audience reaction?

I definitely like to watch the show from near the photographer's pit, to see which looks get the most clicks from the photographers and to see how the audience is responding to the show. It used to be the amount of applause at the end of show would be an indicator to the show's success, now it's silence and all audience members capturing the final walkthrough on their smartphones (please do not use iPads, people). Clapping would indicate that the audience is not taking photos or videos, and I would measure that as not a great response.

What activities take place immediately post show? Interviews? Photographs?

Immediately following the show, we want to get the most important press/influencers backstage interviewing and taking photos of and with the designer. We only have about twenty minutes to a half hour to manage post-show media, get the collection packed up and make the space available for the next show, so it's crunch time in getting the most influential connections, quickly.

After a show, what happens in the next twenty-four hours and during the next days and weeks?

Within the next several hours, our job is to get the high-res and low-res images from the house photographer and the house videographer. These images and video content will be sent out to press and influencers around the world, along with a press release that outlines the collection that was shown and highlights key attendees (celebrities) that were present.

We monitor the show coverage for the next several days and weeks – across all layers of media: print, digital and social. We then do a post-show report that quantifies the coverage. For a catwalk show over one of the 'Big Four', the media coverage ends up being in the tens to hundreds of millions of dollars' worth of exposure, depending on the designer.

How is social media used before, during and after a show? How important is this and which platforms are used?

Social media is almost like breathing. If a brand is good at it, everything that they do will be recorded digitally for their fans to engage with. The possibilities are endless as to what you can do and how much you can engage – it just takes time. Instagram is so

Figure 6.3 Courtney Blackman. (© Courtney Blackman, Founder of Forward PR)

visual; I would say it is one of the most used over a fashion week, and now that Instagram has added stories, it has made Snapchat slightly redundant. Most designers feed their Instagram feed through to their Twitter and Facebook accounts, so all platforms are covered, as you never know what medium your fans prefer. We also work a lot with influencers that use YouTube and Periscope to communicate fashion week to their own fan bases, which is brilliant exposure for our designers, depending on the reach of each content creator. Long story short, social media is important, and it isn't going away anytime soon.

How do you and the designers/brands you work with use material online before, during and after a show?

It varies per each designer. Some create pre-show content, some like to keep everything under wraps until the first look exits onto the runway. If a designer does have material to use pre-show, we'll send out to media for previews stories. During the show, it's mostly imagery and video footage captured during the catwalk show to share on social media, and after the show, it's spreading the professional imagery and video content as far and wide as possible. A lot of PRs try to control who has access to images and video, but once it has hit the Internet, it's out there. You may as well share broadly with the press release to get the intended message across.

To read the full interview with Courtney Blackman please visit http://www.bloomsbury.com/stark-the-fashion-show.

Figure 6.4 The Philipp Plein after show party in Milan, June 2014. (Pier Marco Tacca/Stringer via Getty Images)

The post-show consumer

The loyal consumer, having enjoyed the multiple touchpoints that the show has provided to interact with the brand, has been excited by the build-up to the event and may have responded to teasers and sneak peeks, expressing their anticipation on Facebook, Twitter or WhatsApp. They will have watched the show online, possibly live streamed, devouring the experience of the runway and images of models, celebrities and opinion leaders. They have read tweets, and re-tweeted, responded to images on Instagram and consumed messages and information about the show through multiple media channels. Powerful positive messages have been received by the consumer, reinforcing the brand's value, its unique identity and its personality. They are inspired to continue to invest in the brand. If the show was live streamed with the opportunity to see-now-buy-now, the consumer may already be looking forward to receiving product seen on the runway.

Figure 6.5 For health and safety reasons, striking the set cannot start until the audience has left the runway area. (© Regent's University London, Photographer Tony Rogers)

The after party

The party that follows the show of a well-known brand or designer is an item on the social calendar, reminding us that many things about today's events are reminiscent of the 19th-century shows which formed part of the social season. Today, attended by those who work in the industry and by guests in the form of celebrities, such after parties are glamorous affairs and they are planned with the same level of organization as the show itself. After parties offer further promotional opportunities, rewarding influencers for their involvement with the brand, and reinforcing the personality of the brand as both glamorous and important within the contemporary scene. Parties provide more images with which to feed the celebrity-hungry consumer and stimulate yet more social media traffic as party-goers Instagram, tweet and Snapchat at what the brand hopes is the party of the season.

Striking the set

As some move on to celebrate, the crew will be keen to *strike* or dismantle the set as soon as possible. Sometimes a set will be used for more than one show, particularly during fashion weeks. If not, the set must be dismantled as quickly as possible. This is essential because the venue hire finishes at a pre-agreed time. For health and safety reasons, striking the set cannot start until the audience has left the runway area. At the end of an industry show many guests will move on quickly, some of them getting up and going as soon as the designer has taken their bow. It is well known that Anna Wintour, for instance, likes to be seated so that she can exit a venue quickly once a show is over. However, sometimes it becomes necessary to politely ask guests, in the interest of safety, to leave a venue.

The collection and accessories

After the show the collection, accessories and other items must be packed and returned. If items are not returned that day, they can be stored safely overnight by the transport company, together with any items that have been loaned or hired. If merchandise from a retail outlet or another designer has been used for the show, the organizers must ensure that items are handed back in a good condition with everything accounted for. Any damage must be identified and dealt with in accordance with any agreement signed before the event. Sadly, in the bustle of backstage, it is not unusual for items to go missing, usually an accessory or shoes. If very expensive items such as valuable jewellery have been loaned, one person is usually assigned to oversee these backstage.

Leaving a venue

Once the audience has left, the work of packing and clearing up begins. The contract for venue hire states how the venue must be left. Clearing up after a show is the least enjoyable element and this is a time that is as telling of character as the high-pressure moments earlier in the day. Backstage is usually messy with items such as the remains of styling products, empty drink containers, tags, pins and coat hangers. Front-of-house, guests leave behind programmes, drinks glasses and miscellaneous litter. Rubbish must be disposed of responsibly, with due consideration to recycling, and as agreed in the contract for the venue hire. By designing elements such as refreshments carefully, rubbish disposal can be kept to a minimum. The hire contract might include cleaning and if not, the venue might arrange cleaning for an additional fee. If an event finishes late and the venue has only been hired for a day, cleaning may have to take place early the following morning. All of this is negotiated in advance with the venue management. A deposit is usually paid when hiring a venue, and the cost of any repairs to the building and its contents are deducted before the deposit is returned. Repairs might include repainting walls that have become marked or repairing damage to flooring. Those who produce shows regularly have learned ways of working in a venue without damaging the building.

Congratulating everyone

It is common, immediately after a show, to send congratulations and thanks to everyone who contributed to the event. The designer(s), the creative director and others who played a major part are congratulated and thanked, the production crews and others who were employed to create a great runway experience are also thanked, even though they may have been paid for this work. Volunteers who may, for example, have dressed models or worked front-of-house should be thanked, and it is often valuable for student volunteers to receive a reference.

Figure 6.6 Clearing up after a show is the least enjoyable element. The excitement is over, everyone has worked hard, but there is still work to be done. (© Regent's University London, Photographer Jason Pittock)

Post-show marketing and PR

The event is over, the set dismantled, the venue empty and people have moved on to the after party. However, not everyone is partying – for those in PR and communications and for the photographers and film crew, their work is far from over. Attention turns to getting the story and images into as many publications as possible, while continuing to push messages out to consumers and others through social media. The collection was designed to look fabulous in social media and in post-show images. The show was designed to look even more amazing online than it did live. Through the night and in the days immediately following the show, the team continues to reinforce the brand's key messages, reminding everyone who attended what a great show it was, signifying its importance within fashion and maintaining brand reputation. The consumer is still being fed the dream as media communications continue to keep alive the feeling of excitement generated by the event. Powerful runway and post-show images continue to stimulate desire for a dream coat or a must-have new handbag.

PR teams always want photographs of the show as quickly as possible and house photographers are under pressure to balance quick delivery with the time it takes to choose and edit the best quality hero shots. The sooner great photographs go out, the more likely they are to be featured, but a good photographer knows that the quality of the shot is essential. PR teams send out post-show press releases with powerful runway images, continuing to feed the press with anything that is newsworthy and can be used to get valuable media coverage. PR teams often work late into the night to get material out.

Getting further media coverage

Over the days post-show, attention shifts from communicating straight runway images to photographs of details, quirkier images of the show, more interesting celebrity shots, backstage interviews and pre-arranged shoots. The communications team continues to stimulate interest and to promote brand messages, adding information onto websites: runway shots, celebrities photographed against the step-and-repeat boards, backstage shots and those all-important backstage interviews. Good examples of backstage interviews can be viewed on websites, such as Copenhagen Fashion Week. Meanwhile, the PR team continues to:

- Send out press releases and other copy with images.
- Follow up on conversations before the show and on interviews pre- and post-show to encourage the media to publish material.
- Talk with the media to try to get further coverage.
- Get images to the picture editors of digital media such as Vogue.com.
- Talk with stylists and celebrities to get their feedback post-show and to lend product.
- Hold the collections of the labels they represent in their showrooms.
- Lend samples of garments to the media for shoots that will appear in newspapers, magazines and digital media.
- Dispatch items or deliver them and to make sure that they are booked back in (often the roles of interns).

Having seen items on the runway, the media will call in various items for features they might be creating in newspapers, magazines or online articles and editorials.

Figure 6.7 Dsquared2
SS2014 show in Milan. (Pier
Marco Tacca/Stringer via
Getty Images)

These are loaned to the media and booked out for shoots. For a designer, t[ ]
are clear promotional advantages to this free publicity and great value in t[ ]
products being chosen by fashion editors and stylists as worthy of inclusion [ ]
publication.

Garments seen on the runway are also used in the showrooms immedia[ ]
after the show so that buyers can place orders. They are held in the PRs' off[ ]
and later; for some brands, they are also sent out to trunk shows held in r[ ]
stores, particularly in American department stores where the trunk show has b[ ]
popular since the early 1900s.

Reputation management

While Naomi Campbell's fall on the Westwood runway brought opportune p[ ]
attention, a show that is unfavourably reported in the press can have a detrime[ ]
effect on the success of a company for a season or more. In such cases, the PR [ ]
becomes one of crisis and reputation management. Dsquared2's SS2014 sk[ ]
held in Milan, Italy received a range of negative reviews. One of the mildest [ ]
the following from *Vogue*'s Tim Blanks:

> It takes guts to open your collection with the agonizing sound of a plane c[ ]
> but Dean and Dan Caten have never been shrinking violets. Anyway, they [ ]
> to set up their mise-en-scène of a trio of boykini-clad castaways languis[ ]
> on a desert island. It was as fully realized as all the Catens' scenarios [ ]
> been – the downed plane carcass, the waterfall, the encroaching jungle – [ ]
> it was ultimately as distracting as all those other productions. At some p[ ]
> you want to throw up your hands and cry, 'Boys, give us clothes, not ca[ ]
> (Blanks, 2014)

"The downed plane carcass, the waterfall, the encroaching jungle . . . it was ultimately as distracting as all those other productions. At some point, you want to throw up your hands and cry, 'Boys, give us clothes, not camp!''
Tim Blanks, 2014

Figure 6.8 After the event, sponsors want photographs of their product and/or logo. (© Regent's University London, Photographer Tony Rogers)

At a designer show I will shoot over 1,000 images, maybe 2,000 if it is a bigger collection.

Interview with Simon Armstrong, February 2015

A poorly received show, criticism about zero-size models and complaints about fur on the runway are examples of reputational risk that fashion companies have faced. Dealing with such a crisis means abandoning the planned post-show PR campaign and creating a new strategy fast. There are well-developed strategies for managing crisis communication and they tend to follow a similar pattern:

01. Act immediately by issuing a holding statement; act positively and decisively.
02. Use social media as well as traditional media.
03. Assess the situation.
04. Agree new messages to deal with the crisis. Resist being defensive.
05. Create a strategy and identify media channels to communicate through.
06. Communicate in a straightforward manner, acknowledging negative feedback while setting this within the context of a longer-term, positive track record.
07. Respond confidently to all questions.
08. Enlist the support of a third-party endorsement where possible.
09. Limit the damage where possible.
10. Learn lessons for the future.

Sponsors

After the show, sponsors that have contributed product or services must be thanked for their support. Generally, it is agreed before the event what the sponsors will receive. Sometimes this is written into a formal contract, at other times it is less formally agreed through email exchange or verbally. At the least, most sponsors will expect to receive runway shots, sponsor shots (photographs from the event where their logo was in view) and links to any media coverage that shows or mentions their brands. Sponsor photographs are often agreed beforehand and the photographer will ensure that images are received by the PR team immediately after the show so that they can be sent out to sponsors with a 'thank you'. Material in the coverage books that PRs create for their clients can also be used to present coverage to sponsors.

Photographers

After each show photographers are under huge pressure to get the best hero image of each look to the PR company. Whether the event was part of fashion week or something less high pressure, it is imperative to get ahold of photographs quickly. Photographers will often work with assistants who download images from memory cards while the photographers carry on shooting. During fashion weeks, runway photographers might shoot a ten-minute show every hour. After each show the assistant uploads all of the 1,000 or so images onto a laptop (archiving the material onto hard drives so there is always a backup) and starts to select hero images.

It takes time to upload high-quality images, then a relatively small number are selected as hero images. So, what makes a hero image? A scan through runway images on a website such as Vogue.com reveals that the images for a show capture the models at the same point on the runway and in the same pose. Simon Armstrong, London Fashion Week runway photographer says:

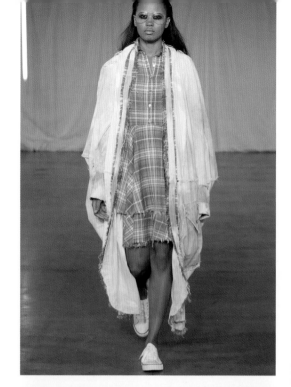

> I am a stickler for what I want from a pose, and I very rarely have to change things. He [my assistant] knows the pose I am looking for and the place on the catwalk. We tweak the processing to make them all look the same if necessary. He will select thumbnails, then he will open those up. Sometimes it looks OK but the focus isn't right or she's blinking, or the hand position isn't right, it could be about the way the clothes have fallen. So out of about five shots, one of them might be right. If not, you have to go back again to get different shots. Once you've got those four or five per shot you can select the hero image and once he's got the whole edit, the twenty looks, there shouldn't be a lot of tweaking but it depends on the collection.

During busy times photographers can work until 4 o'clock in the morning, have two hours of sleep, then start again. Because of the speed of fashion weeks and the quantity of shows, house photographers and their assistants, like many others, have a punishing schedule. Once the immediate post-show work is over, some clients will want further and more plentiful images. Because of the need to control quality (and reputation), a photographer will rarely send all of the images, so a further selection process takes place.

Film

Immediately after the show, the priority for the film companies is to get a live stream feed onto a brand's website. One that is done, the brand might want further edited film for various purposes. The film company produces an edit, also known as a *first cut* or a *preview*, which they show to and discuss with the client. Nick Horrell, videographer, talks about the theory called the *primacy and recency effect*, where what you show at the beginning and at the end is important because the start makes a big impression and what you finish with leaves people with a good feeling. This is used to determine the running order of the show, and it is also important when editing footage to create videos for various uses after the event. Film of the show might be used on YouTube, on websites, in retail stores and for many other purposes. Often several films are created: very short films of about sixty seconds for use on social media, and longer edits created for other platforms.

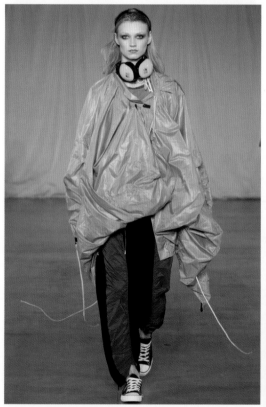

Figures 6.9 and 6.10 Runway photographer Simon Armstrong ensures that the hero poses are all at the same point on the runway. Note the exact positioning of the feet. From the collections of Ailsa Grant and Gabriella Wright at Regent's University London Graduate Fashion Show 2017. (© Regent's University London, Photographer Simon Armstrong)

Industry Insight

Simon Armstrong, runway photographer

Figure 6.11 Simon Armstrong.
(© Simon Armstrong)

How did you become a catwalk photographer?

I worked in advertising. As an art director, I worked with lots of photographers. I'd been developing my photography and I started shooting street stuff. I worked near Carnaby Street, I would go there in my lunch hour and shoot people, trying to capture the moment, tell a story. Everything I've done has been creative, but it has always been about collaborating with different people.

One day I got tapped on the shoulder by a director of the company that owns Carnaby Street. We had an exhibition called 'Catwalk Carnaby'. That's how I got my first exposure. Through that I met a design duo, and they invited me to shoot their show at Amika Club. That is the first show I did. Later, I shot a couple of shows at Fashion Scout. You know the people who don't know what they're doing and stand at the side [of the press pit] – I was one of them!

Who commissions you to shoot a show?

It is not always the designer who contacts me; sometimes it's the PR. Sometimes the PR takes over the production of the show; sometimes a designer is more hands-on. I prefer a more hands-on designer because they know what they want the show and the photos to be.

As house photographer, what do you do before the show?

You are part of the creative team. The first time I worked for Jamie Wei Huang, her idea was for dry ice, but it wouldn't work in the space, so we tweaked the lighting. It was a different look from the typical white catwalk. A lot of people are steering away from the typical white catwalk now. They are using the environment, rather than go somewhere where you create your own environment. That has its ups and downs: it is not as controllable but it's more interesting. Before the show, you discuss the lighting; once it starts you are in one spot and it's about getting the right shots. At the London Fashion Week venue, the lighting is perfect. At a bespoke venue, designed for just one show, you have to do tests with the lighting because you will need to tweak things. I did Joshua Kane's show this season. It was good, but there were LED lights on the catwalk and down the side . . . none behind me on the catwalk. You take a picture to show the designer what they are going to get. The camera sees things very differently from the human eye.

Do you work with the models before a show?

Yes, it's good to be at the rehearsal. Most models walk down the middle of the catwalk, but there's always one who walks on the side. Then I have to move the camera and the audience is in the shot all the way down. You have all clean images and then one that is all audience.

Are you conscious of how your photography is used to promote fashion?

Yes, more so than most because I used to work in advertising, so I understand brands and target audiences and the whole marketing side of things. I understand what they are doing, but I have to concentrate on the quality of the product because that is my specialism.

Do you shoot backstage or audience?

If I'm employed as house photographer, I can't do front row. I am in the wrong position for the front row. And the more important people are, they will either come in before everyone else, or come in very late. I can't do front row. My purpose has to be on the catwalk. I can't be shooting front row two minutes before the show starts with a different camera. I need to be in the pit.

What is it like in the pit?

It is OK. You know most of the people, there is a camaraderie. Generally it is light-hearted. You have a lot of time standing around and you get to know each other. When you are shooting you are concentrating completely on what is in front of you. I am house photographer so I have to make sure my field of view is clear. You can hear the guys behind you going 'can you move over there, just move that way, can you go down a little bit?' Photographers are on boxes, higher and higher . . . shooting over someone's shoulder. Everyone wants to be straight in the middle, so everyone is trying to get that position because that's the picture that you can sell.

So the balance is about speed and quality?

PR is all about speed and about being seen first. For me it is quality first, speed second. I have to try to manage expectations. I have to maintain a business relationship with the PRs. They have to like me, recommend me to their clients. I have to deliver to them, but I also have to manage their expectations. Designers are very different. For a designer it is about the quality.

Figure 6.12 Rick Owens' SS2014 fashion show. (Miguel Medina/Staff via Getty Images)

The press: Assimilating, analyzing and writing

Like the photographers and the PRs, journalists often get little sleep as they juggle attending shows and presentations with writing and other activities. In between shows and writing, they liaise with PRs, photographers, stylists and others. They also plan future work and travel. Fashion weeks are both 'addictive' and at the same time demanding and high-pressure. They must assimilate and analyze show after show: writing copy, selecting images, writing captions, thinking of interesting titles. For many of the press, their reviews of shows must be online within twenty-four hours, hence the pressure on the photographers and PRs to feed them the material they need in the form of images and press releases. In writing about a show, they will consider it within the wider context of the history of the designer and their previous collections. The press must also consider a show within the broader context of what is happening in fashion internationally at that time. They must write about what is relevant and newsworthy while capturing the imagination of the reader.

Lucy Norris, writing for SHOWstudio on 7 March 2016, about the American designer Rick Owens' womenswear show, combined her knowledge of the American designer's previous shows with information provided by his PR company:

This actually felt like a more hopeful collection than some of Rick Owens' other more dystopian offerings. . . . in the basement of the Palais du Tokyo – the regular show spot for Rick Owens – it was lights down as we waited for his new vision to emerge. This collection was an extension of the designer's menswear narrative for A/W 16. It had the same title, Mastadon, and was also very much about environmental concerns. . . . a sweetened version of a print within the men's collection . . . Owens talked in his show notes about a more feminine idea of 'folding into the ether'. Norris, 2016

Industry Insight

Joshua Kane

Figure 6.13 Joshua Kane. (© Joshua Kane)

Figure 6.14 (© Joshua Kane)

Joshua Kane is a London menswear designer. He has produced his own shows but takes a very innovative approach to presenting his collections, also using installations, video and other forms of communication. He talks about how a show is not the end of a collection but a part of the evolution of a collection.

It would be interesting to hear about your involvement in shows.

My experience at Burberry was amazing, it was a privilege to spend just under three years there. I was involved in the shows in Milan. It was an amazing logistical experience: designing it in London, developing it in Italy, getting it made in Italy, styling it in London, casting half in London half in Milan, flying the collection out to Milan, doing fittings in another country.

At Paul Smith, as senior designer, I did London Collections Men. I worked on the Paris show and the London show. The Paris show was traditional catwalk, all the look and the theatrics, very much what I was doing at Burberry. But in London, we did an installation in an art gallery on Savile Row, all based on English traditionalism; it was a show but without models. Now with my own business we do an installation about every eight weeks. We did an installation at Tramshed Restaurant in Shoreditch: summer and winter collections, suspended from the ceiling at two different levels.

So, you view the show in its broader contexts?

For me the show is becoming more about performance, it's a theatre, it's a film. The last show was inspired by a gig so we had a rock band playing and it was live and the next show we are working on is very cinematic, very film inspired. We premiered the sunglasses on the catwalk, then we had a static installation, then we had a moving installation, and we've got a video launch so that's another platform, then we've got the product shops on the e-commerce website, we have Facebook animations so that's another . . . With Facebook and Instagram and Snapchat advertising progressing at such a rate, if you haven't done it, you're behind.

The show is part of the evolution of the collection. Before the last show, I made the finale coat. We looked at the show as a team and it needed more drama, so it was born from another garment in the collection and we made a more extreme version of it. That ability never to let it go . . . the collection is never finished . . . the runway is never ready. Even after the show we continued to design the collection. We showed one winter collection in London and then we re-showed it in Switzerland. Mercedes sponsored a show in a stadium of 10,000 people. We added the camel coat and other pieces, the knitwear scarves and they were so well received we added the bobble hat and the sweater. It is really the same project that has just never ended.

For the full interview with Joshua Kane please visit http://www.bloomsbury .com/the-fashion-show-9781472568489.

The buyers

During four fashion weeks (fashion month), the buyers sit through many shows and attend buying appointments. Shows enable them to get a feel for the season and its trends. They learn about the story of each collection and how it's portrayed on the runway, and they view the full commercial collections through buying appointments in the showrooms. Buyers can spend hours or even days in one showroom and while the runway shows are important for them, time spent in the showrooms is essential because that is where they get close to the product, feel it, see it modelled and even try it on. Large retailers may have analysts working with them in the showrooms, telling them what sold last season, information that can be helpful for the brands as well as the buyers.

Some buyers place orders before the shows, which they might amend after viewing the collections on the runway. Others use fashion weeks to view the collections and then decide what to order. In the showrooms, a buyer can select garments and edit them down to a workable range for their store, placing orders before moving on to the show. A lot of the buying takes place in Paris because fashion weeks start in New York, move to London then Milan and finish in Paris. For this reason, some designers hold their runway show in one city, and then move on to take orders in the showrooms in Paris.

The debrief

After a show, it is the role of PR to gather and assess media coverage, both traditional media coverage and Twitter, Facebook, Instagram, Pinterest and other forms of social media. PRs create coverage books within which they capture and present all of the media coverage achieved for each brand or designer that they represent. In the past interns would spend days methodically scouring magazines and newspapers to find every mention of the collection and the show in the press. Today, there are computer searches for mentions, so that what is written about a brand or a designer is located and, where mentions are via social media, messages are monitored and responded to.

For powerful brands with large budgets, a whole industry has evolved that measures and evaluates a company's media profile, analyzing media coverage and the impact of campaigns in different parts of the world. Key performance indicators (KPIs) are identified such as benchmarking against competitors and brand equity. Messages are assessed, reputation and brand equity are analyzed and competitive positioning is reviewed. In this way, a brand can learn about the response to its fashion shows in different countries around the world. This insight enables brands to assess the successfulness of campaigns and to plan strategies for the future. Competitor analysis is of paramount importance. As Mario Ortelli of Sanford C. Bernstein was quoted as saying in *The Business of Fashion* in October 2016: 'For brands, it's about stealing market share from one another. If you're not a supercool brand, you inevitably lose market share in such a competitive market environment' (Kansara and Abraham, 2016).

For a dynamic industry that produces so many shows, the next runway event is always on the horizon. The debrief is about looking at the client's and the industry's responses and the data from a show, analyzing what was successful and what could have been better and making decisions about what to do next time. Much in fashion is incremental and evolutionary in nature. While it may look to the consumer as if each fashion show is presented in isolation, runway is part of an incremental creative zeitgeist and while one show is taking place, the creative directors and the producers are already thinking about the next event.

Alexandre de Betak has spoken about the 'pressure to outdo himself': 'I put down my Clearcom headset . . . what are we going to do next? . . . Especially if it was a success, because my job is to do it again, and better, or if not better, at least different.'
Anaya, 2013

Activities

01. Backstage interviews

Find and review five backstage interviews:

A. Analyze them and list the messages about the designer or brand that they communicate.

B. Do they all contain similar messages? What are those messages?

C. How do the messages reflect the personality of the designer or brand?

02. Media coverage

Choose two designers or brands and gather as much post-show media coverage as possible. Search all media channels. Having gathered the coverage, analyze it to ascertain:

A. What did reporting comprise – reports by the fashion press, runway shots, backstage interviews or images, celebrity shots?

B. How well were the shows received? Were they reviewed positively or negatively, or were there mixed reviews?

C. Was there common consensus on the success of the events?

D. What did the reviews communicate about the relevance to modern fashion of the collections and the shows?

E. Did one collection and show receive more or different attention than the other, and why was that?

03. Brand messages

Choose two brands and source as much post-show material as possible. Analyze post-show communications by the brands and identify the key messages that the brands were promoting. Compare the messages of the two brands. If you can find a brand that has experienced reputational risk in relation to a fashion show, use that as one of the brands. Assess:

A. How well the brands have communicated brand personality and brand values.

B. How the brands have differentiated their offer through their post-show activities; is this just another show or has the brand communicated its unique characteristics?

C. What the brand has promised through its post-show communications.

04. Images

Choose three fashion designers/brands. Source as much imagery as possible that was communicated before, during and after their shows, by the company and by others (influencers and consumers). Analyze the imagery communicated by each of the designers/brands to ascertain:

A. What were the most popular forms of communication?

B. What was the content of the visual communications?

C. Where was it communicated from – front row, backstage, photographers?

D. When was it communicated – before the event, during the event, after the event?

The future of the fashion show

As the global fashion industry develops, it is likely that some cities around the world will become more influential, just as Tokyo did in the 1980s. In the 1900s, the Paris fashion industry found itself in the position of trying to maintain its dominance as the originator of fashion, and it is quite possible that the Big Four will be equally challenged in the 2000s as the economic balance shifts around the globe.

Population growth, climate change and scarce resources will affect the fashion industry of the future. The rationalization of fashion, with seasonless collections, showing menswear and womenswear together and the abandonment by some designers and brands of excessive numbers of shows could lead to a new approach to shows and to fashion weeks – possibly with fewer people travelling the world using resources and building up those air miles!

With the trend toward experiences and the idea that owning stuff is out, the fashion show will possibly serve a new purpose, selling directly to the consumer, through a truly entertaining shopping experience, either online or at events similar to the Montreal Fashion and Design Festival.

See-now-buy-now from the runway, and product that is available immediately after a show, are likely to continue, particularly amongst wealthier brands that can afford to pre-manufacture. What could be more persuasive than to buy directly from the runway when the consumer's excitement about the product is at its most intense?

New technologies have moved the traditional runway onto digital platforms and brought new techniques to show production, resulting in innovative use of moving image and the creation of virtual fashion shows. The use of fashion film by designers such as Gareth Pugh has resulted in pioneering presentations and innovations such as Instagram video continue to transform communication about the show. It is highly likely that the fashion consumer of the future will watch fashion shows (and purchase from the runway) through augmented reality.

For some, the speed of change has resulted in a nostalgic approach to show production. The St Laurent show in March 2016 was a throwback to the elegant ateliers of the first fashion houses, with gilt chairs, a compere calling out model numbers and models walking through mirrored salons. (View the show on the St Laurent website or on YouTube.) But typically for the fashion industry, there is excitement for the new. The legendary show producer Alexandre de Betak recently advised:

"Enter the creativity by whatever door you want, but, especially at the beginning, be as free and extreme as you can be. Because once you get into the real professional world, you will have to make compromises, it's totally normal, such is life. But when you're starting out, just dream, and never stop dreaming."

De Betak, himself, certainly hasn't stopped dreaming. Asked what his dream project would be, he doesn't hesitate for a second before responding, earnestly and perhaps unsurprisingly: "I would love to do a show in space and hopefully will do that."
(Anaya, 2013)

Bibliography

Agins, T. 2014. *Highjacking the Runway: How Celebrities Are Stealing the Spotlight from Fashion Designers*. New York: Penguin.

Akbareian, E. 2015. 'Tom Ford Debuts New Collection in "Soul Train" Inspired Video Starring Lady Gaga'. *The Independent*, 2 October 2015. Available online: www.independent.co.uk/life-style/fashion/tom-ford-debuts-new-collection-in-soul-train-inspired-video-starring-lady-gaga-a6676846.html (accessed 19 September 2016).

Akeroyd, J. 2015. 'Foreword', in C. Wilcox, ed. *Alexander McQueen*. London: V&A Publishing.

Alessia, B. 2014. 'Greenpeace Activists Protest at Milan Fashion Week'. *WWD*, 20 February 2014. Available online: http://wwd.com/fashion-news/fashion-scoops/greenpeace-protests-7487320/ (accessed 20 February 2014).

Amed, I. 2014. 'Suzy Menkes on Going Digital and Her Top Fashion Moments'. *Business of Fashion*, 12 June 2014. Available online: http://www.businessoffashion.com/2014/06/full-video-inside-suzy-menkes-new-digital-world.html (accessed 2 July 2014).

Amed, I. 2015. 'Why Stage Fashion Shows?' *Business of Fashion*, 2 October 2015. Available online: https://www.businessoffashion.com/articles/week-in-review/why-stage-fashion-shows (accessed 12 May 2016).

Anaya, S. 2013. 'The Creative Class/Alexandre de Betak, Fashion Show and Event Producer'. *Business of Fashion*, 12 July 2013. Available online: http://www.businessoffashion.com/articles/creative-class/the-creative-class-alexandre-de-betak-fashion-show-and-event-producer (accessed 10 January 2016).

ANDAM Award. Available online: http://andam.fr/fr/ (accessed 3 July 2014).

Anya Hindmarch Movies. 2016. 'Anya Hindmarch Spring/Summer 2017 London Fashion Week Show'. Available online: https://www.youtube.com/watch?v=zlJb7jZuabw (accessed 2 May 2017).

Arnold, R. 2009. *Fashion: A Very Short Introduction*. New York: Oxford University Press.

Blanks, T. 2014. 'Spring 2014 Menswear Dsquared2'. *Vogue*, 25 June 2013. Available online: http://www.vogue.com/fashion-shows/spring-2014-menswear/dsquared (accessed 6 September, 2013).

British Fashion Council. 2014. 'London Fashion Week'. Available online: http://www.londonfashionweek.co.uk/ (accessed 27 July 2014).

British Fashion Council. 2017. 'The British Fashion Council Launches Blogger Strategy'. 5 September 2013. Available online: http://www.britishfashioncouncil.co.uk/pressreleases/The-British-Fashion-Council-Launches-Blogger-Strategy (accessed 23 April 2017).

Camera Nazionale della Moda Italiana. 2014. Available online: http://www.cameramoda.it/en/associazione/cosa-e-la-cnmi/ (accessed 27 July 2014).

Cartner-Morley, J. 2012. 'Burberry Brings a Warmth to Catwalk Show After Raining on Its Own Parade'. *The Guardian*, 20 February 2012. Available at: http://www.theguardian.com/fashion/2012/feb/20/burberry-hyde-park-london-fashion-week (accessed 20 November 2015).

Cartner-Morley, J. 2014. 'The Many Faces of Stella McCartney'. *The Guardian*, 6 March 2014. Available online: www.theguardian.com/fashion/2014/mar/06/-sp-stella-mccartney-interview (accessed 15 October 2014).

Clark, H. 1954. 'Chanel Designs Again'. *American Vogue*. February 15.

Cope, J. and Maloney, D. 2016. *Fashion Promotion in Practice*. London: Bloomsbury Publishing.

Desimone, L. (2015). 'Set Design: Explore Erdem's Vintage-Inspired Set Design'. *Architectural Digest*, 31 January 2015. Available online: http://www.architecturaldigest.com/story/erdem-vintage-inspired-set-design (accessed 27 August, 2016).

Diderich, J. (2012). 'Famous Runway Showdown Revisited in "Versailles '73"'. *WWD*, 9 July 2012. Available online: http://wwd.com/eye/fashion/versailles-redux-6056411/ (accessed 28 May 2016).

Diehl, M. E. 1976. *How to Produce a Fashion Show*. New York: Fairchild Publications.

Duff Gordon, L. 2012. *A Woman of Temperament*. Attica Books.

Duggan, G. D. 2001. 'The Greatest Show on Earth: A Look at Contemporary Fashion Shows and Their Relationship to Performance Art'. *Fashion Theory* 3: 243–70.

Euromonitor. 2014. 'New Apparel Research: Part 1 – A Focus on Geographies'. Available online: http://blog.euromonitor.com/2013/03/new-apparel-research-part-1-a-focus-on-geographies.html#sthash.wBpsQMtB.dpuf (accessed 2 August 2014).

Evans, C. 2003. *Fashion at the Edge: Spectacle, Modernity and Deathliness*. New Haven and London: Yale University Press.

Evans, C. 2013. *The Mechanical Smile: Modernism and the First Fashion Shows in France and America, 1900-1929*. New Haven and London: Yale University Press.

Everett, J. C. and Swanson, K. K. 2013. *Guide to Producing a Fashion Show*. 3rd Ed. New York: Fairchild Books.

Fashion Channel Milano. 2012. '"Kenzo" Spring Summer 2013 Paris Full Show by FashionChannel'. Available online: https://www.youtube.com/watch?v=k1lIUIUE9tk (accessed 3 January 2017).

Fashion Design Council of India. 2014. Available online: http://www.fdci.org/default.aspx (accessed 27 July 2014).

Fisher, A. 2008. 'Why Are Catwalks So White?' *The Observer*, 6 April 2008. Available online: http://www.theguardian.com/lifeandstyle/2008/apr/06/fashion.features?guni=Article:in%20body%20link (accessed 26 October 2014).

Fury, A. in Wilcox, C. (Ed.). 2010. *Future Beauty: 30 Years of Japanese Fashion*. London: Merrell Publishers Limited.

Geczy, A. and Karaminas, V. 2017. *Critical Fashion Practice: From Westwood to van Beirendonck*. London: Bloomsbury Publishing.

Grant, K. (Ed.). 2013. 'Vivienne Westwood: Everyone Buys Too Many Clothes'. *The Telegraph*, 16 September 2013. Available online: http://fashion.telegraph.co.uk/news-features/TMG10312077/Vivienne-Westwood-Everyone-buys-too-many-clothes.html (accessed 4 October 2014).

Groen, T. 2014. 'I Say Yes to a Lot of Stuff'. *Frame*, Jan/Feb: 99–105.

Harris, S. 2014. 'Show Business'. *British Vogue*, 8 January 2014. Available online: http://www.vogue.co.uk/news/2014/1/08/show-business (accessed 10 January 2014).

Hills, M. 1923. 'A Seat at the Paris Openings Spring 1923'. *American Vogue*, 61: 39–132.

Hines, T. and Bruce, M. 2002. *Fashion Marketing: Contemporary Issues*. Oxford: Butterworth Heinemann.

International Center of Photography. 2009. 'David Seidner: Paris Fashions, 1945'. Available online: http://www.icp.org/museum/exhibitions/david-seidner-paris-fashions-1945 (accessed 9 May 2014).

Israel, K. 2016. 'Behind the Set: Bureau Betak's Vision for Dior's Cour Carrée A/W 2016 Show'. *Wallpaper*, 8 March 2016. Available online: http://www.wallpaper.com/fashion/behind-the-set-bureau-betaks-reflective-vision-for-diors-louvres-cour-carre-aw-2016-show (accessed 18 February 2017).

Jones, D. 2013. 'Louis Vuitton'. *British Vogue*, 2 October 2013. Available from http://www.vogue.co.uk/fashion/spring-summer-2014/ready-to-wear/louis-vuitton (accessed 13 June 2014).

Kansara, V. A. and Abraham, T. 2016. 'Cavalli Prepares for Radical Turnaround as Peter Dundas Exits'. *Business of Fashion*, 12 October 2016. Available online: https://www.businessoffashion.com/articles/news-analysis/peter-dundas-departs-roberto-cavalli (accessed 13 October 2016).

Kissick, D. 2014. 'Debate: Fashion Shows Are So Last Year'. I-D, 19 February 2014. Available online: http://i-d.vice.com/en_gb/read/think-pieces/1730/fashion-shows-are-so-last-year (accessed 26 April, 2014).

Knight, N. 2015. 'Alexander McQueen: Unseen 2004 Black Show Footage with Kate Moss and Michael Clark'. Available online: https://www.youtube.com/watch?v=PEmfJtyNGH4 (accessed 29 April 2017).

Kotler, P. and Keller, K. L. 2016. *Marketing Management*. 15th ed. Essex: Pearson.

Leitch, L. 2012. 'London to Get Its Own Men's Fashion Week(end)'. *The Telegraph*, 22 January 2012. Available online: http://fashion.telegraph.co.uk/article/TMG9031323/London-to-get-its-own-Mens-Fashion-Weekend.html (accessed 4 July 2014).

Luxury Daily. 2016. 'Burberry Updates Fashion Calendar to Meet Global Demand'. *Luxury Daily*, 5 February 2016. Available online: http://www.luxurydaily.com/burberry-updates-fashion-calendar-to-meet-global-demand/ (accessed 8 February 2016).

Maddison, J. 2011. 'It Costs HOW Much to Stage a Fashion Show? Marc Jacobs Reveals How He Spent $1 Million in Just Nine Minutes'. *MailOnline*, 23 February 2011. Available online: http://www.dailymail.co.uk/femail/article-1359309/Marc-Jacobs-spent-1m-just-9-minutes-fashion-show.html#ixzz34X5x8BHm (accessed 13 June 2014).

Madsen, A. C. 2014. 'Debate: Catwalk Shows Are Here to Stay'. I-D, 19 February 2014. Available online: http://i-d.vice.com/en_gb/read/think-pieces/1718/catwalk-shows-are-here-to-stay (accessed 26 April, 2014).

Marshall, F. 1914. 'Fashion's Latest Word in Smart Creations'. *The Washington Herald*, August 16.

McCord, B. 2014. 'Dries Van Noten: "Is Fashion Art? I Don't Care About That"'. dazeddigital.com. Available online: http://www.dazeddigital.com/fashion/article/19063/1/is-fashion-art-i-dont-care-about-that (accessed 28 June 2014).

McDowell, C. 1994. *The Designer Scam*. London: Random House.

Mellery-Pratt, R. 2014. 'Pitti's Peacocks and the Liberation of Men's Style'. *Business of Fashion*, 19 June 2014. Available online: http://www.businessoffashion.com/2014/06/pittis-peacocks-liberation-mens-style.html (accessed 19 June 2014).

Mendes, V. D. and de la Haye, A. 1990. *LUCILE Ltd: London, Paris, New York and Chicago*. London: V&A Publishing.

Menkes, S. 1993. 'Runways: The Shock of the Old'. *The New York Times*, 21 March 1993. Available online: http://www.nytimes.com/1993/03/21/style/runways-the-shock-of-the-old.html (accessed 25 October 2014).

Menkes, S. 2012a. 'Gucci's Orgy of Gorgeousness'. *The New York Times*, 19 September 2012. Available from http://www.nytimes.com/2012/09/20/fashion/20iht-fgucci20.html?_r=0 (accessed 1 February 2016).

Menkes, S. 2012b. 'IHT Luxury Conference – Rome 2012'. *The New York Times*. Available online: http://www.nytimes.com/video/fashion/100000001908125/iht-luxury-conference-rome-2012.html (accessed 4 August 2014).

Menkes, S. 2013. 'Sign of the Times: The New Speed of Fashion'. *The New York Times Style Magazine*, 23 August 2013. Available online: http://tmagazine.blogs.nytimes.com/2013/08/23/sign-of-the-times-the-new-speed-of-fashion/ (accessed 3 July, 2014).

Messina, B. 2013. 'Sao Paulo Fashion Week the Most Important Fashion Event in Latin America'. *Fashionbi*. Available online: http://fashionbi.com/newspaper/sao-paulo-fashion-week-the-most-important-fashion-event-in-latin-america (accessed 4 August 2014).

Moss, M. n.d. *The Woollands Story – Swinging into the Sixties*. Unpublished manuscript.

Neuville, J. 2013. 'The Creative Class – Thierry Dreyfus, Lighting Designer and Show Producer'. *Business of Fashion*, 27 August 2013. Available online: http://www.businessoffashion.com/articles/creative-class/the-creative-class-thierry-dreyfus-lighting-designer-and-fashion-show-producer (accessed 23 November 2015).

Niven, L. 2014. 'The Evolution of a Beauty Look'. *Vogue*, 3 October 2014. Available online: http://www.vogue.co.uk/article/erdem-spring-2015-the-evolution-of-a-beauty-look (accessed 3 September 2016).

Norris, L. 2016. 'Lucy Norris Reports on the Rich Owens Show'. *SHOWstudio*, 7 March 2016. Available online: http://showstudio.com/collection/rick_owens_paris_womenswear_a_w_2016/lucy_norris_reports_on_the_rick_owens_show (accessed 28 March 2016).

O'Flaherty, M. C. 2014. 'Are Camera Phones Killing Fashion?' *Business of Fashion*, 6 March 2014. Available online: http://www.businessoffashion.com/2014/3/camera-phones-killing-fashion.html (accessed 5 May 2014).

Robson, J. 2011. 'Paris Haute Couture: The New Breed of Young Clients'. *The Telegraph*, 6 July 2011. Available online: http://fashion.telegraph.co.uk/Article/TMG8618008/474/Paris-Haute-Couture-the-new-breed-of-young-clients.html (accessed 10 May 2014).

Schiaparelli, E. 1954 [2007]. *Shocking Life*. London: V&A Publications.

Seabrook, J., 2001. 'A Samurai in Paris: Suzy Menkes'. *The New Yorker*. Available online: http://www.johnseabrook.com/a-samurai-in-paris/ (accessed 1 January 2014).

Segreti, G., 2017. 'Missoni Talks Politics with Pink Cat-Eared Hats at Milan show'. *Reuters Lifestyle*, 25 February 2017. Available online: http://www.reuters.com/article/us-fashion-milan-missoni-idUSKBN1640KX (accessed 29 May 2017).

SHOWstudio. 2003. 'In Camera: Alexander McQueen'. Available online: http://showstudio.com/project/in_camera/alexander_mcqueen (accessed 1 November 2015).

SHOWstudio. 2014. 'Subjective: Kate Moss Interviewed by Nick Knight About Alexander McQueen A/W 2006'. Available online: https://www.youtube.com/watch?v=kWoQqrRk0ss (accessed 6 May 2017).

Shrivastava. N. 2014. 'Ramzan Couture: A New Face of Muslim Fashion'. *Deccan Chronicle*, 28 July 2014. Available online: http://www.deccanchronicle.com/140727/lifestyle-fashionbeauty/article/ramzan-couture-new-face-muslim-fashion (accessed 28 July 2014).

Skidmore, M. 2015. 'Set Pieces: We Speak to the Designers Turning Catwalk Shows into Pure Spectacle'. *It's Nice That*, 8 June 2015. Available online: http://www.itsnicethat.com/features/set-pieces-we-speak-to-the-designers-turning-catwalk-shows-into-pure-spectacle (accessed 27 August 2016).

Smith, R. 2014. 'What It Takes to Put on an Instagram-Ready Show: Fashion Week Relies on a Handful of In-Demand Producers'. *The Wall Street Journal*, 3 September 2014. Available online: http://www.wsj.com/articles/what-it-takes-to-put-on-a-fashion-show-1409786771 (accessed 27 December 2015).

Statista. n.d. 'Chanel Advertising Spending in the United States from 2012 to 2014 (in Million U.S. Dollars)'. Available online: http://www.statista.com/statistics/308514/chanel-advertising-spending-usa/ (accessed 11 June 2016).

Steele, V. 1998. *Paris Fashion: A Cultural History*. Oxford: Berg.

Steele, V. 2003. *Fashion Italian Style*. New Haven and London: Yale University Press.

Steven, R. 2015. 'How Hunter Creative Director Alasdhair Willis Is Transforming a 160-year-old Business'. *Creative Review*, 22 September 2015. Available online: https://www.creativereview.co.uk/cr-blog/2015/september/how-hunter-creative-director-alasdhair-willis-is-transforming-a-160-year-old-business/.

Style.com. 2013. 'John Galliano Stages a Grand Opera for Dior Couture – #TBT with Tim Blanks'. Available online: https://www.youtube.com/watch?v=0TajifB1KWA (accessed 28 November 2016).

The Talks. 2011. 'Yohji Yamamoto: "People Have Started Wasting Fashion"'. *The Talks*, 31 August 2011. Available online: http://the-talks.com/interviews/yohji-yamamoto/ (accessed 10 May 2014).

The Talks. 2013. 'Sir Paul Smith: "I'm Happy to Talk to Anybody"'. *The Talks*, 21 August 2013. Available online: http://the-talks.com/interviews/paul-smith/ (accessed 10 May 2014).

Trebay, G. 2011. At Marc Jacobs, the Show Before the Show. *New York Times*. [Online]. February 16, 2011. Available from: www.nytimes.com/2011/02/17/fashion/17Curtain.html?pagewanted=all&_r=0 [accessed 13 June 2014].

Videofashion. 2013. John Galliano - Fall/Winter 1994-95 - Videofashion Vault. [Online]. Available from: www.youtube.com/watch?v=I6ysNYAC5h0 [accessed 29 April, 2017].

Wallpaper. 2009. 'Prada and OMA Catwalk Collaborations'. *Wallpaper*, 25 September 2009. Available online: http://www.wallpaper.com/fashion/prada-and-oma-catwalk-collaborations#moyFIKJemUzfwDBG.99 (accessed 28 November 2015).

Webb, I. R. 2014. *Invitation Strictly Personal: 40 Years of Fashion Show Invites*. London: Goodman.

Welters, L. and Lillethun, A. (Eds). 2011. *The Fashion Reader*. New York: Berg.

Wendlandt, A. and Fuchs, M. 2011. Out of public eye, Arab women power haute couture. *Reuters*. [Online]. 5 October 2011. Available from: www.reuters.com/article/2011/10/05/us-fashion-middleeast-idUSTRE7942YG20111005 [accessed 20 July 2014].

Westwood, V. 2010. 'Vivienne Westwood Gold Label - Spring/Summer 1994 - Café Society Paris, Part II'. Available at: https://www.youtube.com/watch?v=W2Rb9-aeizw (accessed 2 January 2017).

Wong, Z. 2013. What is resort and why is it important - pre-collections explained. *Vogue Australia*. [Online] 29 June 2013. Available from: www.vogue.com.au/fashion/news/what+is+resort+and+why+is+it+important+pre+collections+explained,26070 [Accessed 3 July 2014].

Woo, K., 2013. *The Joy of Sets, in Dazed and Confused* [Online]. Available at: http://www.dazeddigital.com/fashion/article/15567/1/the-joy-of-sets [accessed 22 November 2015].

Woodhead, L. 2012. *Shopping, Seduction & Mr Selfridge*. London. Profile Books.

WRAP. 2012. 'Valuing our clothes: the evidence base'. *WRAP* [Online}. Available at: www.wrap.org.uk/clothingValuing our Clothes [accessed 14 October 2014].

Young. R. 2014. A Couture Stage Beyond Paris: Destiny, Dream or Delusion? *The Business of Fashion*. [Online]. 3 February, 2014. Available from: www.businessoffashion.com/2014/02/couture-stage-beyond-paris-destiny-dream-delusion.html [accessed 14 March 2014].

Yuniya, K. 2004. *The Japanese Revolution in Paris Fashion (Dress, Body, Culture)*. London: Berg.

Dedication

I would like to dedicate this book to the memory of my lovely father, Frank Stark.

Acknowledgements

I would like to thank my wonderful family and friends for their support during the writing of this book, and in particular Eloise, Josh, Pam and my mother Anne. I would like to extend my gratitude to Iain for patience while I spent many hours writing.

A huge thank you to my colleagues and students at Regent's University London, who have made our fashion shows so vibrant with their creativity and enthusiasm. Many of the photographs in this book show their work. Thanks also to Jason Pittock, Tony Rogers and Simon Armstrong whose photographs illustrate much of this book.

Huge thanks to the many contributors without whom this work would certainly not have been possible.

Finally, I would like to thank everyone at Bloomsbury Publishing and especially Colette Meacher, Hannah Marston and Faith Marsland.

Index